CRACKING
the
MILLIONAIRE
CODE

HARMONY BOOKS

NEW YORK

CRACKING
the
MILLIONAIRE
CODE

YOUR KEY TO
ENLIGHTENED
WEALTH

MARK VICTOR HANSEN

and ROBERT G. ALLEN

HARMONY BOOKS is a registered trademark and the Harmony Books
colophon is a trademark of Random House, Inc.

Grateful acknowledgment is made to the following for
permission to reprint previously published material:

Larry Dossey, M.D.: Excerpts from *Healing Words* by Larry Dossey, M.D.
Copyright © 1993 by Larry Dossey, M.D. Published by HarperCollins, New York.
Reprinted by permission of the author.

Harvard Business School Publishing: Excerpt from "What Makes an Effective
Executive" by Peter Drucker from *Harvard Business Review* (June 2004).
Reprinted by permission of Harvard Business School Publishing.

Houghton Mifflin Company: "Thirteen Most Important Marketing Secrets" from
Guerrilla Marketing: Secrets for Making Big Profits from Your Small Business,
3rd edition, by Jay Conrad Levinson. Copyright © 1998 by Jay Conrad Levinson.
All rights reserved. Reprinted by permission of Houghton Mifflin Company.

Simon & Schuster Adult Publishing Group: Excerpt from *First Things First* by
Stephen R. Covey, A. Roger Merrill, and Rebecca R. Merrill. Copyright © 1994 by
Stephen R. Covey, A. Roger Merrill, and Rebecca R. Merrill. Reprinted by permission
of Simon & Schuster Adult Publishing Group.

LIBRARY OF CONGRESS CATALOGING-IN-PUBLICATION DATA

Allen, Robert G.
Cracking the millionaire code : your key to enlightened wealth /
Robert G. Allen and Mark Victor Hansen.—1st ed.
p. cm.
Includes index.
1. Success in business.   2. Wealth.   3. Millionaires.
I. Hansen, Mark Victor.   II. Title.
HF5386.A5432 2004
332.024'01—dc22   2004028898

ISBN 1-4000-8294-3

PRINTED IN THE UNITED STATES OF AMERICA

Design by Barbara M. Bachman

10 9 8 7 6 5 4 3 2 1

FIRST EDITION

We want to make a difference

(with the people who make a difference that makes a difference)

CONTENTS

INTRODUCTION

IMAGINE THIS . . .

Standing outside your front door at this moment are two prosperous-looking gentlemen. The taller of the two reaches out and knocks. You open the door to find Mark and Bob—the authors of this book—standing in front of you, smiling.

"Congratulations!" we say. "You have been selected as a contestant on our new reality TV show, *Cracking the Millionaire Code*. You and 19 other contestants will be Organized into four separate teams. Each team will be given the task of coming up with a brand-new, million-dollar idea for creating Enlightened Wealth. You'll test your idea and launch it with the goal of earning a million dollars in cash. Your team will donate the first 10% of your profit to the charity you choose before you start. Three other teams will be competing with you.

"The Grand Prize? The team that earns and donates the most 'enlightened' money will win an extra million dollars.

"Still interested?

"You might be wondering why we selected you. Well, actually, you've selected yourself by reading this book. And when you fill out the specially designed questionnaire you'll find on the Internet at **www.crackingthe millionairecode.com,** you'll take the next step in demonstrating that you're not one of the typical get-rich-quick, pie-in-the-sky romantics who are quick to dream but just as quick to give up on their dreams. We've learned that most people are great starters but lousy finishers. We can tell that you realize that wealth is a marathon, not a 100-yard dash.

"Are you ready? Imagine millions of people watching you compete for millions of dollars. Imagine the final week of the show when the four teams reveal their million-dollar creations in prime time. Imagine millions of viewers 'voting with their credit cards' to buy one of the million-dollar products that are offered on national television. Imagine the millions in profit that could be generated from such publicity. Imagine how good it could feel to know that your chosen charity receives the first 10% in profit. Imagine being on the winning team and walking away with an extra million for yourself! Wouldn't that be fun?"

REALITY BEGINS RIGHT NOW

Well, our reality TV show may not be quite ready for prime time, but reality itself starts the moment you finish this book and start to take action. In these pages we'll show you exactly how to turn your enlightened ideas into millions. Then, at our website, **www.crackingthemillionairecode.com**, we will guide you on a step-by-step, 101-Day Plan to your first enlightened million.

This book is divided into two completely different types of content. On the second page of each chapter and continuing along the left-hand pages, you'll find highlighted in light green, real-life stories of ordinary people who cracked the millionaire code and created extraordinary fortunes from a single idea, often in the face of extraordinary challenges. They made millions and gave away millions the enlightened way. We hope their stories inspire you.

In the main body of text, you'll learn how to crack your own personal wealth code. We'll show you how to overcome your personal fears. We'll show you how to gather an amazing team around you. We'll show you how to "soul-storm" not one but dozens of million-dollar ideas. We'll show you an incredible, enlightened way to market your ideas.

Some people make the process of creating wealth look easy. Others seem to struggle for a lifetime and still prosperity eludes them. Here is the way this works.

There is an enormous bank vault filled with amazing wealth waiting for you this very instant. Unfortunately, there is no course in the education system called Wealth 101. Very few of us are taught even the basics of money—how to make it and how to keep it. Yet, there is more to wealth than just learning about money. Where do we learn the essential personal development skills of confidence building, time management, and listening to intuition? This book is designed to show you **how** to crack you own personal wealth code. If you don't want it for yourself, then certainly you would want **it** for those people on this planet who are less fortunate than you. Would you share it with them? You can do so much good if you'll just learn how to crack the four key co**d**es that keep your wealth vault sealed. Let us help you uncover the secrets to your personal wealth co**d**e. Each of us is different. Each of us has unique strengths and weaknesses that we **e**ach need to discover and utilize for our fastest route to prosperity. Let us show you the surest, swiftest, safest paths.

In addition to the real-life stories and code-cracking content, there is a hidde**n** layer to this book. To make your reading more interesting and challenging, other secrets are hidden throughout the book. There are 101 unique puzzles, codes, and **c**iphers distributed in the text to encourage you to think more profoundly about Enlightened Wealth. You may pass right over the codes in the text without missing any of the importa**n**t lessons. However, if you'd like to be challenged to **t**hink more deeply about these wealth concepts, we encourage you to attempt to crack the 101 wealt**h** codes that are scattered throughout the book. Som**e** of the codes are obvious and are displayed in plain sig**h**t. Some of the cod**e**s are hidden. For e**x**ample, the words you have read thus far are part of a hidden message contained in **t**he Introduction. Hint: Some of the previous sentences contain letters in bold typeface. Continue throughout the chapter and copy down each of these special letters and an important message will be revealed. There's a space for your answer at the end. The first hidden code will be easy to crack. As in life, clues will become more challenging as the book progresses. You'll be very wise to stop a moment and go back and crack the first code. Each hidden message that you decipher will bring you one step closer to the prosperity that is awaiting you.

Our goal is t**o** inspire you with *real stories,* and empower you with *real systems,* to motivate you to achieve Enlightened Wealth on the **f**astest route possible.

Can you do it in 101 days? Well, we believe it's certainly realistic that real profits can be flowing into your life in less than 101 days; if not in 101 days, then an extra enlightened million in your lifetime is absolutely realistic.

By the way, you may soon be wondering why we use the number 101 so often? We believe that 101 is an enlightened number and has served both of us very well—one of the most successful series of books in history, *Chicken Soup for the Soul,* contains 101 heartwarming stories. Therefore, we'll use the number 101 in several different contexts throughout this book.

Each of ____ has a certain _____ path. On that _____ are the lessons that we pick up like _____ along our way. Perhaps there are a Few more which you need to pick up before you're ready for your enlightened million. Just because you may WANT to become wealthy _____— or just because it's possible for you to make an _____ million this _____—doesn't mean that you OUGHT to do it. _____ your own _____, enlightened million-dollar _____, which is the one you were destined to _____—is over the _____ a few years off. (#1)

To read the above paragraph, use the words below to fill in the blank spaces.

extra	**perhaps**
personal	**us**
earn	**year**
path	**destiny**
idea	**horizon**
ASAP	**pebbles**

Thgilneergehtuoyeviglliwrewoprehgihthgirsiemitehtdnaydaereruoynehw.

#2_____

Then the concepts in this book could be very helpful to you. First read this book and then log onto **www.crackingthemillionairecode.com** to follow the 101-Day Plan.

How much time will this take on a daily basis? If you were part of an actual reality TV show, you and your team would be jamming 24/7. Since most people don't have the ability to sprint around the clock, we've designed the process to take a maximum of an hour a day. If you don't have that kind of time, then it will just take you longer to reach your goal. According to our rough projections, if you spread the assignments over 101 weeks you would reach your million-dollar goal in just under two years. If you choose to do them in 101 months, you will get there in about eight years. As they say, there's no such thing as an unrealistic goal, just an unrealistic time frame.

YOUR OWN CODE-CRACKING TEAM

Before you launch into the work ahead, we'd like to ask you to share your goal with four other like-minded people. Ask four of your friends, family members, or associates a simple question:

Would you like to become an Enlightened Millionaire?

The five of you will form a team. Instructions on how to organize your team will be given later. For now, just imagine what it might be like to meet with a group of success-oriented people who would like to significantly improve their finances this year. The group could be local or virtual. Your meetings could be conducted face-to-face or by phone or via e-mail with friends, relatives, or associates in other cities.

What kinds of people do you want on your Enlightened Millionaire team? Think of people who are positive-minded, success-oriented individuals with a performance track record. You will be building a network that creates all your future net worth. Friendship equity is a precursor to all financial equity. To find four committed, dedicated, like-Minded friends you may have to share this with 101 people. That's okay. You will find those few significant other people who can make a humongous difference to your success, significance, and future results. It may be hard for you to believe right **now**, but they are looking for and praying for you to show up in their lives, as much as you are looking for them. Encourage each member of your team to invest in a copy of this book. Have them **r**ead, underline, highlight, and discuss with you each and **e**very insight, *aha*, and idea. We have tested this book and discovered that individuals who use this formula start to have money-making ideas. They instantly start attracting the right people into their lives to get the right results right now. Later, we will define this as Serendestiny™, where serendipity and your personal destiny come into easy and almost effortless realization.

> *Two are better off than one, because together they can work more effectively. If one of them falls down, the other can help him up. . . . Two people can resist an attack that would defeat one person alone. A rope made of three* **C***ords is hard to break.*
>
> —ECCLESIASTES 4:9–12

Write d**o**wn the names of 10 possible team members in the spaces below. Then, contact them one by one until your team is forme**d**.

1. _____
2. _____
3. _____
4. _____
5. _____
6. _____
7. _____
8. _____
9. _____
10. _____

Are you ready?

Now let's begin.

#3 _____

_____

Crack this Millionare Code after you have read chapters 1 through 10.

_____ ___ __ ___ ___ ____ _____ ___ ___ ____

#4_____ _____ _ ____ __ ____ _____.

CRACKING
the
MILLIONAIRE
CODE

.

Chapter One

WHY "ENLIGHTENED" WEALTH?

THERE IT IS. CAN YOU SEE IT?

I t's the vault containing everything you've ever wanted. On the other side of the huge door to that vault, a lifestyle of abundance and prosperity, wealth and security, awaits you. Behind that door is literally *anything* you want. But how will you ever crack the code to the vault?

Around you it seems as if others have cracked the code to wealth. You can see them everywhere. They live in the best neighborhoods. They drive new, high-end cars. They work at jobs they're passionate about. They seem to be happy and balanced. Their children go to the finest colleges. They take exciting vacations. They seem to have smart, successful friends. They give time to charitable causes. They have time to do what they want, with whomever they want, when they want. It appears that they have it all. How did they get it? Did they really earn it? Or did they do something illegal or immoral or unethical to get it? Aren't you as deserving as they are? Aren't you more honest, ethical, and hardworking than they are?

A little voice inside you may be saying, "Why do they have so much? It's not fair!" Maybe so. Maybe not. But if you focus on the unfairness of it, envy will consume you. Don't focus on them and what they have. Simply focus on your own vault and claim what rightfully belongs to you. It's the wealth that was reserved for you from before you were born. The truth is that you are amazing just as you are. Be open to receiving abundance right now. You don't need to think that anything is wrong with you. You came into this

Nido Qubein

Nido Qubein is a visionary leader and a great philanthropist, benefactor, and humanitarian who multiplies his giving by asking others to share generously also. He came to our shores as a teenager filled with ambitions to live the American dream. He arrived from Lebanon with $50 in his pocket and no command of the English language, yet full of hope. Each day Nido Qubein memorized 10 words that he had written out on 3" × 5" cards. He exercised immense discipline to master a language that would become his ticket to fortune, fame, friendship, and a future that would make a significant and continuing difference in the lives of millions of people.

Accepted by High Point University in North Carolina, Nido Qubein studied hard and worked 10 hours a day to earn his way through college. On graduation day he was talking to the university president when he was informed that an anonymous donor had paid all outstanding bills for his education. Astounded, he wept, said a thankful prayer, and vowed to help others by becoming a generous enlightened steward. He decided to give other deserving students a helping hand with their education, creating the Nido Qubein Educational Foundation. The first year he gave a $500 scholarship to a student named Glenn Meyers, who went on to earn a PhD.

To increase the funding of his foundation, Nido started asking his friends and colleagues to each give $250 or more annually. To encourage their support, he vowed that 100% of the money would be used for scholarships and that he would not only contribute himself, but he would personally pay all the administrative and other costs to run the foundation. Over 600 scholarships have been granted, and the foundation is still going strong.

Nido Qubein began investing in real estate, starting by buying a duplex with 10% down. He always tithed, saving 10% of whatever he earned, and lived inexpensively. In 1970 his own rent was $15 a month. He saved, and he bought more real estate. After investing in American Bank and Trust at

→

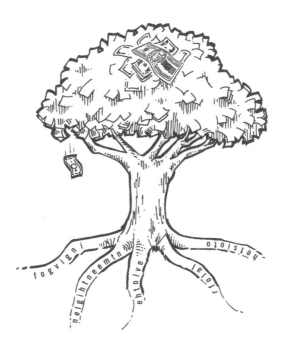

#5 _____

_____

world with all of the necessary talents to open your own vault. Life will teach you some of the essential codes. Others will share with you shortcuts that will shave years off the process. But, essentially, you're the only one who can open the door. You either figure out how to open it yourself or it could remain forever closed.

What if you were destined for a more abundant life? How sad it would be to realize, too late, that you could have lived a more prosperous, abundant lifestyle without sacrificing anything that you now hold dear—your values, your health, your spirituality, your freedom, your friends and family. Here's a shocking thought: You could actually be happier, healthier, more spiritual, more friendly, more free, more able to do more good for the planet if you learned how to crack the code to your own, personalized wealth vault!

age 39, Nido became a board member, catapulting himself into banking prominence. The company merged, grew, and merged again, becoming the 10th biggest bank in America. AB&T now has over 30,000 employees. Nido learned on the job, becoming director on each of the new bank boards and learning from a great leader, John Allison, who is the chairman of this growing conglomerate. Nido recommends that entrepreneurs get paid in stock options, assuming he or she has adequate cash flow to do so; that way one can defer taxes and pay at a lower rate on appreciating earnings.

Nido also invested in the Great Harvest Bread Company and has led it to exponential growth in a time when "low-carb" and "no-carb" diets are the vogue. Reflecting his philanthropic philosophy, at the end of each day the stores give away all of their leftovers to charity and start the next day making fresh bakery goods.

As a professional speaker, Nido talks with great authority about sales, marketing, branding, business, leadership, philanthropy, and education. He has won every honor the industry offers, including membership in the National Speakers Association and Toastmasters International's coveted "Golden Gavel Award."

As a businessman Nido Qubein wants everyone to become fiscally literate, so they know how to earn money, grow it, preserve it, and become wise stewards so they can make a difference and leave a significant and lasting legacy. "Reputation is what others see in you. Character is what God knows about you. Service is the rent we pay while we are on the earth. And we need to be involved and contributing to our community—our city, schools, industry and trade association, and our world. We live in a global village," says Nido. "Philanthropy comes from a Greek word: *Philos* means friend and *anthopy* means mankind, so a philanthropist is a friend of mankind. Everyone can become a philanthropist."

When asked how he does so much and still vacations two to three months a year with his wife and four children, he answers: "It's not time management, it's life management that counts. Life management focuses on the activities that you are passionate about. We have time for whatever we

→

12 21 3 11   9 19 14'20   20 8 5   11 5 25   20 15   13 9 12 12 9 16 14 19, 9 20'19
4 9 19 3 15 22 5 18 9 14 7   25 15 21 18   5 14 12 9 7 8 20 5 14 5 4   7 9 6 20
20 8 1 20   21 14 12 15 3 11 19   20 8 5   20 18 5 1 19 21 18 5.

#6 _____

_____

Does it seem as if you have been locked out of your own vault? Did you blame someone else for stealing your codes? Or maybe you were just never taught them. Perhaps you weren't ready till now. Maybe you told yourself that you didn't deserve them. Or maybe, after trying for years to crack the codes, you have just given up.

In a dramatic experiment some researchers placed a large fish in the middle of an aquarium with minnows to feed on. The fish fed to his heart's delight. Then, the researchers placed a glass partition in the tank, dividing it in two. After the pike had eaten all of the minnows on his side of the partition, he could see the other minnows through the glass but he couldn't get to them. He thrashed, he bumped, he bashed his body against the glass partition, but to no avail. He finally formed a belief that it was impossible for him to get to those fish. He stopped trying. Then, the researchers removed the glass partition and allowed the minnows to swim all around him. He could smell them. He could see them. He could feel them. But he believed that those fish were no longer available to him—that they were forever locked away from him—that it was impossible for him to win. So he starved to death in the middle of an aquarium full of food.

Eholhyh zlwk doo brxu khduw, plqg dqg vrxo wkdw brx duh ghvwlqhg wr eh zhdowkb.

#7 _____

_____

Everywhere you look, people are starving to death in the middle of aquariums teeming with food. Everywhere you look, people are blinded to the prosperity that surrounds them, deaf to the sound of opportunity knocking on their own front door, insensitive to the intuitive feelings that flood their

are passionate about. I have a 'to-do' list, but more importantly, I have a 'to-stop' list. I don't read newspapers in the morning; I read self-help, inspirational, and spiritual literature that uplifts me. I take vacations as an investment in memories with my children."

Recently, Nido's alma mater, High Point University, recruited him to become its president. Once again, he saw an opportunity for stewardship. He instantly committed a gift of $1 million and asked 10 friends to match his contribution. He started his tenure with $10 million raised, and a fine example of leadership in action.

entire being. This doesn't need to happen to you. There is no question that you were destined to be wealthy. One key to the code is understanding that this is not just ordinary wealth we're talking about here.

A NEW TYPE OF WEALTH

Elngitheend waetlh—hwo yuo eran it and kepe ti—si daramtcilaly dfifrneet tahn teh odriarny wlaeth we see, haer, tnihk or raed aobut. It is wtaelh wtih a cpatail W. Het gmae of aqcurniig tarditiioanl "samll w" watleh is auobt cpmoeteitoin, teh sruvvail of teh fttiset, and the fhgit fro the "amghltiy dloalar." Egtenelihnd Wtelah is a ttolaly nwe wya of lokiong at mnoey and watelh adn psropretiy. For srtearts it is MCUH mroe eljonabye, MHUC sfear, and ltsas MUHC lngoer tahn tdaitrinaol wlatelh.

#8

_____

_____

_____

_____

_____

_____

_____

Before we settle in to showing you exactly how to open your personal wealth vault, let us lay down the foundation principles upon which you'll be building the skyscraper of your personal prosperity.

CAN WE TALK?

If you're looking for a "hard-nosed" system for making bundles of quick cash, then this is probably not your book. And if talk of spirituality, faith, or belief in a Higher Power bothers you, then you'd best give this book to a friend. But before you rush off to buy another business bestseller, here's a

MY MANIFESTO OF ENLIGHTENED WEALTH

I believe that I have the potential to create an enlightened fortune.

I believe that wealth creation is a code that I was destined to crack. It is a learnable, teachable, and easily transferable skill. It makes all other skills more valuable, useful, and profitable.

I believe that almost everyone has millions of potential dollars in them awaiting the requisite stimulus—the enlightened spark.

I believe that I have an abundance of enlightened million dollar ideas—seeds that can grow into fortunes. These seeds can sprout in the form of information, books, copyrights, products, services, inventions, licenses, plays, patents, songs, movies, franchises, TV shows, trademarks, processes, etc.

I believe that my richest harvests may arise not from seeds of obvious opportunity, but from seeds of adversity. When I resolve my personal life challenges, others will reward me for helping them pull the weeds from their own adversity gardens of hidden wealth.

I am coded within my DNA to solve and resolve an issue for myself and then to prosper with it by solving it for all others.

I believe that I have been given unique talents. By using my total talents at their highest and best levels I will be happier, healthier and more fulfilled now and my contributions will leave a lasting legacy.

I believe that enlightened profits are the just reward for serving greatly.

I believe that my time is best invested in creating residual income, where I work once and am paid infinitely.

I believe that my dream is more quickly realized by aligning myself with an enlightened team. As a team, we can create multiple streams of enlightened, residual income.

I believe my ultimate legacy is to become an enlightened, residual philanthropist dedicated to doing lasting good works of perpetual philanthropy.

Your Name _____ Date _____

question we encourage you to ponder: How well does traditional business really work?

T 'ΥΥ 'Υφ 'Υ;;"Ωφ´ⲭŸ'Ω ⲭφ Y^ σ'Υ´ϑ'Ω'Γ, ύ¨,ⲭφ'Ω,,ζ

#9 _____

On the website for the U.S. Small Business Administration you'll find this quote:

> **Starting a small business is always risky, and the chance of success is slim. According to the U.S. Small Business Administration, over 50% of small businesses fail in the first year and 95% fail within the first five years.**
>
> ## STOP!!! READ THAT AGAIN...S...L...O...W...L...Y....

No matter how you look at it, starting a business can be a difficult and rocky endeavor. In truth, nobody is 100% sure of the exact rate of business success or failure. A failure rate of 95% is often used, although other research has been more encouraging. As noted small-business researcher David Birch, listed by *Fortune Small Business* magazine as one of the top 10 small-business minds, puts it, "Starting a company is very hard to do. The risks are enormous, the anxiety is enormous. Therefore, the only business you should start is one in which you have a huge interest, or else you won't have the persistence to stick with it."[1]

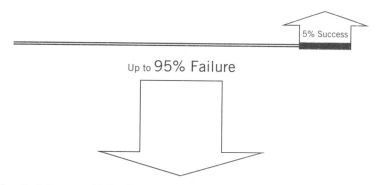

5% Success

Up to **95% Failure**

1. Stephen D. Solomon and Julie Sloane, "The Brain Trust: Top Ten Minds," *Fortune Small Business* magazine, December 1, 2002.

PERCENTAGE AND NUMBER OF COMPANIES THAT SURVIVE BASED ON CENSUS BUREAU STATISTICS

1 year	2 years	3 years	4 years	5 years	6 years	10 years
PERCENTAGE OF BUSINESS SURVIVAL						
81%	65%	54%	46%	40%	36%	25%
NUMBER OF SURVIVING BUSINESSES (OUT OF 1.7 MILLION START-UPS ANNUALLY)						
1.377 mil.	1.105 mil.	.918 mil.	.782 mil.	.68 mil.	.612 mil.	.425 mil.

Alfred Nucci, *"The Demography of Business Closings,"* Small Business Economics.

Every day thousands of new business owners gather at the starting line in the marathon of business start-ups. They're excited. They have high hopes. They've got an idea for a product or service that they feel could change the world and earn them a small fortune. The starter gun goes off and they launch their dream business. However, because they don't first crack the wealth code, few survive.

Why does anyone start a business with those odds? We don't share these pessimistic statistics to scare you but to inspire you to follow a safer and more enlightened path. Some of us simply feel we are destined to be entrepreneurs. The two of us believe that we were destined to transform this 95% failure rate into a 95% success rate for the enlightened entrepreneurs.

So if you're one of the 1.7 million new businesses started each year,[2] how do you turn the odds of success in your favor? You must start by becoming

2. Richard Oliver and the Research Institute for Small and Emerging Businesses, "The Future of Small Business."

an Enlightened Entrepreneur. *Money* magazine echoes this by saying the first step in turning a dream into reality is "seeking something bigger than getting rich."

WHY LISTEN TO THE TWO OF US?

Neither of us is a stranger to business failure. Each of us has had businesses drop dead on us. We've both been legally bankrupt. We know what it's like to suffer the embarrassment of losing everything several times. After being hit "upside the head" enough times, we finally realized that there had to be a better way. We both began to practice these new enlightened business principles and prospered independently of each other. Then, we joined forces and prospered even more. Tens of millions of dollars' worth. This isn't theory. What we'll teach you really works!

DLROWEHT
TIFENEBOTYAWA
TIEVIGOTREGAE
TSOMERAOHWESOHT
OTTSETSAFSWOLFYENOM

#10 _____

_____

_____

_____

_____

We'll teach you a system for creating Enlightened Wealth. But let us warn you before we begin: This is *very* different. It might seem very weird, very strange, very foreign as compared with the world of traditional "business as usual." But the odds of your success will be much, much higher.

This book takes a bold look at how Higher Power would run a business. Frankly, the whole theme of this book is going to be about the Higher Power approach to business success. We're going to go very deep into this—much

of serendipitous opportunities that were somehow absent before the change.

more deeply than almost any business text. No traditional MBA class dares touch on this stuff. It's too touchy-feely. Yes, we will put God and money in the same sentence, although we'll try to do it in a way that doesn't offend anyone.

Let's start with the concept of Higher Power. A lot of words can be used to describe the Supreme Being, depending on your spiritual belief: Universe, God, Goddess, the Creator, Higher Intelligence, Deity, Divinity, Providence, Jehovah, Allah, the Great Spirit, the Supreme Soul, Buddha, Lord, the Wise One, Divine Mind, Universal Life Force, Infinite Spirit, Mother Nature, Godhead, the Holy Spirit, the Almighty, Eternal Father, Father in Heaven, plus a hundred more. We've selected the words *Higher Power* to use throughout this book, although we encourage you to translate the concept into whatever specific words have the most meaning for you personally.

It is our belief that you have been given talents to resolve a specific problem on this planet. Solving this challenge will earn you a literal fortune. We believe that Higher Power knows which problem you were given to solve. Higher Power is waiting to show you the way. Higher Power also knows the shortcut to your enlightened fortune; Higher Power expects you to share some of your profits with those who are less fortunate.

Profits comes first—giving are secondary.

#11 _____ – _____

THE NEW PARADIGM OF ENLIGHTENED WEALTH

—

There is a new sound in the air. It is the sound of a new wind of economic change blowing across the world, an enlightened breeze of hope, of opportunity, of prosperity. Can you sense it? There is a new paradigm of wealth emerging—a new way to look at business, of buying and selling, of Enlightened Entrepreneurship. The old model is giving way to a new way of doing things. Change is on the way, and old-style capitalism is about to be transcended, transformed.

In 1776 Adam Smith wrote the book that changed the world—*The*

Wealth of Nations. Smith laid the intellectual framework for capitalism. He theorized that the "invisible hand" of unbridled self-interest was more powerful than any organized government activity. He envisioned a world where people, pursuing their own self-interest, challenged by the fear of competition and the joy of operating in a free market, would produce better products and services and create a better world. For the most part, he was right. It has created a better world. But the knock on capitalism is that it is so selfish; the self-interested entrepreneur is too often motivated by greed and fear.

BUT ISN'T GREED GOOD?

In 1987, Michael Douglas won an Academy Award for playing stockbroker/corporate takeover specialist Gordon Gekko in the Oliver Stone-directed movie *Wall Street.* The most memorable scene is Gekko's speech to the stockholders of Teldar Paper, a company he is trying to acquire.

> *"The point is, ladies and gentlemen, that greed, for lack of a better word, is good. Greed is right. Greed works. Greed clarifies and captures the essence of the evolutionary spirit. Greed in all of its forms—greed for life, for money, for love, knowledge—has marked the upward surge of mankind. And greed, you mark my words, will not only save Teldar Paper but that other malfunctioning corporation called the USA."*

As the movie goes on to portray, greed eventually reveals itself to be very destructive indeed. There are endarkened ways to create wealth and there are enlightened ways to create Wealth. We think that a new paradigm of Wealth is appearing. And it appears to have the power of science behind it.

A BEAUTIFUL, ENLIGHTENED MIND

In 2001 the Academy Award for best picture was awarded for a movie entitled *A Beautiful Mind.* It portrays the life of John Graham Nash Jr., winner of the 1994 Nobel Prize for Economics. A scene in the movie hints at what Nash's theory would prove. Nash, played by Russell Crowe, and his four buddies watch as a beautiful blond and her four friends enter the room. They all are attracted to her. One of the men says,

> *"Have you remembered nothing? Recall the lessons of Adam Smith, father of modern economics: In competition, individual ambition serves the common good. Every man for himself, gentlemen. And those who strike out are stuck with her friends."*

After pondering the situation, Nash replied that Adam Smith needed some revision. If each of them went for the blond, and blocked one another, then odds are that none of them would get her. This would also offend the other women—who wants to be second best? So the best strategy would be for none of them to go for the blond. The other girls would be flattered and everyone would win.

> *"Adam Smith said the best result comes from everyone in the group doing what's best for himself. Right? That's what he said. Right? Incomplete. Incomplete. Because the best result will come from everyone in the group doing what's best for himself and the group. Governing dynamics, gentlemen. Governing dynamics. Adam Smith . . . was wrong!"*

The movie goes on to show how Nash discovered the game theory that eventually won him the Nobel Prize. In essence, his theory, the Nash Equilibrium—initially applied to game theory—was eventually adopted into a whole range of useful life applications: economics, sociology, politics, warfare, and even biology. In economics, Nash's theory proved that there is a better, more enlightened way than unbridled self-interest. He proved that enlightened cooperation can be more enriching than the invisible hand of competition.

We call this "Enlightened Entrepreneurship." The best result is where every entrepreneur creates wealth for him-/herself *and* the group—but not in that order. In our opinion, the best result comes when the individual entrepreneur creates wealth for the group *first* and then, for him-/herself. In doing so, we believe a divine "invisible hand" orchestrates the Serendes-tiny™ of events to reveal the hidden opportunities for Wealth and perpetual philanthropy.

JUNE						
S	M	T	W	T	F	S
			1	2	3	4
5	6	7	8	9	10	11
12	13	14	15	16	17	18
19	20	21	22	23	24	25
26	27	28	29	30		

JULY						
S	M	T	W	T	F	S
					1	2
3	4	5	6	7	8	9
10	11	12	13	14	15	16
17	18	19	20	21	22	23
24 31	25	26	27	28	29	30

AUGUST						
S	M	T	W	T	F	S
	1	2	3	4	5	6
7	8	9	10	11	12	13
14	15	16	17	18	19	20
21	22	23	24	25	26	27
28	29	30	31			

SEPTEMBER						
S	M	T	W	T	F	S
				1	2	3
4	5	6	7	8	9	10
11	12	13	14	15	16	17
18	19	20	21	22	23	24
25	26	27	28	29	30	

#12 _ .

Enlightened Wealth is the polar opposite of "get rich quick," with its smarmy taint. If you're looking to create Enlightened Wealth in the fastest way possible, keep reading. Contrary to popular belief, we know that it is absolutely possible to earn honest, ethical, enlightened, legal, moral, good money—and to do so even more quickly than if you chose the alternative.

THE PTOLEMAIC MODEL OF ECONOMICS VERSUS THE COPERNICAN MODEL OF ECONOMICS

The sun rises over the eastern skyline every morning and sets in the west at night. For millennia, the masses believed that the earth was the center of the universe (geocentric) and that the sun was a chariot being driven around the earth. That's the way the scientist Ptolemy (ca. A.D. 100) saw it. And that's the way it remained until the Polish astronomer Copernicus (ca. A.D. 1450) changed everything with his heliocentric, or sun-centered, version of the solar system.

In modern economics, Adam Smith is analogous to Ptolemy. Smith said the world revolves around worldly self-interest—the driving force for all capitalistic success. You can see it with your own eyes. Money makes the world go round, right? Apparently so. But just as Copernicus came up with a more accurate view of the way things work, we believe that a better model of economics puts Higher Power at the center—a heliocentric model of economics!

The truth is that everything revolves around Higher Power. What if you operated your enterprise from a Higher Power perspective? What if the products of your enterprise had the Higher Power seal of approval? What if you treated everyone—yourself, your partners, your employees, your customers—as Higher Power would treat them? What if your spiritual activities were not relegated to a special day of the week? What if your enterprise was a living love generator—the evidence of your living principles all week long?

Ptolemaic capitalism puts the earth at the center of the universe—the worship of worldly values fueled by the "invisible hand" of self-interest. Enlightened Copernican capitalism has the earth revolving around a sun that enlightens and gives life to everything. If you make money the center of your universe, the machine will eventually bog down as the sand of greed grinds the pistons to a halt. But if Enlightened Wealth creation, with its love of Higher Power, is at the center of your universe, your economic machine runs far more smoothly. It's not the love of money itself but the love of enlightened *giving* that powers the machine. Compared to greed, giving is godlike.

For centuries people thought the world was flat . . . until Columbus, sitting on his dock, noticed the way boats disappeared over the horizon and then risked everything to prove his theory that the world was round. We, too, perceive a more circular, a different, a more enlightened way to Wealth. Although the clues are very subtle, almost imperceptible, this new world of wealth is waiting just over the horizon—a new world of amazing possibility.

EnLIGHTened Principles

Enlightened Wealth. Do those two words even belong in the same sentence? So many people believe that money and spirituality are mutually exclusive— that one word cancels out the other word. It is our belief that wealth can be enlightened. It can be imagined, created, earned, and distributed in enlightened ways.

Contrary to the widespread belief that money is the root of all evil, we believe that Enlightened Wealth can be the root of an enormous amount of good. It is the unbridled "love of money" for its own sake that has been the cause of much misery and suffering on planet earth.

We don't encourage anyone to love money. We encourage everyone to love the good that money can do. We don't encourage anyone to hoard and stockpile money for its own sake. On the contrary, we encourage everyone to actually give away the first of your financial profits as quickly as possible. At the root of the concept of Enlightened Wealth are five foundation principles that spell the word *LIGHT*.

When you build your finances upon these principles, Enlightened Wealth comes faster and stays longer.

ON YOUR MARK, GET SET, GLOW

To begin your 101 day journey, you're going to need LIGHT for your path.

L overage

I nner Wealth

G iving

H igher Power

T rustee

Let's take a closer look at these five principles.

. —. .—.. ... —-. .... — . —. . —.. .—- . .— .—.. — ....
.. ... —... .— ... . —.. —— —. .—.. —— .... . .—. .— —-.,
.. —. —. . .—. .—- . .— .—.. — ...., —— .. ...— .. —. —-,
.... .. —-. .... . .—. .—- —— .—- . .—. .— —. —.
— .—. ..— ... —

#13 _____

_____

_____

_____

Loverage

WE BELIEVE THAT YOU ACCESS YOUR GREATEST WEALTH NOT BY leverage but by loverage, by doing what comes naturally to you. There are a million ways for you to earn a million dollars, but only a limited number of those routes to the top of millionaire mountain are perfectly suited to you—they tap into your inner talents, skills, passions, values, and destiny.

Yes, we believe that you were not only destined to be financially successful but destined to do it "your way." When you determine what you "love" to do, you access your inner power. In this way, you enlighten your journey by the light of your true passion. One of the first steps toward your million-dollar goal must be to determine which of the many million-dollar ideas that flow into your mind actually fits "who you are."

Just like the surface of each of the cells in your body is covered in "receptor" molecules that let certain substances into your cell—like a lock and key—your emotional body is the receptor of certain ideas, thoughts, and feelings. When you encounter certain ideas, the "receptor" cells on your emotional "body" receive these thoughts and accept them and process them. They just "fit" who you are. They feel natural. Second nature.

In much the same way, you are destined to process the world around you by almost unconsciously receiving, pondering, and processing ideas that are perfectly suited to you. You have enlightened millions waiting for you, if you can just align your emotional body receptors to the floating enlightened concepts swirling around you. We'll cover this in more detail on pages 41–55.

Inner Wealth

A KEY CONCEPT OF ENLIGHTENED WEALTH IS THE UNDERSTANDING that wealth is not just material. Most of the jealousy, envy, theft, and crime in the world today is based on the principle of scarcity. With only a few scarce resources to go around, the rich will obviously get richer and the poor will get poorer.

Richer or poorer in what way?

According to one Harvard study, up to 75% of the value in a major corporation is made up of intangible assets—human capital, organization capital, information capital, culture capital, leadership capital, brand value, and customer loyalty. If most of the value is hidden, why don't we focus on this?

We believe that people will be much happier, more productive, and more successful if they quit focusing on their external assets and focus more attention on internal, intangible assets. Every person in the free world already possesses assets worth in excess of a million dollars.

Skeptical?

Would you sell your eyes for a million dollars? You wouldn't?! Well, since you "own" your eyeballs, but refuse to sell them, then you must own assets that have value in the millions. Would you sell off 20 points of your IQ to the highest bidder? Or your creativity for a million? You already are an Enlightened Millionaire! Even if you don't have a penny in the bank, you "own" assets that are extraordinarily valuable.

It is the wise use of your internal assets that you will "parlay" into millions of enlightened dollars in short order. Inner wealth is the source of all outer wealth. No inner wealth—no external money. Most of us feel "broke" and unworthy to be wealthy, when truth be told, all of us are wealthy. You don't need anything else. We want to show you how to parlay what you already have into millions.

How can we be so bold? Remember our reality TV show?

We see ourselves literally knocking on selected doors all over the world. Inside each home, we will show the occupants how the millions they long for have their source right in their immediate living quarters. Where they currently live! The money is all around them—hidden. The clues to the money are screaming at them—if they'll just learn how to listen.

We want to show you how you are sitting in the middle of riches; invisible assets surround you, million-dollar ideas are swirling around you, angels are anticipating the opportunity to assist you. Literally. For real. No kidding. If 75% of your value is hidden, what are *your* invisible, underutilized assets?

The entire world of business operates off a standard "balance sheet" that lists assets and liabilities, debts and ownerships. But over three-quarters of the value of the entire company resides in the brains, the minds, and the hearts of the people who work there. The brand asset and all of the things that do not exist on a traditional balance sheet are the source of the strength of the entire company. Everyone in the enterprise is already an Enlightened Millionaire, endowed with the incredible talents, gifts, connections, and ideas that, when unleashed inside that enterprise, can unleash enormous fortunes for everyone.

To allow an accountant, CPA, banker, or financier to reduce the wealth of a company to a few simple lines of numbers on an endarkened "out-of-balance" sheet to represent the *real* value of that company is a tragedy. Instead of trying to generate numbers every 90 days to satisfy the needs of people who are chasing the wrong goals, let's focus on more enlightened bottom lines.

In the old capitalism, greed was good. In the new paradigm of Enlightened Entrepreneurship, greed is banished. Let it skulk away back into the shadows.

The G used to stand for greed. The G now stands for giving. The whole purpose for the enterprise—to enlighten that enterprise—is not to get but to give.

—ROBERT COLLIER the means you have, and as you proceed in this spirit the way will open for you to do more.

MORMON • Begin to free yourself at once by doing all that is possible with

Giving

THE THIRD PRINCIPLE OF ENLIGHTENED WEALTH IS GIVING. America is the richest nation on earth because it gives more in public and private philanthropy than all the other nations on earth combined. A billionaire from the last century, John D. Rockefeller, said it best: "Think of giving not as a duty but as a privilege." Why is it a privilege? Because giving lubricates the process of wealth building.

You can see at our website, **www.millionairehalloffame.com,** that our students have earned hundreds of millions of dollars of profits from using our strategies. But more heartwarming are the tens of millions of dollars that these same students have already donated to charitable causes.

We believe that giving is essential to long-term wealth. Givers get. It is our belief that money flows fastest to those who most anticipate the joy of sharing it. Giving primes the pump of the universe.

$$\frac{[(c+a)-7+x] \div (8+18-20)}{(8aw)-1823} = \frac{(8e-n) \times 5+2220}{25a+e78+c^2}$$

#14 _____

In 1975, at age 19, a young man from Seattle founded a company called Microsoft. In less than 25 years, he topped the list as the World's Wealthiest Person. How did he do it? Were he and his partner, Paul Allen, just in the right place at the right time? Was it their extraordinary genius, focus, and drive? Or was it their luck, pluck, and shrewd business acumen? All of this, and more. But rather than asking "how" they did it, here is a more interesting question: "Why" did Gates become so successful?

Did Higher Power know in 1975 that computers were going to be the next "big thing"? Was Higher Power the "invisible hand" that orchestrated the "chance" meetings, partnerships, and ideas that would eventually launch Microsoft? Did Higher Power know that this corporation would eventually employ more than 50,000 people worldwide? Did Higher Power know that the Bill and Melinda Gates Foundation would become the wealthiest charitable foundation in the world, donating tens of billions of dollars toward global health and learning?

Where do million- and billion-dollar ideas come from? From human ingenuity. Where does *that* come from? We believe the source of brilliant ideas is Higher Power who plants them in people who are destined to bring them to fruition.

Which comes first, the chicken or the egg? Does a person first make millions and then get the idea to give millions away or does the idea that launches a successful business get downloaded into the mind of a latent, potential giver—destined to succeed massively and then give vast amounts of the profits away?

Not All Successful Businesses Are Enlightened!

If 95% of new businesses fail in the first five years, what can we learn from the 5% of businesses that succeed? Survivors fall into three camps.

The smallest group of "survivors" is the most visible. The Gordon Gekkos of the world operate their endarkened businesses on "stingy values" and "money-centric" principles. They worship at the altar of increasing profits at the expense of everything else. The front pages of the newspapers are filled with the drama of their rise and demise, giving the impression that they represent all businesses.

The next, and largest, group of the 5% survivors are those stable, ethical businesses that succeed due to a lot of hard work, persistence, and smart business practice. They latched on to a Great Idea and ran with it—without giving much credit or blame to a connection with Higher Power. Many of the recent winners in this group fall under the banner of "corporate social responsibility." Social capitalism is a major trend whereby corporations plan to be better world citizens by being more socially and environmentally responsible. This is proving to be a smart business approach and a useful branding strategy. But this is *not* what we are referring to as enlightened entrepreneurs.

#15
_____

The third and most rapidly growing group are true Enlightened Enterprises. Some of the most successful businesses are built on the foundation of Higher Power principles. To name a few: Newman's Own, The Body Shop, Stonyfield Farms, Ben and Jerry's Ice Cream, and Oprah, and there are hundreds of others. And, more important, lots of new businesses are being born that are purposefully Higher Powered. Their foundation is spiritually based (notice, we didn't say "religiously" based). At the core of the Enlightened Enterprise is the specific desire to bring Higher Power into the boardroom—in a very general way—to ask the question: How would Higher Power run this business? Even if the business doesn't produce an overtly spiritual product, with the right attitude its business can be enlightened.

Do the Best Ideas Come to the Ones Who Are the Biggest Givers?

Why did Henry Ford persist through several bankruptcies to become the icon of the fledgling automotive industry? Where did the idea for Henry Ford's "assembly line" come from? How did Ford recognize it? Did Higher Power know that Henry Ford would eventually set up a foundation that would take the profits from the idea of the motorcar and funnel hundreds of millions of dollars to less fortunate people?

Where did the idea for using oil as fuel come from? How did Rockefeller recognize it? Did Higher Power know in 1870 that Rockefeller would create Standard Oil and eventually create a foundation that would give away hundreds of millions of dollars?

Where did steel come from? How did Andrew Carnegie recognize it? Did Higher Power know in 1872 that Andrew Carnegie would eventually create the world's largest steel company? Did Higher Power know that the profits would eventually be *all* given away to fund 2,800 libraries all across America? We would like to suggest that the answer is yes.

Do the best ideas flow to those who dedicate themselves to the process of becoming the biggest givers? If you got a billion-dollar idea, what would you do with the accumulated wealth? Could Higher Power trust you with it? What would you use it for?

Here's the *real* bottom line: An Enlightened Enterprise needs to be refocused on giving. It reshapes its entire mission to be a company that gives. Its success is based on its desire to give, not its desire to make a profit. Profits are secondary. Giving comes first.

Whether you are a country, a company, or a character, your GDP (gross domestic product, profit, or prosperity) is directly linked not just to giving but to *giving first*. From macro to micro, this rule holds true. It models the Higher Power pattern.

Great givers pattern their life after Higher Power . . . the greatest giver of all. As the scripture says, "And God said, Let us make man in our image, after our likeness. . . . So God created man in his own image, in the image of God created he him; male and female created he them." One of the key "likenesses" we inherited through our divine DNA was our giving nature.

Form the habit that many mega-successful entrepreneurs including Oprah have in common. Give 10% of your money away. But we encourage an even more focused habit—give away the *first* 10% of your profit to those who need it. Do it first. Do it fast. Do it foremost. Do it with a giving heart.

But here's the caveat. Be careful *how* you give.

In a capitalistic society, every expenditure of money can be viewed as an investment. Giving can be mistakenly viewed as a way of depositing your money in the Bank of Higher Power while praying for a better, and more immediate, return on your investment.

4 16 17 24 11 1 16 3 12 15 4 6 19 6 11 4

#16 _____

We suggest that you *don't* treat giving or tithing or charitable donations this way. Don't count your hoped-for profits that Higher Power will deposit into your future bank account. Don't expect Higher Power to "bless" you with more money because you bought a Higher-Powered certificate of deposit. Don't claim your inheritance in heaven as part of the trillion that you will eventually get because you kept the "commandments" here. May we humbly suggest, *don't* think of your charitable giving as a return on your investment.

Today, 1.3 billion people earn less than a dollar to live on. Half of the world's population lives on less than two dollars a day. Compared with them, you're already so wealthy. It is only in comparing your house or car or job to the rich elite in your own city or country that you might feel poor. But to the rest of the world, *you* are the elite rich. Many of the world's poor would sacrifice a kidney to trade places with you—as financially strapped as you might think you are. In truth, because of your health or your citizenship or your education or your opportunities, you've already received a vast fortune from Higher Power. You're already living the "blessed" lifestyle. You've already won the lottery.

Be so grateful for what you have already received that you voluntarily agree to "pay it forward" for the rest of your life . . . without expecting a penny back. It is from this place of overflowing gratitude that your enlightened million-dollar successes begin.

When your giving truly becomes a privilege and not an investment, then Higher Power discerns that you can handle money and will bless you with even more.

Higher Power

THE "H" IN THE WORD *LIGHT* STANDS FOR HIGHER POWER. NINETY-five percent of North Americans believe in a Higher Power, although they may use different descriptions. For most people, even the mention of Higher Power is politically incorrect. Many business leaders, afraid of offending their customers, keep their own spiritual views private. But in our experience, people are hungry for a spiritual approach to business. The world is ready for it.

We believe that business is spiritual. Money is spiritual. Everything is spiritual. Materialism is only grossly material when it is grossly negligent, grossly selfish, and grossly greedy. But material things invested in the most valuable assets—people—in helping resolve their needs, is the most spiritual thing you can do. If your profits are infused with spirit, Higher Power can direct you where the money is to be sent.

Cracking the Wealth Code

Your enlightened enterprise is a locked vault. Higher Power knows the code. Higher Power knows the exact numbers, the exact sequence. Higher Power knows the fastest way to unlock your door.

You can take the slow way to discover that same code for yourself. It's called trial and error. If you have enough time and enough money, you can test a thousand products to find the one that seems to have the greatest market potential. Ninety-five percent of them will potentially fail.

You can also imitate other people's products to borrow the codes that they've cracked through trial and error. You can study the general principles of business and marketing and apply these concepts to your ideas. You can learn a lot from your own experience about which codes seem to work most of the time. Over a lifetime you become a code cracker—able to figure out how to get inside your own vault.

But there is a source for your perfect code right now. Higher Power knows the secret numbers to every vault of your business. Higher Power knows which ideas to focus on and which ideas to forget. Higher Power knows which team members to assemble and which ones you need to let go. Higher Power knows which marketing messages will reach the right people immediately.

The combination of marketing words is every bit as important and powerful as the combination of numbers on a safety deposit box. If done in the right order and the right combination, the words of your marketing message open up vast fortunes much more quickly, much more easily.

So the code is unlocked. It is revealed to you number by number by number, so that you can create a product that is enlightened and will be recognized by those customers who were destined to see it. They say, "That's it. I knew that was it." They follow their intuition, not even knowing why. They literally come to you slowly at first but then bring their friends with them.

"Come. Jim. Kim. Fred. Maria. Come! I found a product! An enlightened product! You have got to see this."

It is enlightened word of mouth. The business starts to grow.

How could it not grow?

The only danger is that the Enlightened Entrepreneur loses sight of where the business is actually coming from. He or she begins to feel it's his or her own brilliance and hard work that brought it all about. The cholesterol of greed starts flowing in their veins and the plaque of pride starts to build up in their arteries. They stop giving and start hoarding, and that brings on the inevitable heart attack. The stroke of selfishness blocks them from the thoughts that could enlighten them.

#17 _____

That's why Enlightened Entrepreneurs need the constant nourishment of nutrients of an enlightened life. The nutrients of humility. The nutrients of gratitude. The nutrients of openness and positivity. The nutrients of happiness and the nutrients of joy. The nutrients of faith. The nutrients of trust. The nutrients of connection with your Higher Power.

Trustee of Residual Philanthropy

THE T IN THE LIGHT PRINCIPLES REPRESENTS THE WORD TRUSTEE. In the legal world, a trustee is someone who holds the assets of a trust to distribute them to the beneficiaries. You are the trustee of your wealth. Your enlightened fiduciary responsibility is to maximize the assets of the trust for your loved ones and for generations of future beneficiaries. Capitalism is all about ownership . . . of real property or intellectual property. With enlightened capitalism, it's not ownership that counts. It's stewardship. Stewardship, or trusteeship, is about achieving success because you don't want to own anything; you simply want to control the flow of it through you. You then become the temporary custodian, not the permanent owner. You make it, enjoy it, use it, take good care of it, maintain it, clean it up, improve it, and then prepare it to hand off to the next generation or the next custodian.

The capitalistic concept of ownership is really based on scarcity: "There is only one of these. I own it. You don't. I have the power. You don't."

Stewardship is very different. It is founded on abundance. When you get a million-dollar idea and realize that you're stewarding it for all the rest of humankind, then it really enlarges you. You are abundantly receiving brilliant ideas so that you can share them as quickly as you possibly can with the rest of humanity.

As Dr. Buckminster Fuller said, "Sharing is having more."

People who become good stewards do it for themselves or family, then their state, then their country, then the world.

The Poster Boy for Enlightened Wealth Is Mr. Paul Newman

In 1982 Paul Newman and his lawyer friend A. E. Hotchner launched a business called Newman's Own. It was dedicated to selling Paul Newman's special brand of natural salad dressing with the goal of donating all of their profits to charity. They broke all of the traditional rules of marketing and good business practices and still ended up earning over a million dollars in profit in their first full year of business. Today, over 20 years later, they are closing in on $200 million worth of enlightened profit . . . and climbing.

Question: Where did the original idea for Newman's salad dressing originate? If you say that it was Newman's fame that made the company successful, then ask a deeper question—where did Newman's fame originate? Did Higher Power know decades earlier when Paul Newman was a *nobody* graduating "magna cum lager" from *nowhere* Kenyon College that he would parlay his eventual fame into an ongoing residual philanthropy that would give away hundreds of millions of dollars?

Newman calls it the "shameless exploitation in pursuit of the common good." This is a model that anyone can duplicate.

The world has known lots of economic models: monarchism, feudalism, socialism, communism, capitalism.

It's time for a new model. The next wave is Enlightened Entrepreneurship, where you come from abundance, you create massive value for other people, and you leave a legacy.

This is a book about creating massive, passive cash flow . . . for yourself and for the world. If you think you can handle the prosperity that Higher Power is ready to shower on you, then read on.

Chapter Two

THE FOUR KEY
WEALTH CODES

Have you ever had a million-dollar idea? Did you ever say to your-self, "Hey, that's a great idea," then let the idea fade away without acting on it, only to discover several months later that someone else had capitalized on "your" idea? Most of us have great ideas yet we simply don't know what to do with them. Ideas are the seeds of future fortunes. Sometimes a simple idea can even grow into billions.

In the summer of 1990, on a train to London, Joanne Rowling got her billion-dollar idea. As she relates it, "All of a sudden the idea for Harry just appeared in my mind's eye. I can't tell you why or what triggered it. But I saw the idea of Harry and the wizard school very plainly. I suddenly had this basic idea of a boy who didn't know who he was, who didn't know he was a wizard until he got his invitation to wizard school. I have never been so excited by an idea."

As soon as she began to write, her life was thrown into turmoil by a series of events: the death of her 45-year-old mother from multiple sclerosis, her marriage to an abusive husband, a miscarriage, the birth of her first child, a divorce, being fired, trying to raise a child on government welfare. Four years after the initial Harry Potter "brainstorm," J. K. Rowling, as she now calls herself, decided to do what she was destined to do and wrote the book that would make her a billionaire and the richest woman in England.

Did you ever have an idea like that? Did you know what to do with it?

In May 1994—the same year that 28-year-old J. K. Rowling was toiling to

Yrma Rico

Yrma Rico has done the impossible. Born one of seven children to migrant worker parents, she knew in her heart that fieldwork offered her no future. She was told that only men needed an education, but instead of going along with that idea she educated herself.

In Fresno, California, 17-year-old Yrma read an advertisement for a dental assistant. When she applied for the position, the dentist asked her if she had training as a dental hygienist; she did not. She countered his quick rejection by saying that she spoke eloquent English and Spanish where he did not—and he needed her because most of his patients were Spanish-speaking. Three days later he called and hired her.

Yrma Rico learned fast and became a great asset to the dentist she worked for.

In the very limited spare time available to a single mom with two small children, Yrma, sometimes working three jobs just to feed her kids, earned her GED—high school equivalency degree. When she took a job selling radio advertising in Fresno, she discovered that she had a great talent for selling. She also saw a gigantic potential in the underserved Hispanic market. She knew from personal experience that even when English-speaking Hispanics get home they want to listen to Spanish-speaking radio and watch Spanish-speaking television and read in their native language. She wisely, actively, and aggressively sought out that market.

Her successes came to the attention of her influential peers. They asked her if she wanted to be an owner and partner putting together independent small Hispanic television and radio stations with print media around the country. She did. Being part of a minority helped her group to buy their first FM station in Fresno. She struggled to put together her $3,000 investment to add to her sweat equity for station ownership. After Fresno, Yrma and her colleagues acquired stations in Dallas, Denver, Providence, and everywhere.

→

finish *Harry Potter*—a 30-year-old researcher was sitting at his desk in a New York skyscraper. As he read reports about the growing Internet phenomenon, an idea struck him. "It was a wake-up call. I started thinking, OK, what kind of business opportunity might there be here?" Fueled by this hunch, he quit his job, borrowed his parents' life savings, drove his wife to Seattle, and launched Amazon.com from their rented two-bedroom house. Five years later, Jeff Bezos was *Time* magazine's Person of the Year as well as a billionaire 10 times over. By this time, billionaire Bezos had sold a lot of billionaire Rowling's books.

Ifit 'sbe endo ne,I t'sd oabl e;th eref ore, youc an doit.

#18 _____

Think of how many success stories begin with a single, simple idea. Michael Dell started his company, Dell, from his college dorm room. Twenty years later he was the world's youngest billionaire. Sam Walton opened the first Wal-Mart store in Rogers, Arkansas, in 1962. Today, Wal-Marts crowd out the sun. This largest retailer in the world gives over $100 million in charitable contributions annually. All this from a simple idea of everyday low prices—and, yes, a lot of hard work.

There are thousands more unknown millionaires and multimillionaires who turned ideas into huge fortunes. Have you heard of these names?

Frank Woodward
Jacob Davis
Ida Rosenthal
Earl Tupper
Margaret Rudkin

Today, either at home or at work, you will most likely pass by one or more of these products:

Over an eight-year period, their little network became Univision, now the biggest Hispanic broadcaster in America. Before going public for $720 million dollars, they offered Yrma Rico a $500,000 buyout package. She did not accept, but gambled and won big-time. That day, Rico was driving to a sales call when shares opened at $16.50, and her net worth instantly soared to $20 million.

The money changed her life, ending all her stress and anxiety about her tomorrows. She bought homes in Mexico and a bigger home in Denver. She opened a marketing agency dedicated to reaching the Hispanic market. She became a major stockholder in Fresno's biggest BMW dealership. She has written a bestselling book called *La Vida Rica,* "the rich life." The assistant who typed the book found it awakened her own aspirations. She started a translating company, got a small business loan, and has built a burgeoning empire of her own. Everyone who gets in Rico's orbit, hears her speak, or reads her books gets inspired to be all they can be, to do all they can do, and to give all they can give.

Jell-O
Levi's
Maidenform bras
Tupperware
Pepperidge Farm

Just as Frank Woodward came up with Jell-O, we believe that you, too, have a million-dollar idea that could eventually be a household name. *Cracking the Millionaire Code* is not just another book on how to turn ideas into millions. This is a book on how *you* can discover the *fastest* possible way for you to create Enlightened Wealth. We believe that you were born to have an enlightened million-dollar idea, an idea that is unique and special to you. Your "enlightened" opportunity can generate fortunes for you and for dozens, perhaps hundreds, of others. It can provide livelihoods for hundreds, even thousands, of employees. It can create residual philanthropy to bless the lives of tens of thousands, perhaps millions of people. The fastest and perhaps the *only* way for you to accomplish this is to build upon the principles of Enlightened Wealth.

HOW TO CRACK THE WEALTH CODES

To transform an idea in your head into a stream of checks into your mailbox, you will need to crack the four specific wealth codes of an Enlightened Enterprise.

Code One.   The Destiny Code
Code Two.   The Prism Code
Code Three. The Angel Code
Code Four.   The Star Code

Each code is essential to your success, although not all of them need to be cracked at once or in any specific order. The following description is just a brief taste. We'll get to the full-course meal in later chapters.

The Destiny Code

TO CRACK THE DESTINY CODE YOU MUST DISCOVER YOUR UNIQUE place in the universe. You arrived here on planet earth encoded with divine DNA—a specific set of talents, gifts, opportunities, connections, and sensitivities. We believe you have a destiny to fulfill. There is music in you, a song you were destined to sing, or an instrument you were destined to play in the symphony of life. Some people discover their destiny quickly. Some take decades to do so, and others never even look for it. When you tap into this pure vein of gold, you become who you were born to be. Psychologist Abraham Maslow called it *self-actualization.* More recently, bestselling author Rick Warren called it *the purpose-driven life.*

4624463 255 958 226 4483.   4483 255 968 226 462 4463.

#19 _____

Whatever you call it, you'll know it when you've found it. You'll just *sense* that you are doing what you were born to do. Money flows faster toward you, but you don't do what you're doing just for the money. Quite the contrary, you would do it for free if they weren't willing to pay you so much. Those who crack the Destiny Code are the truly wealthy. Everyone else is a wannabe. (Aren't we all wannabes until we finally realize who we really *are*?)

The Prism Code

DESTINY IS THE PATH YOU CHOOSE. PRISM IS THE VEHICLE YOU navigate down that path. Prism is our description of the specific product or service that sets you apart—that displays your talents and gifts to the world. When you've discovered your prism, you don't earn a living, you earn a "loving." Your prism refracts your talent into a kaleidoscope of income streams.

The same year that J. K. Rowling was starving to write *Harry Potter* and Jeff Bezos was scrambling to launch Amazon.com, another billion-dollar business was being born. Ty Warner owned a fairly successful toy business but an idea was brewing inside him for a new, inexpensive, cute plush toy. He called it a Beanie Baby. Little did he realize that Beanie Babies would become the fastest-growing collectible toy in history and would land him on the *Forbes* list of the 100 Richest People in the World.

Although you may hear talk of the bursting of the Beanie Baby bubble, the toys still bring in three-quarters of a billion dollars a year. Not bad for a simple idea, brilliantly executed! Now Ty Warner is using his billions to fund other acquisitions and charitable causes. The code he cracked to launch Ty into the stratosphere is what we call the Prism Code. It was a unique way of breaking through the confusion of the toy market. Mr. Warner is a very private person who rarely gives interviews, but if we could interview him we bet he would tell a fascinating tale of how the idea first formed in his mind. The white light of a Higher-Powered inspiration shone through the prism of his talents and experience to shower the world with a rainbow of smiles.

Among the greatest crackers of the Prism Code is George Washington Carver, sometimes called the "inventor" of the peanut. Though Carver was born a Missouri slave, his research developed 325 products from peanuts, 108 applications for sweet potatoes, 75 products derived from pecans, and over 500 dyes and pigments from 28 different plants.

More important, in cracking the Prism Code he achieved his destiny. The products he derived from the peanut and the soybean revolutionized the economy of the South by liberating it from an excessive dependence on cotton. By 1938, five years before his death, peanuts had become a $200 million industry and a chief product of Alabama.

Cracking your Prism Code is a process that you'll learn in Chapter 5 to help you transform your simple idea into Enlightened Wealth–producing products, ideas, and services.

The Angel Code

YOU CAN'T DO IT ALONE. YOU NEED A TEAM. FORTUNATELY, THERE are people who were destined to be on your team. They'll help you fulfill your destiny, and you'll help them fulfill theirs. They bring the missing pieces of the puzzle. Your picture is not complete without them. How do you find them? How will they be attracted to you? How will you know you can trust them? This is all part of cracking the Angel Code.

We've used the word *angel* because it conveys the feeling you'll get when you find the right team players to contribute their expertise and experience. You'll feel as if they are heaven-sent. And who is to say that they aren't? We'll show you how to form an Inner Circle, your core team. We'll show you how to add a Virtual Circle of imaginary geniuses to tap into their brilliance. We'll show you how to create a Winner's Circle of 101 key contacts and resources to help you pull off your idea. We'll show you that every resource you'll need is at most three telephone calls away. We'll show you how to tap into the Circle of Life—the six and a half billion customers who populate this planet. And finally, we'll show you how to access the Eternal Circle—the invisible angel network.

Your team is formed of angels, visible and invisible. Do angels exist? Do they want you to succeed? Will they help you? These are questions that you will answer by cracking the Angel Code.

Speaking of Angel Codes, Oprah Winfrey cracked her code when she created the Angel Network in 1997. Since then her donations from celebrities and viewers of her program have given millions of dollars to charities. She's been given the stewardship of great wealth because she has a Higher Power purpose to use it to enlighten the lives of others.

The Star Code

THIS VERY MOMENT, THOUSANDS OF ENLIGHTENED CUSTOMERS ARE waiting for you to create an Enlightened Enterprise to serve them. If you build it, will they come?

8O, 6W, 2L, 2N, 2T, 1A, 1E, 1D, 1R, 1U, 1Y, 1V

#20 ___ __ _____ __ _____ ____ ___, ___!

If it's your destiny to do it . . . if your idea is Higher Powered . . . if your team is attracted by Serendestiny™ . . . then, yes. They will come. They will most definitely come.

The 1989 movie *Field of Dreams* tells the story of an Iowa farmer, Ray Kinsella, played by Kevin Costner. One day, in his cornfield, Ray hears a voice, "If you build it, he will come." And with it comes a vision of a baseball diamond in the middle of his Iowa cornfield. He follows the voice and builds the baseball diamond and then the "hard facts of life" intrude. Pressured by bankruptcy, Ray is faced with a decision: Should he sell his farm or continue to pursue his dream? At this point in the movie, James Earl Jones delivers a spine-tingling soliloquy.

> *"People will come, Ray. They'll come to Iowa for reasons they can't even fathom. They'll turn up your driveway, not knowing for sure why they're doing it. They'll arrive at your door as innocent as children longing for the past. 'Of course, we won't mind if you look around,' you'll say. 'It's only 20 dollars per person.' They'll pass over the money without even thinking about it—where it is money they have and peace they lack. And they'll walk out to the bleachers in shirtsleeves on a perfect afternoon and find they have reserved seats somewhere along one of the baselines where they sat when they were children and cheered their heroes and they'll watch the game. And it will be as if they dipped themselves in magic waters. The memories will be so thick, they'll have to brush them from their faces. Oh, people will come, Ray. People will most definitely come."*

As the closing movie credits roll, the headlights from a long line of cars are seen flowing toward the isolated baseball diamond in the middle of the Iowa cornfields. People are definitely coming.

That's fine for a movie, but how do you make that happen in the real world? As someone once asked us, "Instead of fishing for customers, how do you get them to jump into your boat?"

Cracking the Star Code is the process of discovering and serving a very special group of customers—treating them like the stars they are. How would

Higher Power treat them so they would keep coming back and bring their friends with them? Of all the codes to crack, this one is the easiest to envision and the hardest one to regularly implement. The success rate of start-up businesses would soar if each new entrepreneur would simply focus on cracking this one code.

Each of the codes requires special "code-cracking" techniques. And imagine how your life will transform when, one by one, you crack them all. Imagine waking each morning knowing that you are on your destined path. Imagine yourself as the leader of an enterprise that earns staggering profits by delivering enlightened products and services.

Imagine an "enlightened word of mouth" that drives an endless stream of new customers through your doors. Imagine a team of people trained to take care of them—not just traditional employees, but angels. For them, work is not work, but sheer joy. Imagine the charitable work you could do with the profits that flow to you. Imagine rising every morning as the sun warms the new day and realizing that your Enlightened Enterprise is blessing you and everyone it serves. You've got it all: friends and fortune, health and wealth, influence and affluence.

Would you like that?

Here's how you'll get it. Destiny. Prism. Angel. Star.

Chapter Three

THE DESTINY CODE

CODES ARE EVERYWHERE.

Zip codes. Gate codes. Area codes. Bar codes. PIN codes. Pass codes. Secret codes. Postal codes. Country codes. Morse codes. Membership codes. Security codes. Color codes. Genetic codes. Entry codes. Exit codes. You can't live without codes.

Codes give you entry to your house, your garage, your car, your office, your telephone messages, your computer, your e-mail. Have you ever been locked out because you forgot or lost a code? Without the right codes *you can't get in!*

There are dozens of types of coding devices: numbered key pads, membership cards, garage door clickers, uniforms, name badges, registration stickers, passwords, tickets. What is the purpose of all of the various coding methods?

To restrict access to Unauthorized people.

In war, messages are encoded (or encrypted) before being sent to protect essential information from falling into enemy hands. Then, the same messages are decoded (or deciphered) when they are received at the other end.

Brandon Barnum

"When you borrow a million, the bank owns you; when you borrow over $100 million, you own the bank," says Brandon Barnum, creative financier par excellence. Brandon has big dreams. He wants to refinance the world's debt and save the world with philanthropy through his new foundation, Giving Globally. Brandon has learned to return by tithing and giving. He is so enthusiastic that he wants to inspire givers to double their giving too, and to help create a trillion dollars in tithing by 2014. He is like Andrew Carnegie, who said, "I'll spend the first half of my life earning a vast fortune and the second half of my life giving it away, while doing the least harm and the most good."

Although he is only 34 years old, Brandon Barnum owns an exceedingly fast-growing company—Integrity Commercial Lending—headquartered in Portland, Oregon, and doing business worldwide. He loves to speak, teach, and inspire people, especially young people, to convey the idea that lenders are your friends and want to serve you and your future. He and his team delight in assisting people to achieve what they didn't know they could. He funds businesses and real estate in innovative ways to provide the money they need.

One example of a company that he is helping to finance is Plantation Timber, a company producing the world's fastest-growing tree, called a paulownia tree. Paulownia trees are unique, lightweight hardwoods that originate in China, where, because they do not rot, they are used to build boat docks. The trees can drink 80 gallons of polluted water per day, cleaning the air and the soil simultaneously through a process called *photoremediation.* Capable of growing up to 30 feet in a single year, paulownia trees are the hope of a world that desperately needs both hardwoods and a clean environment.

According to Stanford biologist Dr. Paul Erhlich, the world currently has a shortfall of 18 billion trees, trees that are the lungs of the earth.

→

. . .

ONE NIGHT WHILE babysitting, a grandfather passed his grand-daughter's room and overheard her repeating the alphabet in an oddly reverent fashion. "What on earth are you up to?" he asked. "I'm saying my prayers," explained the little girl. "But I can't think of exactly the right words tonight so I'm just saying all of the letters. God will put them together for me because He knows what I'm thinking."

Some codes *operate outside* of your awareness. Your computer automatically encodes your e-mail into binary code and transmits it over the Internet to the receiving computer, where the zeroes and ones are unscrambled, reassembled, deciphered, or decoded. Voilà!

Some codes you consciously *create* for yourself, such as the security code for your new burglar alarm system or the PIN code for your new ATM card.

Some codes are *freely given* to you: zip codes and area codes; or the gate code for your new home in a gated community.

The most important codes in life may be the ones you discover. These are the hidden messages floating about you just waiting for you to decipher them, to become aware of them. Higher Power is sending each of us messages every minute of every day. It's our destiny to decipher them. Crack these codes and the world is yours.

Higher Power has a mission for you, if you choose to accept it. First you've got to find it. Flipping through the channels of life's everyday transmissions, you vaguely sense that there is something *big* that you're supposed to be doing with your life. You feel that something is missing in the equation of your life, yet you're not quite sure what. It has something to do with peace and happiness and making a difference. And prosperity. Yes. Lots of prosperity. You were meant to be on TV, not watching TV! The secrets are hidden right in front of you if you could just decode them. Arerzeagaipbteparpa insecrsspostetcountalMorrymembershsesecuripcoltygenetorenticexryphoit computne **(#21)** _____ Rule!

Inspired by the potential in Plantation Timber, Brandon Barnum personally invested in the company and found a clever way to fund it. Plantation Timber presells contracts for future full-grown trees. These contracts are financed by life insurance company annuities before trees are even planted. The insurance companies make lease payments to the tree farmers, our planet gets reforested, global warming is addressed, trees are grown and readied for multiple uses, and money is circulated in a conscious way—everyone wins and no one loses.

Where normal financiers tremble at such thinking, Brandon revels in the possibilities to make the world a better place using our great free enterprise system. Normal loans require backup assets, a financial report and/or equities—stocks, funds, collateral, cash or cash flow—to make a loan. Brandon and his team are dedicated to thinking through all the many possibilities for putting money together and teaching the borrower what to do and how to do it. Brandon happily teaches borrowers how they can go to the bank, make pledges to maximize their personal credit profile and raise their ratings, just as the automobile and real estate industry does. There is no limit, Brandon feels, to how big his operation can become, as he serves ever more people, ever better. He revels in the speed of his loans, some as fast as three days. Some of the current projects he is working on range from a $10 million dollar hotel purchase to a $600 million dollar construction project in Venezuela.

Brandon Branum's vision for the world is his brainchild, Giving Globally. Brandon spent a weeklong vacation in Maui, writing out all his lifetime goals, the biggest of which is to double global philanthropy by January 8, 2020. He is committed to building relationships with the richest and most influential people in the world, challenging them to do more and give more to the world's less fortunate. Giving Globally encompasses all philanthropies and will provide them with cutting-edge Web-based tools to expand their outreach and impact. Brandon has created a dream team that works together to create more financial and volunteer support for needy causes than has ever been raised before. He intends to use the power of

→

What if you could see your life through the eyes of the richest person in the world? Mike Murphy, a retired VP from Microsoft, described what it was like to be in meetings with Bill Gates. "My own mind works like an ordinary spreadsheet—a few columns wide and a few columns deep. Bill Gates's spreadsheet is 1,000 columns wide and 1,000 columns deep *plus* a third dimension of 1,000 columns out. He seems to be able to see it all at once and connects insignificant data in one cell with unimportant chunks of information in another cell. Then, he links the two cells into a brilliant *aha*. It's amazing."

What if you could see your life through the eyes of a billionaire? Well, there's something even better. Imagine seeing it through Higher Power eyes. Imagine that! With infinite awareness, imagine how everything might look different. Through Higher Power eyes, every opportunity you see has infinite potential—because you immediately perceive how to parlay it into the most profitable future. Every product you try to market has infinite exposure because you know the names and addresses of at least 500 million people who want it, need it, can afford it, and are ready to buy it *now*. Every person you meet is six degrees of separation from every resource you need. You don't just see a person; you immediately discern that this is the friend of the sister of the gardener's cousin who is the personal trainer to the president of the company that wants to buy every product you can manufacture for the next 10 years. Higher Power is infinitely aware of every connection.

With so much infinite awareness, why doesn't Higher Power just give us the codes? Wouldn't that be simpler? Easier? Yes, but ease is not what life is all about. Life is a university. We came here to get our doctorate degree. Would you respect a college professor who stood in front of his freshman math class and said the following? "Welcome, class. This is going to be the easiest semester of your life. No lectures. No class work. No homework. The final exam will be a snap. Just take this cheat sheet with you to the test and copy down the answers and you'll get an automatic A."

Students might flock to such a class but once the administration got wind of it, that professor's destiny would be a new career: "Would you like fries with that?"

The term *doctor* comes from Latin meaning "teacher." There are two

publicity and great media to inspire and challenge the world. He plans to introduce people to causes and philanthropies that make a lasting difference for those in need. He wants to take individuals on mission trips so that they can see just how great the need is and experience what a profound difference volunteerism makes both for the volunteer as well as those they are helping. Giving Globally is creating an international communication system to help people connect with a cause they are passionate about and receive updates about the work they are supporting.

One of the philanthropies that Brandon is vitally active in is Northwest Medical Teams International. They send doctors into war zones such as Iraq, Bosnia, and Kosovo to help the homeless, hungry, and hurting. As this is being written he is helping them raise $100 million. Brandon is a great, generous giver who has learned there is a limit to what he can give, but almost no limit to what he can do to inspire others to contribute through his vision, his passion for philanthropy, and his consummate abilities as a public speaker.

types of teachers: informational teachers and transformational teachers. The majority of our teachers are informational teachers. They lecture. You take notes. You take the test and then immediately throw away your notes and forget everything you've learned.

Higher Power is a master transformational teacher. The notes you take in HP's class are written on your heart and imprinted in every cell in your body. Discovery is the prime method of teaching. Questions prod discovery. Sometimes it is not very fun. Most of the time it's not very easy. Yet, it's always highly instructive. To help you discover the hidden codes of your destiny, Higher Power gives hints and clues. Higher Power knows your perfect path but won't deprive you of the joy of figuring it out for yourself.

· · ·

A THREE-YEAR-OLD BOY is playing outside in the backyard. He walks to the back screen door and tries to open it, but the door handle is just out of his reach. He can see his father inside on the couch. His father doesn't immediately get up and open the door. His father gives encouragement through the screen door. "You can do it." The child tries over and over again to open the door. In frustration, he begins to cry for help. The father comes over to the screen door and points to a wooden box next to the door. "Get the box and drag it over here." With great effort the boy drags the wooden crate and stands on it to reach the door handle. Then, he reaches his small fingers into the door crack and pries with all his might until the door finally opens wide enough to let him in. He rushes into his father's arms triumphantly. "I did it!" The father smiles. "Well done, my son. I knew you could do it."

MONEY FLOWS TO GREAT IDEAS

So what does all of this talk about destiny have to do with making some serious money? Well, as Robert Schuller (he's the famous televangelist of *The Hour of*

Power and the Crystal Cathedral) put it, "Money flows to great ideas." Do you want money to flow to you? If so, you need to discover the *Great Idea* that will define your life, the idea that you were destined to find. For MVH it was *Chicken Soup*. For RGA it was *Nothing Down*. Although we didn't know it at the time, we now realize how each of these ideas were downloaded into our minds—they were Higher Power–sent. These were not ordinary ideas. They were *mega*. Those two crazy ideas have generated over a billion dollars *each*. (That's gross income, not net! Substantial, nonetheless.)

nto;;osmy ofrsd vp,r gtp, Hpf ejp [;smyd yjr, om yjpdr [rp[;r
(omv;ifomh upi) ejp str frdyomrf yp ntomh yjr, yp gtioyopm/

#22 _____

_____

THE PATH TO GREAT IDEAS IS
THROUGH GREAT QUESTIONS

—

How do you recognize *your* Great Idea, the one that will flood your life with prosperity? That's a great question, isn't it? The primary methodology for discovering destiny-driven, million-dollar ideas is asking specific, targeted questions to a mind that is prepared to receive the Highest answer.

Your brain is the most powerful, versatile computer on the planet. Touch your forehead and say to yourself, "This is the most powerful computer on the planet!" Your powerful computer brain is activated and energized by asking powerful questions. If you constantly ask yourself, "Why am I so bad with money?" your brain will oblige by giving you a host of reasons. If you ask yourself instead, "How can I get better at handling my money and make it grow?" your brain will also help you uncover solutions. As Jean Houston, codirector of the Foundation for Mind Research, has said, "The primary purpose of your brain is to do *exactly* what you tell it to do." If you ask yourself disempowering questions, you will receive answers that reinforce your sense of powerlessness. If you ask yourself empowering questions, you will get powerful answers. If you ask yourself, "Why haven't I discovered my destiny yet?" your brain will catalogue a list of excuses. If you ask yourself questions like, "What do I love to do? What am I good at? What is important to me? What does Higher Power want me to do with my life?" the vague outline of your destiny will begin to materialize in the fog. Sometimes the answer distills on your soul like dew. Sometimes it comes in a flash of blinding insight.

How did an overflowing bathtub cause Archimedes to shout, "Eureka! I have found it"? How did a falling apple shake the concept of gravity from the brain of Sir Isaac Newton? What is it going to take for your destiny-saturated million-dollar idea to get shaken loose?

Here are a few questions: What does your million-dollar idea look like? Could you recognize your enlightened million-dollar idea if it flashed in front of your eyes? Do you have a sense that you were destined to be the conduit for some ideas that could improve the world? Does Higher Power know what your ideal million-dollar idea is? Are you the kind of person to whom Higher Power could entrust an enlightened million-dollar idea? Would you be charitable with the profits? Have you ever talked yourself out of acting upon a million-dollar idea? How could you be more receptive to the ideas that you're not noticing? Where have you been successful? How could you be even more successful? What do you need to do to take a quantum leap forward in your progress? The answers to these questions come when you pay attention to the Big Rocks.

THE BIG ROCKS

Stephen Covey shares a story in his book *First Things First* that made a profound impact on us.

> *I attended a seminar once where the instructor was lecturing on time. At one point, he said, "Okay, it's time for a quiz." He reached under the table and pulled out a wide-mouth gallon jar. He set it on the table next to a*

completeness must be understood by you and experienced in your thoughts as your own personal reality. —WAYNE DYER *platter with some fist-sized rocks on it. "How many of these rocks do you think we can get in the jar?" he asked.*

After we made our guess, he said, "Okay. Let's find out." He set one rock in the jar . . . then another . . . then another. I don't remember how many he got in, but he got the jar full. Then he asked, "Is that jar full?"

Everybody looked at the rocks and said, "Yes."

Then he said, "Ahhh." He reached under the table and pulled out a bucket of gravel. Then he dumped some gravel in and shook the jar and the gravel went in all the little spaces left by the big rocks. Then he grinned and said once more, "Is the jar full?"

By this time we were on to him. "Probably not," we said.

"Good!" he replied. And he reached under the table and brought out a bucket of sand. He started dumping the sand in and it went in all the little spaces left by the rocks and the gravel. Once more he looked at us and said, "Is the jar full?"

"No!" we all roared.

He said, "Good!" and he grabbed a pitcher of water and began to pour it in. He got something like a quart of water in that jar. Then he said, "Well, what's the point?"

Somebody said, "Well, there are gaps, and if you really work at it, you can always fit more into your life."

"No," he said, "that's not the point. The point is this: If you hadn't put these big rocks in first, would you ever have gotten any of them in?"

What Are the Big Rocks of an Enlightened Day?

Each day is a microcosm of an entire life. The alpha of your day is when the sun rises, giving birth to a new day. The omega is when night falls and you close your eyes to sleep. In between alpha and omega is your time to create a life. So start each day with alpha and end each day with omega. And everything else will just fall into place. When the sun rises and sets on your life, the Big Rocks will be in your jar.

↓|← ←···→↖↘ →‡ → ↘↖   ←···→|←↓↓ ←↖←↓↓ ↔↑↖←···→|←‡↘

#23 _____

Alpha begins by recognizing your eternal being, inseparably connected to your Higher Power. Your first meaningful act upon rising is to honor your Higher Power by studying and pondering the sacred words meant to mentor you to a more meaningful life. Then, meditate and/or pray to see the perspective of your life through Higher Power eyes.

When we use the term *Big Rocks* it represents a daily regimen of preparing your mind to question, receive, recognize, and act upon empowering, enlightened ideas. The three essential practices involve the three B's: your being, your brain, and your body. We call this regimen 3B.

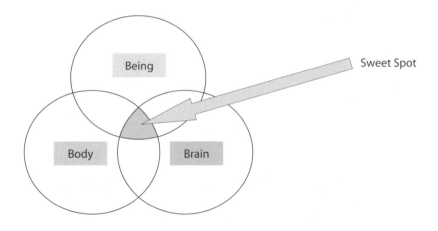

3B or Not 3B? That Is the Question

You say you want to be financially successful? How can you hope to create wealth without connecting with the Author of all Wealth? If only 5% of start-ups succeed, you need HELP!

At every juncture of civilization's progression, there are million-, billion-,

52 | CRACKING THE MILLIONAIRE CODE

and trillion-dollar breakthrough ideas. Higher Power has already reserved *your* shining star idea. Higher Power has galaxies of star ideas waiting to illuminate the world.

Being

Your being, your spirit, your essence, your life force—that spark of eternity that resides in you—is so wise. Where did your spirit come from? Was your spirit ignited into existence from the union of sperm and egg? Or did your spirit exist before the union? As Wordsworth wrote:

> *Our birth is but a sleep and a forgetting;*
> *The soul that rises with us, our Life's Star,*
> *Hath had elsewhere its setting,*
> *And cometh from afar;*
> *Not in entire forgetfulness,*
> *And not in utter nakedness,*
> *But trailing clouds of glory do we come*
> *From God, who is our home.*
>
> —WILLIAM WORDSWORTH,
> "ODE: INTIMATIONS OF IMMORTALITY"

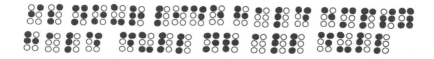

#24 _____

What kind of glory did we drag with us? What genius school were we pupils of? Are our talents and gifts just DNA-coded genetic blueprinted tendencies . . . or are they "learned traits" from previous existences? We believe that the genius of your spirit is immeasurably wise, unfathomably profound, and indescribably brilliant. How do you tap into your genius?

_____prayer   _____deep thought   _____spiritual retreats

_____pondering   _____asking   _____church

_____candles, incense   _____dreaming   _____near-death experiences

Body

The next rock is your body. Take care of it. Your body is such an amazing machine made up of trillions of cells. The wisdom in each of these microscopic cells is staggering. At your conception, the division of your first few cells—the so-called stem cells—contained the entire blueprint for your entire body. The "you" that emerged is miraculous. Your lungs breathe 20,000 times a day. Your heart beats 100,000 times a day. Your blood circulates around your body 1,000 times a day. All of this just happens without a single conscious thought on your part. Imagine how little you would get done if you had to consciously direct the systems of your body—circulatory, immune, respiratory, nervous, digestive, elimination, lymphatic. When you exercise, you enliven, invigorate, and endorphin the magnificent systems of your magnificent body. How do you tap into your body wisdom?

_____exercise   _____sports   _____massage

_____shower   _____breathing   _____jogging

_____bath   _____walks in nature   _____stretching

Brain

The gnarled, three-pound mass of mushy tissue inside your skull regulates everything. Is everything you've ever experienced permanently recorded in your cerebral computer? You can draw from your vast inputs to conjure up wisdom and intuition and thoughts. What can you do to fine-tune this quantum space?

_____visualization   _____certain fragrances   _____multimedia

_____listen to music   _____other-handed writing   _____reading biographies

_____nutrition   _____questioning   _____journaling

54 | CRACKING THE MILLIONAIRE CODE

> *Some of the greatest battles will be fought within*
> *the silent chambers of your own soul.*
>
> —EZRA TAFT BENSON

Brain × Body × Being. It's "you" cubed. When you stretch your brain, your body, and your being, a sacred space is created for receiving enlightened ideas Destined to change your world and the world around you. Thus prepared, you're more Highly sensitive to the best ideas—more aware of the opportunities hidden all around you. If codes are designed to keep out unauthorized people, 3B activates your membership code. You're a member. You belong.

Who got the idea for flight?
> Wilbur and Orville Wright. It was a trillion-dollar idea.

Who got the idea for the telephone?
> Alexander Graham Bell. It was a trillion-dollar idea.

Who got the idea for electricity?
> Thomas Edison. It was a trillion-dollar idea.

Who got the idea for personal computers?
> Jobs, Wozniak, Gates. It was a trillion-dollar idea.

Are you ready for an idea like that? When you get up in the morning, put the Big Rocks in first. Create your own special ritual. For MVH, it is an hour of meditation most mornings at 4 A.M. followed by some treadmill time or weight training while watching empowering videos. For RGA, almost every morning starts out the same: up at 6 A.M., 30 minutes of scripture study, 15 minutes of kneeling prayer, followed by a two-mile walk on the treadmill while talking journal entries and *aha*s into a mini tape recorder.

Endeepen, enheighten, enbroaden, enwiden, enbrighten, and enlighten yourself. Triangulate your life to spark the best ideas. Calibrate your soul to vibrate at the pitch of the Tuning Force of the Universe. Ask your Higher Mentor empowering questions and wait for the still, small answer.

More often than not, Higher Power answers your questions with another question—the still small question—and sends you back to do some more research.

Most people don't do this. They just open their eyes in the morning and dodge the onrushing cars on the freeway of life. There is a peaceful place that you can reach, that separates you from the onrushing traffic—gives you breathing room (take a deep breath) and centers you, grounds you, prepares your perspective.

In the sweet spot between the overlapping layers of body, brain, and being, a Great Idea is brewing. It could take money . . . serious money . . . to launch your Great Idea. In the next chapter we'll show you where to find it. It might be closer than you think.

#25 _____

_____

_____

_____

#26 _____

QUOTE ON BUILDING AT BRIGHAM YOUNG UNIVERSITY, UTAH • The value of your network is

Chapter Four

HOW TO TURN YOUR BURIED
TREASURES INTO MILLIONS

O ne thing can stop your Great Idea cold: lack of money. True? It takes money to make money. Right? The biggest reason why 95% of start-up enterprises fail is because they are undercapitalized. Agreed? We'll revisit these questions at the end of this chapter, but for now, let's assume the obvious. The typical underfunded start-up business just runs out of cash before it gets to its destination. *If* that's true, do you have enough resources to launch your Enlightened Enterprise? Let's find out.

HOW MUCH ARE YOU WORTH?

How are you doing financially? Let's do a financial checkup. 26 Don't skip over this. It's essential. Every time you borrow money for a car, house, or business, your banker checks you out based on the four C's of wealth: cash, cash flow, credit, and collateral. In the financial world this is called a financial statement—a list of your income, your assets, your liabilities. Assets are things you own like cash, real estate, stocks, and so on. Liabilities are debts you owe, such as loans and mortgages. How much you *own* minus how much you *owe* equals your "net worth." If you want to be a millionaire, your assets will need to exceed your liabilities by a million dollars. Find out your "net worth" by completing the following basic financial statement:

Duvall Hecht

The three-hour commute to and from Orange County to Los Angeles by car was becoming tedious for Duvall Hecht, even with the radio on. With a Stanford University education and a body honed by the successful pursuit of an Olympic gold medal in rowing, which he won in Australia in 1956, he was looking for a way to put those hours in the car to good use. He discovered that an electronic engineer named Robert Halverson on the East Coast had taken *The Decline and Fall of the Roman Empire* and other public domain classics, taped them, and was selling the eight-audiocassette book for $80. Duvall listened, learned, and was positively hooked, but he believed rental was the key to large-scale distribution.

An idea bloomed in his mind to record full-length readings of all the great and bestselling books and call it "Books on Tape." He was busy and successful in the securities business, but the idea kept bugging him. He had the energy, vision, and desire to make his vision happen on his own. He acquired subsidiary rights for a handful of books; the publishers, not seeing their value, sold them for virtually nothing. He hired out-of-work Hollywood actors with great voices to record bestselling books in unabridged audio editions. He then rented them through the mail with an enclosed return envelope. 10 This combination of elements had never been tried before—and, as it happened, rent-by-mail, credit cards, 800 numbers, Walkman recorders, and car tape decks were all simultaneously becoming available. The agents and publishers who agreed to work with him helped the start-up by granting rights for extremely modest front payments.

The first year, working late into the night, Duvall Hecht grossed $17,000, using one-inch ads in the *Los Angeles Times*. The press was friendly and started creating momentum. By year eight he had a company that was generating a million dollars a year, and Books on Tape had a commanding lead over the competition. 47 When Random House came

→

My Traditional Financial Statement

ASSETS (I OWN)   LIABILITIES (I OWE)

Cash, Bank Acct _____	Credit card debt _____
Savings Acct _____	Personal loans _____
Cars _____	Car loans _____
House _____	House mortgage _____
Other real estate _____	Other mortgages _____
Stocks, bonds _____	Debts, unsecured _____
Mutual funds _____	Installment debt _____
Life insurance _____	Loans on life ins. _____
Retirement accts _____	Unpaid taxes _____
Value of business _____	Business loans _____
Pensions_____	_____
Jewelry, etc. _____	_____
Furniture, etc. _____	_____
Other assets _____	Other liabilities _____

My Total Assets $ _____   My Total Liabilities $ (_____)

My Total Net Worth (assets minus liabilities) $_____

INCOME (I EARN)

My monthly income $_____

My monthly outgo   (_____)

My monthly net income $_____

CREDIT (MY REPAYMENT HISTORY)

My Total Credit Score
(Pull a credit report at www.creditreport.com) _____

Signed this _____ day of _____, 20_____

My signature _____

knocking at his door in 2001 and bought his company, it was a booming $25 million-a-year business with 125 employees and over 6,000 titles.

Duvall Hecht loves the thought that he has encouraged more nonreaders to experience books than anyone in history, and he is elated by his role in bringing more enlightenment to his customers through the wonderful world of audio books.

With your net worth and cash flow in front of you, now you're ready to make some "traditional" projections. 22 Just for fun, let's see how long it will take you to become a traditional millionaire. Go to **www.crackingthe millionairecode.com** and click on the Free MoneyPower Financial Analysis. You'll be asked to input five simple numbers: your age, your projected retirement age, your current savings, your monthly investment amount, and your projected interest rate. A detailed summary will be immediately calculated of how much money you might have at retirement, plus some other fascinating facts.

yURIEw zSSETh oIKv yURIEw nROORLMh zRv fSELESh
fNTIo wUt fk zNw kUg gl tOOw fSv.

#27

For example, a 40-year-old with $25,000 in savings and $250 a month to invest at 10% will have $595,412 at age 65. To reach a million would require an additional $311 per month. It's all there in black, white, green, and red. It's free. It's fun. It's fast. It's eye-opening. Stop reading right now and go check it out. It'll astonish you. Follow the plan you see there and in time, with discipline and consistency, you can become a traditional millionaire.

This book is about more than making a million. 20 This book is about cracking *your* code to personal Wealth (with a capital W). It's not about making *a* difference but *the* difference *you* were put on this earth to make. Now let's have you prepare an "Enlightened" Wealth Statement. Don't skip over this. It's essential. Your banker, your employer, your friends, your family—almost everyone you know (including yourself) undervalues your true worth and overvalues your temporary net worth. 11 Let's see to it that you don't make the same mistake.

Your Enlightened Wealth Statement

HIDDEN ASSETS (I Own)	LIABILITIES (I Owe)
Life _____	Debts of Gratitude to
Spiritual beliefs _____	Higher Power _____
Destiny _____	Ancestors _____
Skills _____	Parents _____
Life experience _____	Veterans _____
Body and body parts _____	Teachers _____
Sight _____	Children _____
Hearing _____	Disorganization _____
Smell _____	Low self-esteem _____
Taste _____	Bad habits _____
Touch _____	Addictions _____
Citizenship _____	Blind spots _____
Intuition _____	Fear _____
Sense of peace _____	Anxiety _____
Talents _____	Poor health _____
Values _____	Enemies _____
Passions _____	Bad relationships _____
Eternal retirement plan _____	Internal critical voice _____
Friends _____	Laziness _____
Family _____	_____
Health _____	_____
Character _____	_____
Courage _____	_____
Persistence _____	_____
Creativity _____	_____
Joy _____	_____
My Total Assets $ _____	My Total Liabilities $ (_____)

My Total Enlightened Net Worth (assets minus liabilities) $_____

FUTURE INCOME (I WILL EARN)

My future monthly income	$_____
My future monthly outgo	(_____)
My future monthly net income	$_____

CREDIBILITY (MY HISTORY OF INTEGRITY)

My Total Credibility Score (Ask 10 friends to rate you on a scale of 1–10) _____

Signed this _____ **day of** _____ **, 20** _____

My signature _____

Your Enlightened Wealth Statement consists of many hidden assets that you take for granted because everybody has them. 11 But what if you didn't have them? What do you possess that you wouldn't sell for a million dollars? For example, you "own" your eyesight, but would you sell your eyeballs for a million? Would you sell your kidneys for a million? Would you sell your citizenship for a million? Would you sell one of your children? (There's a special dispensation for teenagers—you might *pay* someone to take them!) Would you sell your best friend for a million? Would you give up your belief in God for a quick million? More than likely, there are things you possess that you wouldn't part with for any amount of money. 20 These are assets that you own, and therefore they are listed on your Enlightened Wealth Statement.

By the same token, there are many hidden liabilities on your Enlightened Wealth Statement—obligations and indebtedness that we often overlook. Most of our "debts of gratitude" don't have a monetary equivalent and can be repaid by being grateful, vowing to improve our lives, or agreeing to "pay it forward."

Many of our hidden liabilities have serious financial consequences, however. For example, suppose you could go back five years and erase a major fear that has always held you back, such as fear of failure, or of rejection, or looking foolish, or being less than perfect. How much more profitable would the last five years have been without the burden of your fear? Would you have earned an extra million or two? Suppose you don't eliminate that fear for the next five years. 22 How much will that fear cost you? When you add the money you've lost plus the money you could lose as a result of fear, the total is staggering. Fear is expensive! And fear costs far more than money. It destroys relationships, health, and self-esteem. Put a price tag on those losses.

80 92 95 82 95   91 81   99   77 85 82 88 96   85 94
96 91 94 94 95 82 95 86 97 95   98 95 80 77 95 95 86
88 86 93   99 86 96   88 86 93.

#28 _____

_____

Other hidden liabilities are just as costly. How much does a nagging, critical internal voice cost you? Self-doubt keeps you from pursuing an opportunity when intuition tells you to take the leap. How much could that chance have been worth? You'll never know—you missed it. People with "poor" attitudes don't come up with many million-dollar ideas—precisely because they don't think they have what it takes to implement them. 5 This feeling of poverty extends to their self-worth; they feel they don't deserve to be wealthy, much less capable of dreaming up million-dollar ideas. So let's make sure that this kind of "stinking thinking" (as Zig Ziglar taught) is out of your mind. Putting in the Big Rocks first is a step in the right direction every day.

An essential step in cracking your Destiny Code is to unlock the chains that bind you. Having a million-dollar idea is one part of the equation. Having the courage to pursue it is equally important. 16 Go down the list of your hidden liabilities and notice the one key log in the logjam of your life. Remove that one log and the logjam will break loose and clear the river flowing with prosperity.

Sometimes just being aware of the cost of our liabilities is enough to crack the code. Without question, we all have blind spots. Try as we might, from time to time we just can't seem to see a way out of our predicament. That's why it takes a Higher Perspective, a Higher Prescription. In addition, during the 101-Day Plan posted on **www.crackingthemillionairecode.com** we'll guide you with some step-by-step exercises to rapidly "pay off" those internal liabilities.

Yet, our hidden assets are far more valuable than our hidden liabilities. Your Enlightened Net Worth is incalculable. This very second, you possess assets that are worth millions. The ordinary high school graduate is vastly more educated than 99% of the people who have ever lived. And speaking of living, the life expectancy in the year 1900 was only 48 years. Today it is 78. How much is that extra 30 years worth to you? You may be broke, but how could you possibly think that you are poor? Two billion people earn less money in a day than you probably spend on a skim decaf. Now, *that's* poor. Compared with the 90 billion people who have lived on this planet in the past 10,000 years, you are unbelievably wealthy, vastly rich, privileged beyond belief, extraordinarily free, lavishly lucky. You don't need to play the lottery. You've already won!!!!

Just in case you think that this is fluffy New Age nonsense, read this quote from a scholarly book called *Strategy Maps,* by Robert G. Kaplan and David P. Norton, published by Harvard Business School Press:

> Intangible assets—those not measured by a company's financial system—account for more than 75 percent of a company's value. The average company's tangible assets—the net book value of assets less liabilities—represent less than 25 percent of market value.
>
> What's true for companies is even truer for countries. Some countries, such as Venezuela and Saudi Arabia, have high physical resource endowments but have made poor investments in their people and systems. As a consequence, they produce far less output per person, and experience much slower growth rates, than countries such as Singapore and Taiwan that have few natural resources but invest heavily in human and information capital and effective internal systems. At both the macroeconomic and microeconomic levels, intangible assets drive long-term value creation.

Did you get that? Even Fortune 500 companies undervalue their real assets by 75%. Their financial balance sheets should actually be labeled "out-of-balance" sheets.

When it comes to corporate America, most employers don't value the vast amount of experience that lies in the hearts and minds of their people. 30 The knowledge capital of each employee equals an enlightened net worth in the millions. But how is it valued in the "real" world? On October 7, 2004, AT&T announced it would lay off 7,000 people. The very next morning its stock price spiked up 3%. Went up?!!!

_11) ~417`# -17. -17 @17`# !$ _11)*`^ ~6 -174 %1467`$.

#29

From the point of view of the stock market, short-term profits would go up (the 25% visible value), ignoring the long-term consequences to the enterprise (the 75% invisible value). When 7,000 loyal, hardworking, honest, knowledgeable employees are let go, the *true* value of the company goes down—dramatically! Its enlightened balance sheet is hit hard. The remaining employees are shell-shocked. 11 The company is not enriched, it is impoverished. This happens almost every day.

Think of all the poverty, misery, pain, and disillusionment that flows directly from the devaluation of hidden human assets. This is the root cause of almost all poor health, sadness, failure, suicide, murder, death, divorce, crime, anger, argument, and jealousy. The forces of endarkenment are smiling. 6 Their plan is working.

> *He who destroys but a single life is as if he had destroyed the whole world.*
> *He who saves but a single life is as if he had saved the whole world.*
>
> —The Talmud

But we've got a plan to cheer you up. Let's look more closely at your Enlightened Wealth Statement.

YOUR GENIUS IS WORTH MILLIONS

What?!! You? A genius? Yup. There's nobody like you. Never has been. Never will be. You are a genius at being you. Just the way you are. You could teach classes on it. 24 As Ashleigh Brilliant, the famous cartoonist, writes, "I may not be perfect, but parts of me are excellent."

So how much is your genius worth? Catalogue the things you're good at. Make a list of 101 skills, talents, and abilities you possess and ask yourself how much you'd have to pay someone to provide all that for you. OK, let's suppose all of your combined talent isn't worth millions. Maybe we got carried away. Let's say you calculate it's only worth $10,000. Write that number down. We're not finished yet.

YOUR LIFE EXPERIENCE IS WORTH MILLIONS

—

Former President Bill Clinton was reportedly paid $10,000,000 for his memoir. How much would someone pay you for your memoir? Ten million? OK, how about $10,000? Let's start with that figure and show you how you might perhaps parlay it into $10 million. Your "memoir" is worth far more than you think it is.

Look back over your life. 7 Think of the knowledge you've accumulated. What would someone find useful? Skills. Experiences. Lessons. Realizations. Hobbies. Tips. Strategies. Techniques. Systems. Practices. *Aha*s. Procedures. Proficiencies. Aptitudes. Abilities. Know-how. Shortcuts. Competencies. Expertise. Knacks.

Could someone improve their life by learning from one of your successes? 20 Could you help someone avoid some future trauma or pain by learning from one of your failures? (As they say, "We're all good for something, even if it's only serving as a bad example.") How much would that be worth to them—to avoid the potholes that you hit? Would someone pay you a hundred bucks to mentor them through a crisis that you've already learned from? Would someone pay you a hundred bucks to show them a shortcut to a success skill that you've already mastered?

On Day 8 of the online 101-Day Plan at **www.crackingthemillionaire code.com** you'll find an Experience Capital Survey of 101 valuable experiences. We challenge you to complete this survey itemizing at least 101 lessons you could teach someone that would be worth at least $100. When you're done, you'll see that your experience is worth far more than $10,000.

Tout il y a fortune une dans.

#30 _____

There are almost seven billion people on this planet. If you could reach 10,000 of them with just *one* of your valuable $100 lessons, that could earn you a million dollars! A million bucks from just *one* item of your experience capital. Shouldn't you have at least 10 chunks of knowledge like that? Touch your forehead with your index finger and say: "There are millions of dollars' worth of experience in here." Touch yourself at heart level and say: "I'm worth millions."

YOUR PROBLEMS ARE WORTH MILLIONS!

—

This is going to be a tough one but we promise if you'll do this exercise, in 30 minutes you may feel better at the end of it. 2 Just promise us that you'll complete this or don't even start. Just move on to the next page and return to this when you have more time. Once you've made the promise, take out a blank piece of paper and scan back over your life and draw an "autograph" of the ups and downs of your life. Highlight at least three major ups and three major downs. Let us give you an example.

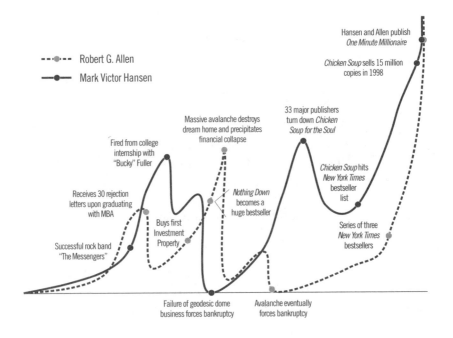

Look over your time line. It's like the graph of a stock price, isn't it? If you could go back in time and buy some stock in your life, where would you buy the most? At the lowest point, right? Is it time to buy some more?

Examine the lessons from your chart. Objectively, where did you learn the most? From your successes or from your failures? In our cases, we learned much from both. The births of our children—that was wonderful stuff. The failures were valuable, too. We didn't like any of our downs at the time, but there were upsides to our downslides. In fact, some of our most devastating moments actually "set up" our comebacks. Lessons learned there served us well.

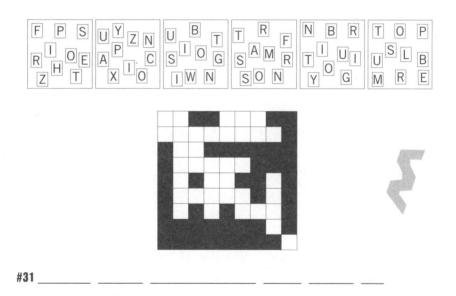

#31 _____ _____ _____ _____ _____ ___

_____ ___ _____ _____.

Every life pulses to the rhythm of its natural ebbs and flows. If you look back on your life and think you're not a winner, maybe it's because you haven't learned the lesson from your setback yet. Once you learn the lesson from a failure, you're a winner . . . because you turned what appeared to be a strikeout into a home run. You transformed what many feel was an experience to avoid into a valuable one—turning lemons into lemonade.

We want you to go a step further. Take another 30 minutes and scan back over your entire life and jot down a list of 101 moments of failure, unhappy times, personal challenges, accidents, rejections, defeats, near catastrophes, embarrassing moments, sad times, sicknesses, deaths, crises of faith, disappointments. Don't let this depress you. We can all do this all too easily. That's life. Just catalogue it. You can go to **www.crackingthemillionaire code.com** to download a "Failures Are Worth Millions" worksheet.

For instance, suppose one of your favorite pets was killed by a car. Yes, it hurt . . . maybe it still does. How could you make that experience valuable? Perhaps you could write a small book to help other people cope with the pain of losing a pet. Maybe you could donate all of the proceeds from the book to a charity to help pets. 40 It won't bring your pet back but you might turn this major tragedy into a minor triumph, or perhaps something greater. You might become a powerful advocate of animal rights and improve the lot of many lives. The loss you suffered can take on meaning. Something good can come out of it.

In other words, you can learn *something* from *everything* that you experience—the good and the bad. Many people look back on their life and assume that it was all bad . . . rough childhood, abuse, drugs, crime. 7 Yes, this does not make for an easy life, but if people learn, admit, accept, change, and transform their "before" stories into "after" stories, they can become truly extraordinary.

And once the lessons are learned, what are they worth? Put dollar amounts on them—and all your other lessons. Add 'em up. There's more value in those downtimes than you might have calculated, perhaps. And that's just what the past is worth. What about the future? Will there be trials, problems, challenges ahead? You can either dread the future or see through the pain to the wisdom and value gained. The future can be a place of hope, not fear; a place of joy, not disappointment. The future can be a wealth of predicaments instead of a poverty of problems.

In truth, all problems are profits in disguise. Every problem is a prospective opportunity. 5 What appears as a problem to one person is an obvious chance for someone else. Don't devalue your problems. There's a fortune hidden in there!

. . .

A car accident almost killed me on March 15, 2003. I skidded off a California freeway during a pounding rainstorm and smashed into a tree at full speed. You can see the photos of the car on our website and wonder, like I do, how anyone walked away from that alive. The healing process was painful. Still is. Yet, I would not trade that experience for all the money I have earned or will ever earn. It simply changed my life. It softened me. Turned me from a guy who was mostly head-oriented to one who is much more heart-oriented. The word gratitude didn't mean much to me before. Now, I find myself driving down the freeway whispering under my breath, Thank You! Thank You! Thank You! Thank You! I thank God every day for just one more grateful day.

—ROBERT G. ALLEN

ARE YOU SURE ABOUT YOUR LIABILITIES?

——

Take another look down your liability column of the Enlightened Wealth Statement. Aren't there some problems that would be worth millions to you if you would just solve them? Suppose your "before" picture has you 100 pounds overweight. What would your story be worth if you lost 100 pounds and then wrote a book about how you did it? There's got to be a million in that story somewhere. What about a divorce? Or a disability? Or a bankruptcy? More than a million Americans a year declare bankruptcy. Would they give you a $100 to tell them how to smooth that bumpy ride? Or even just to tell them that things will eventually smooth over!

There's a fortune in every one of your problems. In fact, the liability column should be relabeled. It's not liability but "lie ability"—the ability to "lie" about how bad things are, when the truth is that they're only bad if you haven't learned anything from them. 17 As soon as you deposit your wisdom dividends, those liabilities transform into your most precious assets.

I have not failed. I've just found 10,000 ways that won't work.

—THOMAS A. EDISON

I hear and I forget, I see and I remember, I do and I understand.

In fact, *everything* that happens to you is an asset—provided you learn the lesson.

Who knew there was so much profit in your problems!!!

YOUR CONNECTIONS ARE WORTH MILLIONS!

You already know 101 successful people. Successful? Just what does it mean to be successful? Do you know someone like this? Educated. Employed. Self-employed. Talented. Gifted. Skilled at something—anything.

Many people you know have completed 12 years of high school education. Some have gone on and completed college. Many have special job training or experience. A few have attained advanced degrees.

Think of all the people you know who have successfully been hired for good jobs. 16 They've got to be valuable—someone felt they were worth a regular paycheck.

Scan through all of your contacts. 16 Pull out your Christmas card or holiday greeting lists, or your e-mail files.

In your educational life, do you know 20 good teachers?
> *(kindergarten, elementary, middle school, high school, college adult education)*

In your work life, do you know 20 successful fellow employees or bosses?
> *(secretaries, supervisors, coworkers, bosses, counterparts in other divisions, people in your e-mail file)*

In your consumer life, do you know 20 competent service providers?
> *(insurance salespeople, meter readers, pest control people, carpet cleaners, repair people, day care providers, landlords, mortgage or real estate brokers)*

In your personal life, do you know 20 people who have achieved success?
> *(successful married couples, daughters, sons, aunts, uncles, cousins, friends, mentors)*

In your group life, do you know 20 people who've been successful?
(churches, civic groups, sports or fan groups, adult education classes, ad hoc committees, political action groups, hobby groups, travel enthusiasts)

Make a list of 101 people who have achieved some level of success. Go ahead. You'll see how valuable this list will be when you're done. (You can download a blank list called "101 People with Enlightened Capital" at our website **www.crackingthemillionairecode.com.**)

#32 _____

_____

_____

_____

OK. 13 Now, look at this list and ask yourself how much this list is worth. Remember to not only look at traditional financial statements, but at Enlightened Wealth Statements. You'll see that people on this list may not realize it, but they, just like you, possess more than 100 assets that they would not sell for a million dollars. Then, when you add up their genius, their experience, their problems—we're talking some serious value! 13 This makes up your first tier of successful contacts.

But we're not finished. Each of these 101 people also knows another 101 successful people. This is your second tier of impressive contacts.

But we're not done yet. Each person in your second tier of successful contacts also knows another 101 contacts with Enlightened Wealth Statements worth millions. 16 This makes up your third tier of 101 successful contacts. All told, from your own home phone you have access to *a million* people in the three tiers of successful people encircling you. (101 × 101 × 101 = 1,030,301)

We know that this may sound ridiculous, so go back and review our assumptions; you'll see that even if we're off in our valuations by a multiple of 100, this list is *still* worth well over a million dollars. 50

Just think about this for a minute. In the three concentric circles of successful people surrounding you *this very second,* the answers you are seeking are there. How much is the right contact worth? Your connections truly are worth a fortune to you . . . if you know how to mine the diamonds in your own mine.

We'll show you how to do this later, but for now, realize that Higher Power already knows which connections you could make to accelerate your success at "enlightening" speed. That's another reason to put Higher Power first.

Oh, we almost forgot. Remember the questions we asked at the beginning of this chapter. Does lack of money stop your Great Idea cold? Does it take money to make money? 11 Is the biggest reason start-ups fail due to lack of financial resources?

Absolutely not! Why do most businesses fail? Here is our answer—which will be scoffed at by most "bottom-line" financial analysts. Businesses fail because they fail to access their hidden resources! You have enough resources on your Enlightened Wealth Statement to accomplish *any* goal you set for yourself.

Let's summarize.

You are sitting on a gold mine. 6 You control buried assets worth millions. Now, with this true perspective, let's show you how to mine your mind for the Great Idea that you are destined to make happen.

#33 _____

#34 _____

Chapter Five

THE PRISM CODE

"It just takes one idea to live like a king
for the rest of your life."

—ROSS PEROT

IS THIS GLASS HALF FULL OR HALF EMPTY?

I t's neither. This glass is neither half full nor half empty. It is 100% *full*.
The bottom half is filled with a "visible" liquid. The top half is filled
with an "invisible" substance called air. The entire glass is full. The
secret to cracking your wealth code is to learn to see the invisible—to perceive what no one else can see even though they are looking directly at it.

Look around you right now. Where are the opportunities that are hidden
in plain sight? They are there, we guarantee you. Every object you see this
very instant has made, is making, or will make someone a fortune. In fact, the
seed idea for every physical object around you—a table, a chair, a glass, a
lightbulb—has probably been responsible for hundreds if not thousands of
fortunes.

Monte Greenawalt

D r. Monte Greenawalt has made a fortune by discovering solutions to problems no one else sees. He has enormous fun in the process, employs an ever-expanding number of people, and uses affirmations regularly to inspire ever-greater success. He is ambitious in his philanthropic outreach and intends to leave a lasting legacy. He believes most other people could think like he thinks, work like he works, and become self-fulfilled major contributors to life.

A chiropractor, Dr. Greenawalt built a substantial practice, and in the process noticed that patients enjoyed more lasting benefits from their chiropractic adjustments when they were confined to bed. Standing and walking seemed to have a negative effect on the holding power of the adjustments. This idea captivated him and inspired him to wonder whether it had something to do with an individual's feet.

Dr. Greenawalt tested hundreds of patients and discovered that patients didn't need as many adjustments and stayed well longer if their feet were balanced by a proper foundation in their shoes. He tested his new invention, called Foot Levelers™, on hundreds of patients. It had such powerful healing effects that he put it into a double-blind study to rule out any placebo effect. Foot Levelers™ worked perfectly every time and patients held their corrections.

Three things helped Dr. Greenawalt's invention take off. He taught chiropractors why and how Foot Levelers™ worked, how much patients liked and wanted them, and how easy it was to create a perfect foam footprint impression to make the Foot Levelers™. Chiropractors made the patient's foot impression in foam and sent it in to Dr. Greenawalt's company, and a week later the patient would have new shoe inserts. It was simple, easy, and a fast-growing new profit center for doctors. The Foot Levelers™ business boomed.

Affirmations are part of the fabric of Dr. Greenawalt's being. He gave us permission to share one of his favorites: "I am a happy healer. True friends surround me. I have boundless energy. I have great wisdom. I am a true

→

ARE YOU AWARE OF THE HIDDEN
OPPORTUNITIES ALL AROUND YOU?

If you've ever been to a 3D movie, you have an inkling of what we're talking about. Once you put on some special glasses you are transported from a flat-screen world to a world alive with holographic depth and fullness.

That's the way the two of us see the world of opportunity. It's not a 3D world but a 3B world buzzing with spirit. Every day we notice new opportunities, read them in the newspaper, watch them on TV. They're everywhere. Give us 10 minutes in your living room and we'd point out at least three of them.

We didn't used to think like this. We remember how absurd it sounded when our mentors boasted of being inundated with opportunity. Too much opportunity?!! How ridiculous! Overwhelmed by pressures, all we saw was the opportunity for another stressful day.

#35

But, despite some very serious "downtime" in each of our lives, neither one of us has ever been much of a pessimist. We knew that something good was going to happen if we just kept moving forward. Eventually, through experience, we created our own set of opportunity glasses. We began to be aware of the opportunities that our mentors had been seeing—and they were right; the opportunities are everywhere.

Have you ever driven off a car lot in a new car and suddenly you begin to notice how many other cars on the freeway are exactly like yours—same

leader. I am filled with God-given creativity and dedicated to helping human-ity. The spirit of the Lord goes before me and makes easy and successful my way. I have faith in myself and all that I do. My creative mind comes forth with new and productive ideas. Day by day, in every way, I am getting better and better. I attract true leaders, who can help achieve my mission to better serve humanity. I praise God from whom all blessings flow. I will leave the world a better place than when I found it."

Monte Greenawalt's philosophy is that to be successful in business one needs to be surrounded by the right people, and then anything becomes possible. These people must be working with you, not for you. As Monte says, "Imagine a plant; it can only grow as large as the pot it's in and then it becomes root-bound. Give it more room and it expands." Likewise, a busi-ness that is shared with the right people becomes unlimited.

Great business success has allowed him to realize his every dream, hope, prayer, and desire. Today, he employs 30 scientists to push back the fron-tiers of science. His scientists have invented an algorithm that can diagnose and recognize prostate cancer and breast cancer, noninvasively with 100% accuracy. Ultimately, he thinks it will detect cancer anywhere in the body noninvasively, which would be the health breakthrough of breakthroughs. This will read out in three dimensions and have the equivalent of a "global positioning satellite." His next machine can noninvasively measure the diameter of a blood vessel in the heart with no dyes or pain. His scientists have created a new computer simulation allowing one to look at an individ-ual's entire physiology and anatomy, watch the blood flow and take the body apart piece by piece and put it back together one element of one sys-tem at a time. One can learn what's working and what's not. And it's much better than reading and studying *Gray's Anatomy.*

As Dr. Greenawalt puts it, "When you look in a mirror you are looking at the most important person in the world. You need to ask: 'Who am I? Where am I going?' People spend weeks planning a good vacation and little or no time asking what they are going to do with their lousy lives. You can do anything you want to do. The biggest thing is to define success for your-

→

color, same make, same year? You wonder, "How many purple Pontiacs can there be?" A few hours earlier, there were hardly any. But now they are everywhere. Did everyone buy the same car on the same day? Or did you just become more aware of what was already there?

By becoming more aware, what amazing ideas can you find in your life at this very moment? What million-dollar ideas are you overlooking, underlooking, or looking through, around, or beyond? How can you increase your awareness so these ideas become *obvious* to you? How can you make what's invisible to you at this moment, visible? As Antoine de Saint-Exupéry wrote in *The Little Prince:* "What is essential is invisible to the eye." We hope to teach you a way to turn what is essential from invisible to visible, if not to the eye then to your intuition.

So let us say it again: Everything you see made someone a fortune. Everything. If you look more closely, everything you see could make *you* a fortune. Everything. That's right—*every single thing!*

Every object around you is buzzing with aliveness—whispering its subliminal secrets.

"Improve me! Invent me! Reinvent me! Enlighten me!"

Select any object within 10 feet of you. How about that ordinary telephone over there. It was once just a thought in the mind of Alexander Graham Bell. He cracked the same four codes you'll need to crack: Destiny, Prism, Angel, and Star. And the world has never been the same.

That original "telephone" idea has morphed in a thousand directions, from wall phones, to cordless phones, to cell phones, to satellite phones, to Internet phones. Each variation comes in different colors, sizes, shapes, and with ever more useful features—with PDAs, digital cameras, and MP3 players, not to mention accessories such as carrying cases, identification stickers, straps. And different services—insurance, answering messaging, phone coverage, e-mail, repairs, directory assistance. Plus a variety of information products to teach us how to use them—manuals, checklists, instruction books, information exchanges, Internet websites.

self. Success is doing what you truly enjoy doing and having it provide the quality of life that's acceptable to you, but leaves you wanting a little more. Money will not make you successful. Doing what you truly enjoy doing is the ultimate success, because happiness comes from within."

Monte is an insatiable giver. He believes that giving is the way to increase one's value, self-respect, and self-esteem. Giving allows you to keep moving forward and to become more of who you really are. His life is devoted to helping and serving others. He owns the second-largest home in Las Vegas, which is no small feat. It is laden with beautiful antiques, artwork, tapestries, and mementos from the Who's Who of the world. Every month, he has a different charitable function at his home to raise funds for what he deeply believes will be of great service to his friends and community. For this purpose he cheerfully supplies his exquisite mansion, complete with food cooked by his French chef, Andréa. Everyone in Vegas knows, loves, respects, and cherishes his friendship, his brilliance, his genius, his natural sense of humor, and his generosity. Monte Greenawalt wants to fulfill his destiny and make the world a better place than it was when he got here. He believes that nothing makes us feel better than helping another person.

Since the idea of the telephone first popped into Alexander Graham Bell's 29-year-old head well over a century ago, it's staggering to contemplate all of the tens of thousands of companies worldwide employing tens of millions of people focused on the telephone. How many of these companies were launched by individuals just like you, sitting in their living rooms looking at the phone and wondering . . . "I wonder if I could make it smaller, bigger, cheaper, faster, slower, more colorful, more exciting"?

What will the telephone be like a century from now? Radically different. Unimaginably altered. Yet someone is going to do it. Why not you?

The truth is, *every* object in your home is a hidden million-dollar idea (MDI) waiting to be released from the straitjacket of solid form and morphed into something marvelously profitable.

Do you still doubt this? OK. Put on your opportunity glasses. Select something really ordinary. How about that wastebasket over there? In the last 1,000 years on this planet, how many thousands of enterprises were successfully launched to manufacture, distribute, warehouse, market, advertise, and sell wastebaskets in every shape, size, color, price, construction, material, and/or design? People can throw their trash in a free paper grocery sack or crush it in a $1,000 trash compactor, with countless choices in between.

Who designed the very first garbage can? Perhaps some caveman fashioned one out of animal skin for the corner of his cave. Then, a visiting caveman saw this new "waste collection system" and said, "Hey, that's a good idea. Tell you what—make me one of those and I'll give you a woolly mammoth tusk." And pretty soon every cave was equipped with one.

How many wastebaskets have you bought in your life? How many will you buy in the next 10 years? You might need another wastebasket right now. After thousands of years, has the flow of new "wastebasket" ideas dried up?

The array of opportunities from one clear product category is amazing. For example, take the product category "motorized transportation." Just think of all of the support businesses that have sprung up to provide extra products and services for the owner of a car—service stations, insurance companies, tow trucks, car detailing—the list is endless. The millions are also endless.

4v2iii1v4iii1v 2iv4iv 3iv1v5ii1v4iii 1i3iv
3v4i4i3v4iii4v5i3iv2iv4v5v 5iii2iv4v2iii3v5i4v
4iv3v3iii1v3v3iv1v 4v3v 4i4iii3v2i2iv4v 2i4iii3v3iii 2iv4v.

#36
_____

_____

_____

PRISM PATTERNS

—

As you explore the world of millionaires, you discover that they earned their fortunes by profiting from patterns in the world around them. An enlightened idea is a ray of pure intelligence beaming down from Higher Power—a moment of clarity—the eureka moment. This ray of light can now be refracted through the inventor's prism into a spectrum of possible . . .

P   rimary Products

R   elated Products

I   nformation Products

S   ervices

M   edia

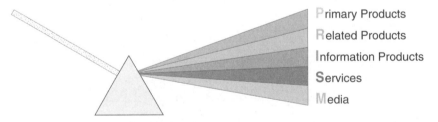

Since we love to create acronyms, we've designed the word *PRISM* to represent the patterns of profit—the Primary Products, Related Products, Information Products, Services, and Media. The first profit pattern is to have a primary product—in this case, the ordinary, run-of-the-mill automobile. The second profit pattern is to create additional or related products to enhance the primary product—such as a radar detector or car polish.

rather as the ordinary man with nothing taken away. The average man is a full human

THE PRISM CODE | *83*

PRISM Profit Patterns

PRODUCT-PRIMARY	Automobile
RELATED PRODUCTS	Radar detector, spare parts

INFORMATION PRODUCTS AND PROCESSES

Data	Kelly Blue Book
Information	Owner's manual
Directional signage	Stop signs
Consulting	Management consultant
How-to systems	Training car dealers how to sell more cars

SERVICES

Manufacturing	Factory
Design	Aftermarket upgrade
Distribution	Trucking
Marketing	Ad agencies
Sales	Fleet purchases
Protection	Car shades, window covering, from heat and UV rays
Enhancement	Deodorizer
Humor	Bumper stickers, sayings, poems, etc.
Advertising	Magnetic signs
Safety	Car insurance
Packaging	
Maintenance	Service department
Repair	Auto body shop
Renovation	Upgrade shops
Spare parts	Pep Boys
Inspection	Smog inspection
Improvement	Gas mileage
Conversion service	Converting it to home use, business, handicapped, etc.
Foreign language	Export product or make available to domestic foreigners

MEDIA

Entertainment	Car racing (adult toys)
Experience	Driving in the pace car at the Indianapolis 500
Hobby	
Toys and Games	Toy cars (kid toys)
Association	Car collectors
Business opportunity	Car club for Corvette enthusiasts
Personal endorsement	Car dealerships

being with dampened and inhibited powers and capabilities. —ABRAHAM MASLOW • If a man is called to be a street sweeper,

The third profit pattern is to add information products or processes to support the primary product, such as maps, owner's manuals, training systems, directional signage, and so on.

The fourth pattern, and perhaps the largest, is to add services to support automobile owners, such as insurance, car detailing, repair, maintenance, advertising, and so on.

The fifth profit pattern is to create media—experiences, entertainment, or personalities—that enhance the ownership of a car. This includes events like watching the Indianapolis 500, toys, hobbies, associations, and so on. The combination and permutation of opportunities swirling around a major primary product (like an automobile) is endless. Do you get the picture?

Where is *your* enlightened million-dollar idea (EMDI) going to come from? As you explore the patterns of profit that swirl around your existing lifestyle, a few patterns will begin to emerge. The experience may be similar to viewing those images that were so popular a few years ago. At first you think you are looking at a flat piece of art; then, upon intense, concentrated focus, a new and completely different 3D image explodes into your perception. "I see it!"

Look at the following illustration. How many cubes do you see?

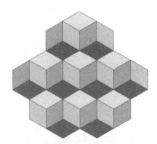

Some people see seven cubes. Other people swear that they can see eight. Which is it? Seven? Or eight? (Note: If you have difficulty seeing either seven or eight, turn the book upside down and look at it from a different perspective.) The truth is that there are both seven AND eight cubes—a total of fifteen cubes in this image—depending upon your perspective.

Millionaire patterns are very much like this. As your awareness increases, new patterns just pop out at you from daily life. The idea for television existed "in the ether" since the days of the cavemen, but it wasn't until the early 1900s that societal infrastructure and scientific wisdom allowed Philo Farnsworth to discern the opportunity of a lifetime. Accordingly, on September 7, 1928, the first television signal was transmitted in a laboratory in San Francisco and the era of television was born. Just calculate, if you can, the patterns of profit that cascaded on the millions of entrepreneurs (and shareholders of their companies) as a result of launching that one single idea! Are other "television" ideas floating around your head (or someone else's head) this very instant just waiting for your prepared, enlightened mind to recognize them and manifest them into reality?

HOW TO SEE THE PATTERNS OF PROFIT

Imagine that the three of us are actually sitting inside your residence at this very instant. Look around your environment and count how many physical objects are visible. For example, in a fairly modest home or apartment, there should be at least 101 specific objects, products, services, and commercial patterns. (At **www.crackingthemillionairecode.com** we've listed the 101 basic items, from toilet paper to a chair and a bed.)

koloraennoorevvoebahhtgourrdenuninuroadybndabyonedyorudeianulituyoesehetlilimnostiofefrsouy

4.4.2.4.5.7.5.2.6.2.3.6.4.4.5.3.3.3.8.2.6.3

#37 _ _ _ _   _ _ _ _ _, _ _, _ _ _ _ _, _ _ _ _ _ _, _ _ _ _ _ _ _,

_ _ _ _ _, _ _, _ _ _ _ _ _ _, _ _, _ _ _   _ _ _ _ _ _   _ _ _ _

_ _ _ _   _ _ _ _ _ _ _ _ _   _ _ _   _ _ _   _ _ _ _ _ _ _ _ _

As we look at the patterns of your life, we notice the prisms through which profits can flow. Every area of your life—from transportation to procreation to recreation to wealth creation—offers a completely different prism. If you like to cook, the cooking prism refracts into 101 or more cooking ideas and products. If you like to fish, the fishing prism refracts into 101 or more common, ordinary objects and ideas needed for success in fishing.

Here are some questions we'd ask you: "What fascinates you about life? What are your hobbies, interests? What do you get excited about? What television programs do you watch?" We'd wander around your house and notice where you seem to focus particular attention, whether it's a special collection of books—fiction or nonfiction—or whether it's a certain style of clothes hanging in your closet. You naturally gravitate to certain things in life. They just become "you."

Our questions to you would revolve around four key concepts: passion, talent, values, and destiny. What do you love to do? What are you good at? What is important to you? What were you born to do with your life? Answers to these questions reveal some of the clues to cracking your Destiny Code.

Destiny Code Clue Finder

PASSION

What do I love to do?

_____
_____
_____
_____

TALENT

What am I good at?

_____
_____
_____
_____

VALUES

What is important to me?

_____
_____
_____
_____

DESTINY

What was I born to do?

_____
_____
_____
_____

Eventually you begin to figure out "who you are," what you like and what you dislike—your first nature. When you begin to look at the world through your "purpose" eyes, moments of "clarity" begin to occur with greater frequency. Possibilities begin to open up to you—"What could happen if I actually . . . ?"

Whether overtly or unconsciously, you "lean toward" certain tendencies that define you. If you want a great book on the subject that comes with a very detailed analysis of your strengths and weaknesses, pick up a copy of *Now, Discover Your Strengths,* by Marcus Buckingham and Donald O. Clifton, PhD. Their book includes a wonderful program that shows you how to develop your unique talents and strengths.

These prism possibilities tug at you, draw you toward them—as if you have been "prepared" since birth (or perhaps before birth?) to make this your life's work. You sense that your destiny intertwines with certain objects, ideas, associations. Did you form a pact in a previous life? Absurd! But still . . . it's as if you've heard all this before, but you can't remember when. You mutter under your breath, "I've seen these concepts drawn out on a blackboard before. In a science lab—sometime, somewhere—I did experiments on this stuff." You just "know" things that other people simply don't know.

Certain objects and products and concepts begin to glow with a special aura. The intelligences that comprise this quantum field seem to be calling you. "Morph me. Improve me. Make me better. Help me serve the world in a more loving way. Refine me. Take away my impurities. Help me bless more people. Make me less expensive yet more effective. Please help me." And as you do follow your passion, groping toward a greater clarity about your new "calling," you become more attuned to the messages that are flowing through you from Higher Power. You become more courageous to be able to act upon them. You begin to live on purpose.

That was quite a philosophical detour, wasn't it? Let's get back to work. Remember, we're still sitting in your living room trying to show you where the money in your house is hidden.

LET'S SEE IF WE CAN MILLIONIZE SOMETHING

—

Let's make some assumptions. We've determined that you've been putting in your Big Rocks every day searching for your personal Great Idea. We have a hunch that you're a natural-born entrepreneur. You're ready to create some-thing and market it. We've discovered (let's say) that ever since you were a child you have been fascinated with writing instruments—all kinds of pens and drawing instruments, both new and antique. It's your hobby. You even have displayed a nice collection of unusual pens in a cabinet. You subscribe to the *Pen Collectors International* magazine and go to Pen Collectors semi-nars and workshops. You never thought you could make any serious money from it. You're just a pen "nut."

#38 _____

How many fortunes do you think have been created by this simple object? There must be 10,000 companies worldwide today that reap the bulk of their profits from the pen prism. If your life depended on making a million dollars with a totally new "pen" concept by this time next year, could

your rent? (Better pay up before you receive your eviction notice.) —ROBERT G.

THE PRISM CODE | *89*

you do it? (Notice how the previous question galvanizes your mind.) What if you didn't know anything about the pen business—or about *any* business for that matter—but you still were "under the gun" to launch a successful product from "scratch." What would be your first step?

Step One: Pick a Team

YOU NEED TO INVOLVE A TEAM OF COMMITTED INDIVIDUALS. THE selection of your soul-storming team members—who, how, when, where—will be shared with you in Chapter 7, "The Angel Code." We'll share with you daily exercises and processes designed to prepare these "other sets of eyes" to discern and capitalize on the prism patterns around you. For now, let's just assume that you have been joined by at least four other highly motivated, talented people who want to help you succeed.

Millionairium: See Through Different Geniuses' Eyes

To prepare your team to be flooded with enlightened million-dollar ideas, let's set the stage for you. Imagine a brightly lit space set in the center of a large room. On this stage is a sturdy, ornate pedestal, about three feet high. On the top of the pedestal is a flat shelf where each EMDI will be displayed under a brilliant spotlight. We call this the Imaginarium of Wealth . . . or the Millionairium. Step up onto the stage and walk around the pedestal. Although there is nothing yet on it, you can imagine what it will be like to see your EMDI from all angles.

As they begin to focus, your team is going to come up with many flashes of insight, strokes of genius, enlightning strikes of ideas for improving the world. We call these million-*aha*s! (Our hope for you is that your life will be flooded with million-*aha*s from this moment forward.) To access your sixth sense (*aha*-ability), we recommend that you involve all five of your senses. Your Millionairium is as multisensory as your imagination. (Remember, we're from California so some of these ideas are going to seem a little "out there." But as Einstein said, "For an idea which, at first, does not seem absurd—there is no hope." Welcome to the land of the absurd.) Here are some definitions to learn:

MILLION-*AHA*S. How do you know if an idea is an enlightened million-dollar idea? Flashes of creative brilliance will connect the hidden dots. It's that Eureka! moment when a good idea floods into your mind. You say to yourself, "Now *that's* a million-dollar idea!"

MILLION-EARS. How do you know what an EMDI sounds like? It just resonates within you. You just know it. To increase your audible awareness, add some music to your Millionairium. Let each team member choose his or her favorite creativity-inducing music. Play it for one another to find the music that seems to produce the best result.

MILLION-AIRS. What does an EMDI smell like? That's a crazy thought! Heighten your olfactory awareness by adding fortunate fragrances to your Millionairium. Just which aroma will most stimulate your imagination? Maybe it's a spicy incense, a burning candle, a flower bouquet, or a natural potpourri. Experiment. Find just the right combination of scents to ignite your senses.

MILLION-UMMS. What does an EMDI taste like? Awaken your gustatory sensitivities by adding some titillating tastes to your Millionairium. What flavor on the tongue inspires the imagination? What savor heightens your sensory apparatus? Experiment. Find just the right combination of luscious, healthy snacks.

MILLION-ARMS. What does a brilliant thought feel like? Is it warm? Is it cool? Does it vibrate or is it still? When you have a Great Idea, where do you feel it? Does it feel good? If a million-dollar idea brushed by you, would you notice it? Put your arms around your idea. Feel it. Fondle it. Nuzzle it. Caress it. Give it a hug.

MILLION-EYES. What does an EMDI look like? Does it give off a certain glow—an aura? Sharpen your focus. See everything through enlightened eyes. Shine an enlightened spotlight on it.

Your EMDI is ready to be coached out of hiding by just the ideal combinations of sights, sounds, smells, tastes, and touches. There it is!

On a personal level, when your awareness is heightened and fine-tuned, you become a sensing mechanism for tuning into the hidden messages that the world around you is subliminally sending you. On a team level, when you and your team are disciplined enough, you become an amazing million-dollar idea factory that receives, processes, and improves the world around you.

Million-eyes	How to see the invisible clues hidden all around you
Million-ears	How to hear the inaudible hints
Million-airs	How to smell the imperceptible signals
Million-umms	How to taste the unsavorable signs
Million-arms	How to feel the inscrutable traces

It only gets better with focus and practice. As John Steinbeck wrote: "Ideas are like rabbits. You get a couple and learn how to handle them, and pretty soon you have a dozen."

Let's assume that you've prepared your mind, assembled a crack team, and are ready to turn on your million senses.

#39 _____

_____

_____

Step Two: Pass Your Product
Through the Millionairium

AS PART OF YOUR TEAM SOUL-STORMING, YOU WILL BE PROCESSING your idea through the four million-dollar filters of the Millionairium. Each filter refines, screens, and amplifies your ideas—similar to refining gold ore to leave you with an ingot of pure 24-karat gold. (Three of these filters are discussed in this chapter; the fourth is in Chapter 6.)

For most of us, our ability to "daydream" has been in decline since kindergarten. Therefore, the Millionairium is designed to "loosen" up rigid, inflexible thinking. To help you discern the patterns of profit, you and your team will access several contributing sets of "eyes." In the chapter on the Angel Code, you'll learn how to add potent circles of influence to your Millionairium.

INNER CIRCLE. This circle is composed of you and your team of 5–10 players.

VIRTUAL CIRCLE. On the imaginary side you can add enlightened "virtual" experts, by visualizing a conversation with Leonardo da Vinci, say, or Thomas Edison. Don't you think these two inventors would have something to contribute?

WINNER'S CIRCLE. Your team has physical, real-world contact with many players: enlightened customers, partners, family, friends, associates, suppliers, vendors, mentors, consultants, and coaches. Don't you think at least one of them might have an insight on how to "enlighten" your "pet pen" project?

ETERNAL CIRCLE. On the spiritual side, are there enlightened angels, emissaries from Higher Power to help you visualize a new approach?

NOW, THE MILLIONAIRIUM

Imagine gently placing your selected object—the pen, for example—on the brilliantly illuminated pedestal in the center of the stage. The pedestal is surrounded by concentric circles of chairs. The first circle of chairs—the Inner Circle—is occupied by the members of your team. Don't forget to include the first and most important team member in your enlightened deliberations: Higher Power is the ultimate mentor, guide, teacher.

The second row of chairs is to be occupied by your virtual team—26 imagined experts invited to lend their collective wisdom to the process (more on this in Chapter 7). The third row of imaginary chairs is occupied by your winning team. Each team member is encouraged to prepare a list of 101 successful people that they know in their life. The Winner's Circle is made up of hundreds of relationships that may provide essential resources later on. In Chapter 7 we'll explain how the concentric circles of influence around your team reach as many as 5,000,000 people. For now, imagine that several million smart eyes are focused on your pen.

The First Filter: Patterns of Profit Overlay

AS A WARM-UP EXERCISE, DISCUSS WHICH OF THE FIVE CATEGORIES of the PRISM relate to your chosen idea by asking five PRISM questions:

Pattern 1: Primary Product—How could this pen be dramatically improved?

Pattern 2: Related Product—What add-on product would make a pen more useful?

Pattern 3: Information Product—Who needs valuable information about a pen?

94 | CRACKING THE MILLIONAIRE CODE

Pattern 4: Service Product—Who needs help with their pens or pen businesses?

Pattern 5: Media Product—What experience could you create with pens?

The purpose of this exercise is to stretch your mind to alternative opportunities. For example, your initial impulse was to create, manufacture, and market a revolutionary pen product. But in soul-storming, you and your team realize that you don't have to start from scratch. Perhaps you could be a distribution service arm of the hundreds of existing pen manufacturers worldwide. You love pens. They love to make pens. You market their pens. It's cheaper, simpler, easier, faster. Everyone wears destiny smiles.

This alternative possibility may remain as a backup idea. It could be the first spin-off idea when your Great Idea hits the Great Time. That brings us to the second filter of the Millionairium, which we call the Million-Eyes process.

The Second Filter: Million-Eyes

THIS PROCESS CONSISTS OF A SERIES OF NINE EMPOWERING QUES-tions designed to stretch the team imagination to see the world through different eyes. The soul-storming as a team is also called soul-utionizing. The ground rules are simple; assuming that this product never existed, how would you create it or re-create it from scratch if you were looking through more powerful eyes?

Eternalize: How would Higher Power transform and enlighten this?

Billionize: How would a billionaire (of unlimited resources) redesign it?

Futurize: What will this look like 100 years from now?

Hypersensitize: How could this be multisensitized? (Add smell, taste, touch, sound, light.)

Expertize: How would the world's leading scientists and experts improve this?

Globalize: Where in the world could we take this? What in the world could we bring here?

Childize: How would a five-year-old child improve this? (Ask 101 childlike questions.)

Blindsize: What if we could see like the blind and hear like the deaf? (Disability in one area gives superability in the other areas. What do they perceive that we can't?)

Nostalgisize: What if we could bring back the past?

In our experience, amazing, exhilarating mind shifts occur while soulutionizing your product idea through these questions. Your problem will not be too few ideas but many dozens of interesting ideas—so many that you could be drowning in opportunity. This is where most people flounder. They don't know how to focus these ideas into one, viable, profit-producing chunk or stream of bankable cash.

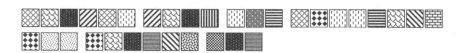

#40 _____

The Million-Eyes voting process is important. As each of the nine Million-Eyes questions is asked there is a five-minute group discussion. Then, each team member writes down the idea they believe has the greatest potential for enlightened profit. Accordingly, at the end of the session, each team member will have nine total ideas. Then, with intuitional inspiration, each team member takes a few minutes to select their top three business ideas—and to write each idea on a single sheet of paper. Assuming a team with five members, there will be 15 potential million-dollar ideas. The

15 notes are collected and stacked one on top of the other to make a single pile.

Remember this is still creative ideation. You haven't yet settled on the final product.

The Third Filter: Great Idea Grid

A LEADER IS CHOSEN TO TAKE 1 OF THE 15 IDEAS FROM THE TOP of the pile and compare it with the next idea underneath it. A conversation ensues to score each of the competing million-dollar concepts based on six key factors: enlightenment, simplicity, speed, ease, cost, and investment. (See the Great Idea Grid on page 97.)

In deciding the winner, keep in mind Occam's razor, the scientific theory posited by William of Occam in the fourteenth century. Stated simply: The simplest answer is the best answer. For example, suppose one of the first two competing ideas is to create a space-age pen that works through telekinesis— what you think is automatically written down on the page in front of you. (If someone creates this pen, it *will* make him/her a billionaire, but that's not the point.) The development of this idea will take, as our partner Tom Painter says, "millions of dollars and thousands of lives." The second idea on the list is to make a million dollars by giving pens away for free. Whoa! How would *that* work? The team finds a corporate sponsor who would supply free pens for every college student in the world—on two conditions: one, the sponsor (giver) of the pens would emblazon an advertising logo on the pen, and two, the recipient (givee) of the free pen would agree to receive an e-mail blast from the sponsor once a week for 52 weeks. The sponsor would have to be convinced of the profit potential of this kind of "free" publicity. As for the students? Why pay for pens when someone else will give them to you?

When these ideas are compared side by side, the winner is the one that would be the simplest to implement. Unless you're privy to an easy, simple way to develop a pen that automatically writes down your thoughts, our vote would be the "free" pen idea—simply because it's simpler.

But there are other criteria to consider also. They actually form a grid.

THE GREAT IDEA GRID

	Low	Medium	High
ENLIGHTENED	2	4	6
SIMPLE	1	2	3
FAST	1	2	3
EASY	1	2	3
INEXPENSIVE	1	2	3
LEAST INVESTMENT $	1	2	3

Total Grid Score

Each competing idea is ranked on a scale of low to high in each of the six criteria. Note that an enlightened idea is weighted double, because, although it may appear to us mere humans to be difficult, Higher Power already knows the simplest, fastest, easiest, cheapest way to bring an idea to fruition. If you sense an idea is enlightened, it scores more.

Circle the score for each of the criteria and add up the score. Then, with this as backdrop, have each member of the team vote on which of the two competing ideas should be kept and which one shelved (for now).

The winning idea is then compared with the next idea on the pile of 15. After the scoring is complete, a vote is taken and the winning idea is then compared with the next one on the pile. And so on, until the final three ideas remain, ranked in order from one to three.

The three ideas that survived the Grid are the result of enlightened win-novation: refined, polished, fine-tuned, seasoned and perfumed, and ready for the next filter. But before we continue, let's review how we got here.

STEP ONE. You picked an object that had a purpose "glow" about it—a pen.

STEP TWO. You explored the PRISM variations of profit as a way to loosen up your group.

STEP THREE. You asked the nine Million-Eyes questions, and team members wrote down their best ideas for improving your Great Idea. Each idea was written on a sheet of paper and the stack of 15 ideas was ready for the Great Idea Grid.

STEP FOUR. The top two ideas on the stack were passed through the Great Idea Grid to come up with a score. The team voted on which idea would be the better idea. The idea with the highest score won. The winner was then compared with the next idea on the stack. The winner of this duel is compared with the next idea. This continues until the final three ideas are left ranked one, two, and three.

STEP FIVE. Now you have three viable ideas.

In the next chapter we'll show you how to run these ideas through the Wheel of Wealth, which is the fourth filter in the Millionairium.

Chapter Six

WOW

In 1960 Rosser Reeves, the advertising guru, in his seminal book *Reality in Advertising,* coined an acronym that has been on the lips of marketers worldwide ever since: USP. It stands for Unique Selling Proposition. When someone sees an ad for your product, they've got to say to themselves, "WOW! I want one of those. *Now!*"

Reeves is responsible for one of the most famous ads in history, for M&Ms: M&M candies melt in ____ _____, ___ __ ____ ____.

Similarly to M&Ms, your product has to melt in their hearts, not in their minds. This chapter teaches you a process we call the WOW—the Wheel of

John Paul Dejoria

John Paul Dejoria is a Horatio Alger character. He emerged from rags to riches and became a great philanthropist along the way.

J.P., as friends call him, started his flourishing hair care enterprise while sleeping in the back of his car. J.P. was the businessman and his partner, Paul Mitchell, was the hairstylist. In 1980 they had a dream; they wanted a company established by hairdressers for hairdressers. Their venture was dedicated to the success of individual stylists, their salons, and the professional beauty industry as a whole. Their marketing strategy was to travel extensively and conduct no-cost product demonstrations for salon owners. They also guaranteed the salon owners that they would sell all the products they purchased or get a full refund. This practice was a first for the beauty and hair care industry. With only $750 in borrowed dollars between them, the two men courageously started what has become the fastest-growing privately owned hair care business in the world, doing close to $700 million a year in 45 countries with approximately 15,000 salons. In the beginning they faced challenge after challenge. "We should have gone bankrupt perhaps 50 times during that first year," says Mr. Dejoria.

John Paul Dejoria started by asking bottle manufacturers to give him bids on 10,000, 50,000, 100,000, and 500,000 bottles. He made the same request to the printer and the manufacturer. He asked them all for 30-day terms. (Essentially, he started with no money down and a supplier-financed deal, with 30 days to pay.)

The artist creating the labels would not agree to wait 30 days to get his pay, so John Paul negotiated the artist's fee down from $1,000 to $750, which was his total available cash. Then, while learning to eat on less than three dollars a day, J.P. went from beauty shop to beauty shop asking for their business. Four out of five stores rejected him. He was unfazed. He asked beauty salons for dozen-unit orders and cheerfully accepted twos and threes as samples. Having accumulated enough orders, he went to a manufacturers' representative organization and convinced them that he had the

→

Wealth. It shows you how to enliven every product with a Unique "Souling" Proposition—to give your product the soul of uniqueness, originality, differentiation.

Reeves also wrote another famous ad, "How do you spell relief? R-O-L-A-I-D-S." If you're a budding entrepreneur, long on ideas but short on cash, how do *you* spell relief? W-O-W. The Wheel of Wealth answers the question, "How can I create a product that will *wow* the world?"

Ruoy tcudorp tsum tlem ni rieht straeh, ton ni rieht sdaeh.

#41

If you're an intrapreneur working inside someone else's enterprise, your job depends on what you contribute. If it were your company—if you called the shots—how would you wow your customers? Use the WOW to find new ways to refresh an existing product or to electrify a new product.

In the previous chapter we selected an ordinary "pen" for our case study. But before we run the pen through the WOW, let's limber up your mind. Take a trip to your mailbox and see if you received any mail order catalogues today. If you don't get much junk mail (lucky you!), you might need to visit the local post office or recycling center and cull through the bins where people have discarded their tons of junk mail. Digging through the trash might seem a bit creepy (especially if those empty aluminum cans look tempting) but remember this is serious research! You'll find catalogues specializing in almost anything. For our case study, you're looking for a catalogue that has something to do with pens.

Looking through a competitor's catalogue opens your eyes. It might be a bit discouraging to see a catalogue filled with so many items similar to the ones you're about ready to bet your life savings on. (And frankly, a good scare is not a bad thing since the success rate of start-ups is so low—unless, of course, you implement the strategies in this book.) But studying the successes of others shows you what is working. Each item had to go through a

initial business and that they had a no-lose opportunity if they took on his line. Of course, they had to prepay their order, which funded his company. And the rest, as they say, is history.

As just one example of J.P.'s regular, hands-on philanthropy, he was invited to talk at a women's correctional prison in Texas. Speaking to more than 1,000 female felons, he encouraged them to start their own businesses when they got out. As he put it, "You can start your own honest business for essentially zero. All you need is a cell phone, a P.O. box address, some cards and stationery, and you're in business for less than $29. And if you want a career in cosmetology, my company is offering scholarships, and when you graduate, I can promise you some job offers."

Bob Circosta

In the 1970s Bob Circosta was a radio talk show host, sharing with listeners in Clearwater, Florida, his thoughts on politics, national events, and everyday life. One day Bud Paxson, the station's owner, came into Bob's office with a box of electronic can openers he had just accepted as payment for radio airtime. Bud told Bob, "When you come out of the news, I want you to sell these can openers."

Bob was uncomfortable, but he had a family to feed and a radio station to keep on the air. After Bud explained the relationship between selling the can openers and getting a paycheck, the can openers started to look pretty good. By simply telling listeners the benefits of the openers, and inviting them to call now, reserve one, and come down to the station and pick it up, Bob Circosta sold 112 can openers. In that moment an industry was born.

For five years Bud and Bob used the radio to sell everything from jewelry and gadgets to expensive computers. At one point Bob went to Bud and said, "I despise selling." Bud gave Bob advice that would change his life. Bud said, "Sales have nothing to do with selling. Sales have everything

→

dozen hurdles just to make it into the catalogue, and many won't make it into the next one. Call your would-be competitors and ask to be put on the mailing list for their catalogues. Every few months go through the stack and notice how products come and go. There are a few perennial winners. There are lots of flashy losers that fade and disappear. The question that is running through your mind is, "Why do the winners win?"

Now take that catalogue you dug out of the trash bin at the post office. Go through it page by page, stopping at each item to ask yourself, "What is the USP of this product? What makes this product successful?" In other words, why would a catalogue risk valuable space to display this product when there were 1,000 different products competing for the same space? What is unique about it? Which of the following features make it stand out?

____Price	____Brand	____Style
____Name	____Effectiveness	____Design
____Size	____Quality	____Availability
____Solution	____Color	____Marketing
____Speed	____Material	____Sale
____Ease	____Beauty	____Promotion

Which of these features will set *your* product apart? What will be your Unique Souling Proposition? Here's the bottom line: You can sell enough of any product to make a living, but if you want roaring success, your product has got to WOW them. That's what this next exercise is about.

THE FOURTH FILTER OF THE MILLIONAIRIUM: THE WOW PROCESS— WHEEL OF WEALTH

———

In the previous chapter you came up with three broad product ideas for a pen. The WOW consists of a final series of 21 questions designed to assay each of the three ideas to see which one gets the gold, silver, or bronze medal.

to do with helping another person." Fortified by this new perspective, Bob was ready to help a lot of viewers out with the next product or service.

In the 1980s, when America got wired to cable TV, Bob went on camera with what he considered an unsellable item, an AM/FM radio toilet paper dispenser. After simply using his newly developed benefits formula he sold an astounding 4,000 in five minutes. The business he founded on the strength of this success, The Home Shopping Network, would grow into a $7 billion-a-year international behemoth, offering customers 65,000 different products over the next several decades!

And Bob Circosta has an offer for you when your enlightened product is ready for the marketplace. Go to **www.crackingthemillionairecode.com** and learn how Bob Circosta can show you how to get your product on TV. He declares. "If it's a fit we can sell your product or service on the air, or do a joint venture."

Wealthy beyond his dreams, Bob takes pleasure now in helping others become successful. He wants to share his knowledge, expertise, and awareness to help ever-increasing numbers of people. To this end Bob asks everyone he meets to take the following exercise.

Write down the five things you'd like people to say about you at your funeral. Of these, how many are you working on today? Here, in your own words, is the blueprint to making your journey meaningful, important, and truly capable of making a difference.

☀ *WOW 1. Enlighten it.*
How can we enlighten this in the most unique way?

THE SOUL OF ENLIGHTENED ENTREPRENEURSHIP IS TO ALLOW THE clear beam of Higher Purpose to flow through you in the form of products, services, and experiences that spread joy to every customer. Then, you share the first profits from your service and designate a worthy cause to be the perpetual, residual recipient. Soul-storm with your team, "How will we share the wealth? How can our PRISM be a source of profits to benefit a specific charity?" This enlists the help of the charity, the heart of the buyer, and the blessing of Higher Power. The prime example of this is Newman's Own; with revenues in excess of $100 million a year, it donates 100% of all profits to a long list of charities. Nearly $200 million has already been donated to worthy causes since the launch of the company in 1984.

Most businesspeople start businesses to earn a profit. We encourage you to start a new enterprise with the **primary** goal of raising funds for residual philanthropy.

The sun icon is to remind you to soul-storm with your Inner Circle ways to enlighten your ideas.

E	A	Z	Y	P	Q	Y	W
V	N	W	O	W	T	O	A
E	D	I	U	S	P	U	N
R	X	N	R	A	X	T	T
Q	W	E	A	L	T	H	X
V	C	O	U	L	D	E	Y

#42 _____

_____

WOW: The Wheel of Wealth Questions

WOW 1. Enlighten it.	*How can we enlighten this?*
WOW 2. Infinity it.	*How can we residualize this?*
WOW 3. Multiple stream it.	*How can we create additional streams of income from this?*
WOW 4. Combine it.	*How can we combine this with something else?*
WOW 5. Plus it.	*What can we add to this?*
WOW 6. Subtract it.	*What can we subtract from this?*
WOW 7. Multiply it.	*How can we multiply this?*
WOW 8. Exponentialize it.	*How can we make this grow exponentially?*
WOW 9. Divide it.	*How can we divide this?*
WOW 10. Minimize it.	*How can we make this smaller?*
WOW 11. Maximize it.	*How can we make this larger?*
WOW 12. Focus it.	*How can we focus this?*
WOW 13. Trend it.	*How can we attach this to a trend?*
WOW 14. Time it.	*How can we improve the timing of this?*
WOW 15. Rabbit it.	*How can we speed this up?*
WOW 16. Turtle it.	*How can we slow this down?*
WOW 17. Undo it.	*How can we undo/reverse parts of this?*
WOW 18. Connect it.	*How can we connect this to something else?*
WOW 19. Sex it.	*How can we redesign this to appeal to gender?*
WOW 20. Yin/yang it.	*How can we attract its opposite?*
WOW 21. Recycle it.	*How can we make this more "planet-friendly"?*

∞ WOW 2. *Infinity it.*
How can we residualize this?

RESIDUAL INCOME MEANS "MAKING MONEY WHILE YOU SLEEP." Residual philanthropy means "giving money while you sleep." The left side of the infinity icon represents money flowing to you in this life for efforts you have already expended—money while you sleep. The right side of the infinity icon represents the money that flows perpetually to your favorite philanthropic entities.

One of the main reasons why most businesses fail is that they don't plan for either residual earning or **residual** giving. They don't have a 101-year plan. They're lucky to have *any* plan. They hope to make next week's payroll. Before you open your doors, your Big Picture road map should be clear in your mind. The enterprise you launch must make it because the philanthropic cause you're committed to *needs* it. People are counting on you. Long after you're gone, imagine the acorns that are falling from the forest of oak trees that you planted. Shade is being enjoyed by future crowds of grateful people. Can't you see them there? Will you work smart? Yes! Because your vision demands it. We'll explore the concept of residual income and residual philanthropy more deeply in Chapter 11. The infinity icon is a reminder to ask the question, "How can we residualize this?" Is your potential product ready to bring in residual profits?

 ## WOW 3. *Multiple stream it.*
How can we create additional streams of income from this?

MOST BUSINESSES FAIL BECAUSE THEY RELY TOO MUCH ON ONE stream of income. When that stream dries up, so does their **business.** But with several streams of income to count on, the loss of one stream is merely a temporary setback. Multiple streaming is a defensive strategy as well as an offensive strategy. Gotta have it.

So, let's consider our pen case study. As soon as the pen finds a viable market, and money is flowing in, the next step is to launch your Plan B product. Then, your Plan C. You can never tell when the B or C product will catch hold and outpace Plan **A** by a mile. Apple used to sell nothing but computers; now most of the company's profit comes from iPod, its MP3 player.

A+B *Wow 4. Combine it.*
A + B. How can we combine this with something else?

AN OBVIOUS EXAMPLE IS THE TWO OF US. MARK VICTOR HANSEN IS the coauthor of the number one series of right-brain heart books in the world—*Chicken Soup for the Soul.* Robert Allen is the author of some of the all-time bestselling money books—*Creating Wealth, Nothing Down, Multiple Streams of Income.* It would appear that the two of us don't speak the same language. Truth is, Mark has a brilliant business mind and Robert is no slouch when it comes to right-brain creativity. But the mixing of the two of us gives both of our databases a fresh approach. *Chicken Soup* books find a new market in Robert's database. And who doesn't want to earn Multiple Streams of Income? As they say, we're greater than the sum of our two parts.

The A+B icon is a reminder to ask, "What could we combine with our product to create a much bigger, better product?" The cell phone and the PDA represent a marriage of communication and organization. The cell phone and the digital camera are a marriage of communication and entertainment. The marriage of two equal products makes the combination massively more useful to certain customers.

$$\text{Near}: \frac{\text{Near}}{\text{VIE+G}} + \frac{24}{7} + \frac{\text{Pe}+(\text{r}+\text{t})}{\text{Re+Sid}} + \text{U}-\text{all}=\text{Y}$$

#43 _____

✚ *Wow 5. Add it.*
What can we add to this?

SOMETIMES JUST ONE ADDITIONAL INGREDIENT CAN MAKE A PROD-uct unique enough to become an entirely new product. What billion-dollar business could you **create** when you add a simple ingredient to ordinary aspirin? The added ingredient is caffeine. The product is named Anacin. It's been around for 75 years.

Think of all of the cereals that made their name—Special K or Total—by adding vitamins to their products. Notice all of the cosmetic and hair care products that add vitamins and/or minerals. What about Ivory soap? What did they add to the "soap that floats"? Bubbles. (Discovered by mistake.) Speaking of soap, what do they add to Dove? Moisturizers.

Speaking of additives, here's a blurb from the Chevron website:

> *Gas is gas, right? Not quite! Fact is, all gasolines contain additives. Some additives are better than others are, but none surpass the proven power of Techron®. And only Chevron gasolines contain Techron® . . . based on a family of compounds called polyetheramines. These compounds function like highly effective detergents for removing and preventing deposits (dirt) in engine fuel systems.*

Do you know what Techron® is? Do you care? Well, some people do. They've gotta get their Techron®.

The all-time classic in WOW lore is the Post-it Notes story. Post-its were discovered by the addition of a weak adhesive to an ordinary notepad. The world has never been the same.

The plus icon is there to remind you to ask, "What can we add to this product?"

▬ *WOW 6. Subtract it.*
What can we subtract from this?

SOME PRODUCTS BECOME EVEN MORE SUCCESSFUL BY WHAT THEY subtract. Speaking of gasoline, what is more expensive than a gallon of gaso-

—ROBERT G. ALLEN

line? A gallon of water. What?! Do you remember when cheap water from the faucet was good enough? How did a gallon of fancy bottled water get so expensive? It started by what they took out—the impurities. They sucked the water out of the ground from the deepest, purest places and delivered it to us in clean, pure, stylish containers. Then, having subtracted the impurities, they added to the water minerals, vitamins, highly charged oxygen molecules. The result? Highly profitable water.

Do you remember when the fat-free craze hit in the 1980s and food products began to boast of their low-fat content—whole milk, 2%, 1%, no-fat milk? Then in the 1990s the Atkins Diet hit and everyone began to brag about low-carb content. Fat free. Carb free. Sugar free. Caffeine free. What will they take away next?

Make your product special by either adding **to** or subtracting from it. Or both.

✖ *WOW 7. Multiply it.* *How can we multiply this?*

SHOPPING AT A NORMAL STORE USED TO BE A "ONESIES AND TWOSIES" experience—you buy one of this and two of that. Then starting in 1976 the first huge warehouse store, Price Club, opened up in San Diego, followed in 1983 by the first Costco. The idea was simple: Come into our warehouse; we'll charge you a yearly fee; instead of a shopping cart we'll give you a flatbed on wheels and instead of a pack of gum we'll sell you a whole carton of gum—cheap! The Great Idea worked. Multiple sales took off. Now, there are hundreds of similar stores all over the world with over 100,000 employees and close to $50 billion in annual sales.

An entirely different method of multiplying sales was launched in 1984. Millions of dollars' worth of products are moved each day through "in your face" television marketing from the two channels that specialize in it—QVC and Home Shopping Network—and the myriad of knockoffs. On page 102, you can read the story of how Bob Circosta helped launch HSN. How it came about is amazing.

failure, success for success: What you project is what is reflected back to you.

safe landing.   —ROBERT G. ALLEN   • Life is a hailstorm of distraction.

WOW | *111*

On a smaller scale, Sherry Granader uses the multiplication concept to multiply her profits. She is the author of *Soy You Wanna Lose Weight?* about the health benefits of soy. She has become an expert and public speaker in her niche market. Eventually, she discovered that soy product manufacturers would pay her extra to have her promote their products during her public speeches. Each company pays her approximately $1,000 to mention their product and its benefits. She mentions about 10 different products per talk. That doubles her fee and makes for a great bonus income. In addition, she gives free samples to every audience member—like Lean Routine and Bite Bars Nutrition 21. The attendees leave smiling because they receive instantly usable information and valuable product samples.

Sherry believes that almost every "want-to-be" speaker and writer can multiply their income like she did—by conquering a little niche and becoming its spokesperson.

The multiplication icon reminds you to think of ways to multiply your sales.

X^2 *WOW 8. Exponentialize it.*
How can we make this grow exponentially?

MULTIPLICATION IS NICE BUT EXPONENTIAL MULTIPLICATION IS even nicer. What does this mean mathematically?

Here is a chart that shows the difference.

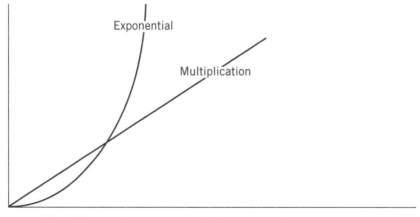

The difference between multiplied growth and exponential growth

"Word of mouth" helps multiply sales, but exponential growth is "word of mouth on steroids." Sales go ballistic.

Case in point: Hotmail. The company was launched on July 4, 1996, with $300,000 of borrowed money. It was sold on December 31, 1997, to Microsoft for *$400 million*! What happened in those 18 months was exponential! When you get deeper into the story, you get a sense that this was a Higher-Powered idea drenched in destiny. Steve Jurvetson was the venture capital partner who lent the initial $300,000 to launch Hotmail. In the December 1998 issue of *Wired,* in an article titled "Hot Male," Po Bronson wrote about Jurvetson and his memory of the day when Sabeer Bhatia and his partner, Jack Smith, came in to pitch their idea: "He brought in these revenue estimates showing that he was going to grow the company faster than any in history. We dismissed the projections outright, but he insisted. 'You don't believe we're going to do that?' He had hallucinogenic optimism. He had an unquenchable sense of destiny. But he was right. He grew the subscriber base faster than any company in the history of the world." From 100 subscribers in the first hour to over 10 million in just the first year!

$$\div 2 \times P+0+18+T+L!$$

#44

Please *don't* file this story under "Sure, everything was easier in those dot-com days." Instead, count up the WOW principles that were converging to exponentialize this idea.

- (WOW 6. Subtract it.) First, they made the service free. They subtracted the price. That was brilliant.
- (WOW 4. Combine it.) Second, two essential products were combined—snail mail (U.S. Postal Service) with the computer—to **make** sending mail easier and cheaper. Brilliant!

- (WOW 8. Exponentialize it.) Third, it was contagious. When something is fun and fast and free, no wonder it's *hot!* The name Hotmail was originally spelled HoTMaiL as a play on words with the Internet programming language HTML. Soon this was forgotten and Hotmail became the most unforgettable USP in only seven letters!

Every time someone used Hotmail, it spread the message like a virus—because an advertisement for Hotmail was at the bottom of the e-mail. Brilliant!

As we continue, try to figure out how many of the 21 WOW principles are present in the great idea for Hotmail.

It was a brilliant Higher-Powered recipe. A cup of WOW, a dash of destiny, a pinch of patience, a teaspoon of tenacity. Delicious!

÷ *WOW 9. Divide it.*
How can we divide this?

AN APARTMENT BUILDING DIVIDED INTO INDIVIDUAL OWNERSHIPS is called a condominium. Converting ordinary rental apartment units into condos can double or triple the value of the entire property. On one day, the building is worth X. On the next day, it's worth 3X. All because of the WOW principle of division.

How does this relate to the marketing of products? Paul Hartunian used this WOW principle when he bought a stack of old lumber being hauled from a construction site at the original Brooklyn Bridge. He then cut up the wood into one-inch-square pieces and sold them to tourists under the banner, "New Jersey man sells the Brooklyn Bridge for $14.95." It brought in $7 million in orders in the first year. That's a lot of money to divide up. Division is a beautiful thing.

The concept of division can itself be divided. Division #1. You divide up a product like the Brooklyn Bridge. Division #2. You divide up the market into smaller and smaller segments—geographic, ethnic, religious, special interest. That's exactly what *Chicken Soup for the Soul* has done. Volume I was a huge bestseller. Then, the idea was divided into Volume II (*A Second Helping*) and Volume III (*A Third Helping*). Then, they had the "bright" idea to reach more hearts one story at a time. Where do the brightest ideas come from? By subdividing the original idea into specific markets. *Chicken Soup for the Pet Lover's Soul* (special interest), *Chicken Soup for the Canadian's Soul* (special geography), *Chicken Soup for the African American Soul* (special ethnic group). Brilliant!

A cartoon hanging in the Chicken Soup offices illustrates how thinly this idea can be sliced.

Copyright Steve York/CartoonResource.com

■ *WOW 10. Minimize it.*
How can we make it smaller?

WOW 11. Maximize it.
How can we make it bigger?

JUST ONE EXAMPLE CAN ILLUSTRATE BOTH WOW 10 AND WOW 11. Take the classic Post-it Notes we talked about earlier. Shrink them down to the size of a postage stamp or blow them up to giant flip chart size. Now you have two new products for two new markets. Can **your** product be made more successful by minimizing it? Or maximizing it? Or both? That's the idea behind mini golf courses and IMAX theaters.

Get even more ridiculous. Make it so small you have to see it with a microscope. Or blow it up to the size of a hot air balloon. Imagine that its shape is elastic enough to morph into any size. Play with it. Why would anyone want it that way?

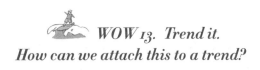 *WOW 12. Focus it. How can we focus this?*

GROW RICH IN A NICHE. THAT'S WHAT THIS ICON MEANS. SHARPEN your focus. Narrow and deep is much more viable than broad and wide. The product segment needs to be narrow enough to make the customers feel unique and special enough to sustain a successful enterprise. USP is the mantra of marketers: Unique Selling Proposition. Make sure it also means Unique Sliver of People.

Gymboree only deals with exercise for kids. Harley-Davidson only deals with a certain kind of biker. What is your niche?

WOW 13. Trend it.
How can we attach this to a trend?

HOCKEY GREAT WAYNE GRETZKY SAID HIS SUCCESS WAS GOING WHERE the puck was going to be, not where it had been. Do you know where the puck is going? People move on invisible tides. Can you tell which way the tide is running? Small groups may travel in tribal units. Can you tell where they are going to be in 10 years? Will you be there waiting for them with a warm fire and hot chocolate when they arrive? If you're riding a trend, sales come almost effortlessly; the current sweeps you toward easy street. If you're fighting a trend, you're swimming against the current.

eno nac rof efil ruoy evlos yenom melborp gnivlos smelborp!

#45 _____

_____

A host of experts are predicting what the future will bring. You'd be wise to read what they have to say before you launch your new product. Ken Dychtwald, a leading "age wave" expert, characterized the 10 physical, social, spiritual, economic, and political crises we will face as we age in the twenty-first century in the following list. (You can learn more at **www. agewave.com**.)

1. A Pandemic of Chronic Disease
2. Mass Dementia
3. The Caregiving Crunch
4. Coping with Death and Dying
5. "Gerassic Park"
6. An Inhospitable Marketplace
7. Changing Markers of Old Age
8. Financial Insecurity
9. Age Wars
10. Elder Wasteland

Let's hear what Dr. Dychtwald has to say about one of these issues. What about "Gerassic Park"? As Dychtwald writes,

All future-oriented public policy in America, including policy regarding Social Security and Medicare, is based on the assumption that there will

be no meaningful breakthroughs that will affect longevity or biological aging. So what happens if we wake up tomorrow morning and there is a breakthrough?

Might it be a "Gerassic Park" in which, instead of cloning entire humans, we find a way to clone organs? What if we learn to manipulate the body's immune system to increase longevity? Can we imagine a future without cancer, a world without Alzheimer's or heart disease? It is possible. . . . The biotechnology century is coming; we should expect the unexpected.

—Dr. Ken Dychtwald, "the 10 physical, social, spiritual, economic, and political crises the boomers will face as they age in the 21st century," american society on aging (www.asaging.org)

There are dozens of major trends and hundreds of minor ones. Massive trend waves—positive and negative—will crash on the shore of humanity in future decades whether we like it or not. The fortunes created by being "tipped off" to the future will be enormous. The billionaires of 10 and 20 years from now are ordinary people, just like you, who will be thrust onto a destiny path that will transform not only their lives but your life. That's right, *your* future will be affected by ideas that someone else is going to bring to the world—ideas that may not have yet been showered down on the earth. They are still "out there" in the ether. Someone is going to have them. Would you like one? Why should Higher Power let you have one of them? Are you ready? Could you be trusted with one? What would you do with your newfound fortune? Would you let it overwhelm you? Would you snort it or strut it or squander it? Would you tithe it? Would you put Higher Power first? Would you steward it for the greatest good of the largest number of people?

Perhaps you weren't destined to discover an idea that will change the *entire* world. It's a *big* world. But there are enough ideas for you to massively affect a part of the world. Millions can come from it. Hundreds of millions.

The trend icon is there to remind you to discern the trend.

WOW 14. Time it.
How can we improve the timing of this?

REMEMBER THE WAY IT USED TO BE? BUSINESSES OPERATED primarily Monday through Friday. The mail carrier only delivered mail during the weekdays. Nine to five were normal business hours, except for banks that always closed at 3 P.M. Nothing was open on Sunday.

Hard to believe how the world has changed in 25 years. In the next 25 years, 24/7 will be the rule rather than the exception. That's the way it is right now on the Internet: anything you want, anytime you want, anywhere you want. Right to your front door.

Doctors used to make house calls. When did that practice stop? The anything/anytime/anywhere world is going to bring back the house call. Soon everything will come to your house—not just because it's more convenient but because we won't have time to go out and get it. The world will flow to us. Mobile fitness comes right to your door. Mobile phones to go with your mobile life. Mobile hair and nail salons. Mobile waiters will bring mobile meals. Mobile car detailers. Mobile dent repair. Mobile everything. 24/7.

Think about your Great Idea. Is it ready for a 24/7 world?

WOW 15. Rabbit it. How can we speed this up?

IT'S NOT ENOUGH TO GET IT 24/7. WE WANT IT FASTER. A POSTAGE stamp costs less than a half a buck. Who would have ever thought that someone would pay *25 times* that amount to get something when they absolutely, positively had to have it overnight? Every expert in the world told Fred Smith he was nuts when he told them his Great Idea. Federal Express now brings in *billions* of dollars a year as proof that all the experts were wrong.

It's not size that's important. It's speed. Speed is leverage. Forget one-hour photo. How about one-minute photo? The business world is trying to run a faster four-minute mile. World records will be broken as businesses compete to shave a few hours off a day, a few minutes off an hour, a few seconds off a minute, a few milliseconds off a second.

Can you get your product to your customer in the blink of an eye?

7183 6974 0487146 57286322 5919 59 343153 43283719
068916564906

#46 _____

 ## WOW *16.* Turtle it. *How can we slow this down?*

S . . . L . . . O . . . W D . . . O . . . W . . . N . . . !!!! R E L A X.
Smell the roses. Your life depends on it. That's what they say. So just like modern foods have been stripped of vital nutrients, modern life strips vital ingredients of a life worth living—hugs, beauty, serenity, luxuriance, comfort, romance. Whole industries will rise to revitalize, renutrient, reacclimatize, restore bodies and minds and souls. Information, processes, and systems for slowing things down will become more and more popular. Products will tout their magical ability to slow down the aging process with revolutionary anti-aging ingredients.

Can your product slow down the rat-tat-tat-tat-tat of a machine-gun life?

WOW *17.* Undo it.
How can we undo/reverse parts of this?

YEARS AGO, WHEN YOU MADE A TYPO, YOU HAD TO CRUMPLE UP YOUR letter in a ball and start over. Then, in 1951 a 25-year-old single mom had a Great Idea. Bette Nesmith was a secretary who kept making mistakes with her new electric typewriter. She started painting over her typos with a mixed-up concoction of water-based paint poured into an empty nail polish

#47 _____

mark on it forever. —FRANÇOIS MAURIAC • *No man becomes rich unless he enriches others.* —ANDREW

bottle. Other secretaries took notice and she started selling a few bottles a week. She called her brainstorm Mistake Out. It became Wite-Out, and eventually morphed into the product you've heard of—Liquid Paper. In 1957 IBM refused to buy her idea, so she continued undaunted until Gillette purchased her company in 1979 for $48 million. Not bad for a secretary! Unfortunately, Bette didn't live long enough to enjoy most of it. She died a young 56, leaving a legacy of about $50 million. Half went to a surviving son. The other half to **philanthropy.** Good for her.

With the arrival of the computer, the need for Liquid Paper was replaced by a simple click of a mouse. On the Microsoft Suite of software programs such as Word, PowerPoint, and Excel, if you make a typo, you just highlight the error and type in the new text and voilà, it undoes what you just did. No fuss. No muss. It's instantaneous.

The WOW icon represents the "Undo" function of a business—to reverse or undo your actions and return things to the way they were. In a metaphorical sense, this icon doesn't refer to "whiting out" your mistakes but to reversing life to the way things used to be.

Whole industries will be returning to the good old days. Take the health care industry. It's a mess. The richer you get, the more you hate it . . . waiting in lines with the RAMS—an old navy slang term for the ragged, aimless multitudes. You've got the money and you're willing to pay for the right kind of attention. You don't want to wait a minute longer than you have to. Let the doctor wait for *you.* You can afford it. Doctors used to have it good. Then, HMOs wiped out that lifestyle. Now doctors have hooked up with voracious HMOs. They take their cool 150 grand and act like a time-clock employee. Service has gone to hell. Well, to heck with that!

Don't you want to reverse it—click a button and go back to the way things used to be? When did you start pumping your own gas? Don't you want the gas station attendant to know your name and to wash your windshield and to check your oil without being asked?

Don't you want 10-cent Saturday matinees and safe neighborhoods and bake sales and Main Street square dances? Some of the innocent past is gone forever, but don't you want the best of yesterday brought back? Don't you

thing that will ultimately fail. It is better yet to succeed at something worth failing for.

WOW | *121*

want to undo the parts of today that make life unbearable? Don't you want less stress and less pollution and less crime and fewer school shootings? How much would you pay for it?

Can your product reverse the slide? There's a fortune in there somewhere, and perhaps you'll find it.

@ *WOW 18. Connect it.*
How can we connect this to something else?

E-MAIL HAS TAKEN THAT STRANGE SYMBOL @—THE "AT" SIGN—AND made it something very different from what it was all those years it lay hidden on the keyboard. Now it means the connection of a single person to an ISP (Internet Service Provider), for example, **markandbob@crackingthe millionairecode.com.** When you see the "a" with the swirl around it, you know it means that that person is connected through something legitimate. The world is isolating us from each other faster than we can believe. Forget about loving your neighbor, do you even *know* your neighbor? Maybe in the heartland of America they still pass cookies over their backyard fences, but in most metropolises anonymity is king. We watch television and let it tell us what to think, becoming more disconnected by the day.

But our souls cry out for connection. Joining something—anything—is something that we need. Way. Down. Deep. Products are going to fill that void, bringing people with the same interests together. "Your child is in kindergarten? Mine too!" "You've got tickets to the Indianapolis 500? Man, I dream of sitting in the stands at the Indy!"

Enlightened products will offer a web of associations that people are missing. One major theme will be satisfying philanthropic yearnings. "You're going to Africa with a group of customers of XYZ Help-the-World Enterprise? You know, I've always wanted to do something more than just send a few dollars. Do you think they have any more spaces left?"

Memberships are "in." American Express, Costco, Sam's, and so on. Online dating services are "in."

It's going to be stars@yourenlightenedenterprise.com with all of you linked up for Higher Purposes. It's coming. "Mark" our words. "Bob" our words. It's coming.

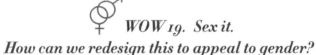

WOW 19. Sex it.
How can we redesign this to appeal to gender?

MARLBORO CIGARETTES ARE AMONG THE BESTSELLING CIGARETTES in the world (this is a great case study but not a particularly enlightened one). Did you know that from 1924 until the late 1940s Marlboro was a woman's cigarette? Yup. The motto for Marlboro used to be "Mild as May." True story. The Marlboro Man was really the Marlboro Woman! But women didn't want it, so the product died. It was resurrected when someone had the idea to market it specifically to men. Billboards started showing pictures of rugged men living a rugged cowboy life. And sales went through the roof. Actually, today, even though it's marketed primarily to men, it is also one of the world's leading cigarettes for women! They didn't want it when it was targeted only at women, but they want it now, when it's only meant for men. You see, when you decide exactly who you want as a customer *and* who you don't want, *everybody* is attracted. But when you try to be all things to all people it often means that *nobody* wants it. Here are some examples: *Sports Illustrated* swimsuit issue; Victoria's Secret; men's clothing stores; women's clothing stores; MPC—Maximum Prostate Care; Prime Factor for Women; Prime Factor for Men; and Secret deodorant.

So the male/female icon, WOW 19, is there to remind you that sex sells. Your product might be more marketable and more desirable if it is targeted only to the opposite sex. You don't see many men smoking Virginia Slims. You didn't used to see very many women entrepreneurs. But women are flooding into business, bringing with them the heart to conduct Enlightened Entrepreneurship in ways that men haven't been able to get their heads around. Enlightened Entrepreneurship is a natural for women. And men are going to love getting used to it. It's been long overdue. There's been too

— DOUGLAS

dream world, and there are some who face reality; and then there are those who turn one into the other.

EVERETT

much testosterone flowing through the halls—"Just win, baby!" Well, a softer side is a better side. No matter what your gender.

Can your product be more successfully targeted to a specific gender?

🌓 *WOW 20. Yin/yang it.*
How can we attract its opposite?

EVERYTHING HAS ITS OPPOSITE. GOOD AND EVIL. LIGHT AND DARK. Pleasure and pain. Expansion and contraction. Hot and cold. People are either running toward something positive or running from something negative. Those are the two great marketing drivers and they always will be. Your product either leads a person to Higher Power or it leads a person away. The icon for WOW 20 is there to remind you to make sure you are speaking the language of *all* of your customers. Some people are not attracted to positive messages. The light repels them. But enlightened products need to speak to everyone. The **goal** of a truly enlightened product is to reach the yin and the yang of every audience. A Chinese text from the third millennium B.C. by the mythical Yellow Emperor explains:

> *The principle of Yin and Yang is the foundation of the entire universe. It underlies everything in creation. It brings about the development of parenthood; it is the root and source of life and death. . . . Heaven was created by the concentration of Yang, the force of light. Earth was created by the concentration of Yin, the forces of darkness. Yang stands for peace and serenity; Yin stands for confusion and turmoil. Yang stands for destruction; Yin stands for conservation. Yang brings about disintegration; Yin gives shape to things.*
>
> —PATRICIA EBNEY, *CHINESE CIVILIZATION: A SOURCEBOOK*

The yin/yang icon is there to remind you to balance your marketing (and your life).

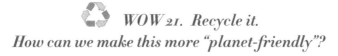

WOW *21. Recycle it.*
How can we make this more "planet-friendly"?

IS THERE ANYONE WHO DOESN'T KNOW WHAT THE RECYCLING symbol means? Is there any enlightened business that doesn't want its negative impact on the earth to be lessened? Is there any product that can't be made more ecologically friendly? Ecology has become too political. Forget politics. Treat the earth better no matter what your political ideology. It's an enlightened strategy. It's a smart strategy. It's a rich strategy. Make your products smart, rich, and enlightened. Anita Roddick of The Body Shop taught the whole world how a focused effort to be kind to the earth could reap a billion-dollar payoff. Emulate Anita's best dance moves.

Does your product promote clean air? Does your manufacturing facility use free energy from the sun? Do your employees use safe cleaning products? Are your paper goods recyclable?

If not, start now.

Well, that's the WOW—21 questions for enlightened products of the twenty-first century. It's the last of the four processes of the Millionairium. Here is a review:

> The PRISM
> The Nine Million-Eyes Questions
> The Great Idea Grid
> The WOW

You started with one Great Idea and ran it through the Millionairium. By the end, you expanded your single idea to three possible candidates. You're now ready for the final vote. Your job as a team is to tally up the scores and hold up the cards like they do at the Olympics to indicate gold, silver, and bronze.

The deciding factor on a close call? Go with your gut.

Which one do you feel Higher Power wants you to start with? We'll explore how to find customers for it in Chapter 9, "The Star Code."

Whew! That was a lot to chew on at one sitting. Let it settle for a few days and come back to this again. You'll notice things you missed the first time.

Here's the bottom line of what you should have learned over the preceding two chapters: Any product can be improved, often dramatically, often radically. To compete in the shorter product cycle of a fast-paced world, your product needs to be remarkably robust. A product that passes through the Millionairium will be better prepared to make it in the real world.

Now, let's explore the team of angels that is going to help make your product fly.

#48 _____

Chapter Seven

THE ANGEL CODE

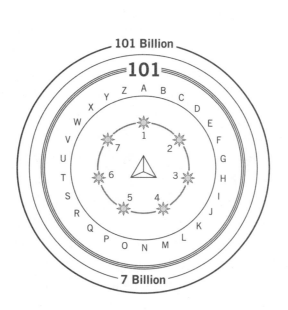

O K, you've got three great ideas bursting to be shared with the world. Your heart is pumping. Your mind is racing. This could be your ticket to the kind of financial freedom that most people don't even dare dream about!

*H*old your horses, pilgrim.

As Edison would tell you, "Genius is 99% perspiration and 1% inspiration." Having a brilliantly inspir*E*d idea is the small part of the equation. The rest of this book is about the other 99%. Luckily, you don't have to supply all

Wendy Robbins and Jorli McLain

With no money, no experience, no knowledge, no clients, and no MBA, Wendy Robbins and her business partner, Jorli McLain, decided that they could build a fortune using a product that they had developed and patented called The Tingler®. The Tingler® is the ultimate head massager. At the time, Wendy was $10,000 upside down with credit card debt, but she believed fiercely in her product. As she describes it, "Imagine 10 long fingernails gently tickling and massaging your whole head at the same time, giving you goose bumps from the tip of your toes to the top of your head. Just one touch of these copper fingernails and stress is instantly transformed into relaxing laughter. With one-quarter of all prescription drugs Americans take aimed at controlling stress, we provide a much-needed antidote to a h*U*ge problem!"

In 1999, Wendy, formerly a documentary filmmaker, and Jorli, a landscaper, went to Ace Hardware for the necessary materials to make their first prototype. With it in hand they were ready to sell their way to success and profitability. Wendy was "ignorance on fire." When she boldly walked into a Fred Siegel store, the buyer asked her to leave the store. Wendy's reply? "I will not leave without an order; besides, you look stressed out. Try our Tingler® and I promise you'll feel better right away." The store buyer loved it and gave them an order for 144 Tinglers every two weeks.

That first order gave the two entrepreneurs the confidence to attend the L.A. Gift Show, where in one weekend they received orders worth $12,500, followed by the New York Gift Show's orders for $25,000 more. They were in business, yet they didn't have an order form, or the ability to accept credit card payments, or even a manufacturer! But the enthusiasm that got them started kept them going and growing. Ultimately they created so much business they had to hire manufacturers in America and China just to meet the ever-expanding demand. In the first year they grossed $199,000. After the second year sales jumped to $1.4 million. Then they

$\rightarrow$

of the perspiration. In fact, you *can't* do it by yourself. The myth of the self-made millionaire is just that—a myth. Edison didn't do it alone, either. You need a team. And they need you.

Stephen Covey teaches that any effort worth undertaking is like launching a spaceship. A massive amount of preparation is required in advance of the launch. Then, on launch day, it takes enormous thrust just to escape the earth's gravitational pull. On a typical moon launch, more energy is expended in the first 50 miles than in the rest of the 500,000 mile round-trip!

That's what launching your enterprise will be like. It will take a team of enlightened people to help you launch it. Somewhere in the circles of people surrounding you are a few "good" people endowed with the seeds of greatness and destined to help you in cracking the Angel Code.

Every resource you need for success is most likely found in the circles of people you'll have around you. Everything you need. Your team will help poLish your Great Idea until it has been added, subtracted, multiplied, and maximized. You can see it there, pulsating inside the tetrahedron on the pedestal of the Millionairium. All eyes are on it. Millions of eyes.

IT'S A SMALL WORLD

Perhaps you've heard about Six Degrees of Separation, the theory that any one of us is connectEd to any other person on the planet by an average of only six acquaintances. In 1967, *Psychology Today* published the results of an experiment conducted by psychologist Stanley Milgram.

> *Milgram sent 60 letters to various recruits in Wichita, Kansas who were asked to forward the letter to the wife of a divinity student living at a specified location in Cambridge, Massachusetts. The participants could only pass the letters (by hand) to personal acquaintances who they thought might be able to reach the target, whether directly or via a "friend of a friend."*

—"THE SMALL WORLD PHENOMENON," ARTICLE IN
WIKIPEDIA, THE FREE ENCYCLOPEDIA

were featured in *InStyle* magazine and sold $500,000 worth of Tinglers®
in two weeks!

The dynamic duo discovered how to get product placements on TV
shows and in films. Then, to enc*O*urage celebrities to use The Tingler®
they went to their personal publicists, who cheerfully gave them to their
clients as gifts, unless they were told not to. Soon The Tingler® was featured on shows like: *Will and Grace, Sex and the City, Ally McBeal,* and
even on CNN. With a patent on The Tingler® and catalogue sales rocket-
ing, *Inc.* magazine wanted to do a feature story on them. When the magazine did a financial valuation, they discovered they were worth $10 million.

On *Fir*c with success, Wendy and Jorli are now bringing a new product
to market called Toilet Trees.™ It's a pretty plastic tree that provides an
attractive solution to the problem of where to put that unsightly toilet
plunger. For every one sold, they are planting a tree. They also want to *R*aise
more money for charity than has ever been raised before. We predict that
once again they won't take no for an answer, because, as Wendy Robbins
puts it, "There is no separation between you and the source, God, who can
do anything through you and me."

#49

_____

_____

_____

_____

_____

Here's the good news. It only took four days for the first lEtter to arrive. The bad news is that only three letters ever made it. Ninety-five percent of them failed to get through. Still, the word began to spread about "the small world" phenomenon that eventually spawned a Broadway play, a movie by the same name, a game called Six Degrees of Kevin Bacon, and a recent bestseller by Malcolm Gladwell called *The Tipping Point.*

By the way, did you know that Kevin Bacon can be linked to any other actor in any movie that's ever been made? (For example, Bacon is connected to Marilyn Monroe by two steps because she was in *The Misfits* [1961] with Eli Wallach. Kevin Bacon and Eli Wallach aCted together in *Mystic River* [2003].)

Yeah? So what? If everyone is linked to everyone else by six degrees of separation, then why are so many people struggling? Because for most people it is six degrees of *separation.* So what if we're separated from everyone by a chaIn of six anonymous acquaintances!? What we really need is six degrees of *connection.* How do you build an enlightened network of the right people? How do you crack the Angel Code? In this chapter, we'll show you that you are much closer than you think to the resources you need. For many, they are right under your nose.

The first step to cracking the code is to acknowledge your blind spots. Which blind spot are you hiding behind?

LEFT-BRAIN BLIND SPOT:
I HAVE TO DO EVERY DETAIL BY MYSELF

——

Many left-brain entrepreneurs think that six degrees is a fairy tale. They don't need people. They're so chronically independent, most of them never look up from their work long enough to ask if there might be an easier, faster way to go. They are self-reliant *to a fault.* They just can't seem to delegate. Many of them have an obsessive need to assimilate every lesson, make every decision, and control every function. Self-reliance is their motto. Their theme song is "My Way" by Sinatra. They get so busy and so overwhelmed and have so many irons in the fire that they put their own fire out. "What's the deal?" they ask. "Aren't I working hard enough?"

RIGHT-BRAIN BLIND SPOT:
GOD'S GOING TO DO IT ALL FOR ME

——

Then, there are the "wannabes." They believe in six degrees *too* much. Since they believe they're so connected, they're waiting for someone to show up at their doorstep with a big check. Their dream is so real they won't come back from the future to plant the first seed. They're waiting for God to dro*P* the winning lottery ticket in their lap. They believe. They have faith. They deserve it. They're entitled to it. "What's the deal?" they ask. "What's taking so long?"

Frankly, we need to get these two people on the same team. Between these two blind spots lies the truth.

For you right brainers, here it is: It will take longer than your plan calls for. It will be harder than you expect. It will be more expensive than you hope. You'll need to risk everything you've got. It will take every ounce of dete*R*mination you can muster.

For you left brainers, here's the truth: It will be more serendipitous than you expect. It will be more coincidental than you can imagine. It will be more spontaneous, magical, and "out-of-the-blue" than you're prepared for. You'll need to surrender your mind and your heart. It will take every *O*unce of faith you can summon.

For both of you, here's the whole truth and nothing but the truth: If you can handle the workload and can shoulder the belief load, the mother lode is yours. Can you handle the truth?

For help you need to turn to an Inner Circle.

THE FIRST CIRCLE: YOUR INNER CIRCLE

Which comes first, a Great Idea or a Great Inner Circle? There is no easy answer. Perhaps your Great Idea arrived first, downloaded into your mind, all wrapped up like a Christmas present. If so, you need to convene an Inner Circle to help you unwrap it. Perhaps you have a burning desire to do something great with your life but you have no idea what that is. Then the team's first task is to help you soul-storm a Great Idea into existence.

Inner Circles are idea in*C*ubators. Heaven knows that the world of business is hungry for more enlightened soul-utions. In keeping with the enlightened theme of this book, we've decided to give a nickname to members of your Inner Circle. Actually, it's borrowed from the world of the New York theater: Investors in a Broadway play in New York have long been referred to as "angels."

Inner Circle

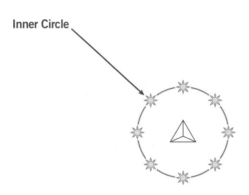

Angels in your Inner Circle are people who "invest" their resources—time, talents, ideas, and so on—to accomplish a specific task.

The >< || the 6°of][& the 6° of ( ) is inyestersden!

#50 _____

_____

Who Needs an Inner Circle?

THERE ARE 24 MILLION BUSINESSES OPERATING IN NORTH AMERICA and millions more on the drawing board. Whether you are an entrepreneur, an intrapreneur, or an extrapreneur, you need an Inner Circle.

ENTREPRENEURS. You own your own business(es) and are already bringing in streams of income. Two-thirds of existing businesses are solo entrepreneurs with only one employee. Everything else is outsourced. Of all businesses, 98% have fewer than 100 employees and bring in less than $1 million a year in revenue. If you want to break your business into the 2% stratosphere, then you've got to form Inner Circles inside your enterprise and unleash them to bring more to your bottom line. In the next chapter, we'll go into more deta*I*l on how to form Inner Circles in your enterprise to help build a "better" business.

INTRAPRENEURS. You may be an employee or executive working in one of these 24 million businesses owned by someone else. You enjoy your job. You are pleased with the career you've carved out for yourself and hope to keep growing with this company for the duration. Starting your own company is the furthest thing from your mind. You make up 90% of the people in the workforce. Still, you must learn to think like the boss—to be on a constant lookout for ways to improve the bottom line. As long as the bottom line keeps expanding, your job should be safe. The next chapter is for you as well.

EXTRAPRENEURS. On any given day in North America, 10 million Americans are attempting to start their own businesses; one-third of these individuals will actually get a business off the ground. Does this describe you? You *don't* like your job. You hate going to work every day. In fact, the thought of working for someone else always chafes at you. You hope to build an ex*T*ra stream of income to supplement your current job income, with the goal of eventuall*Y* forming your own enterprise. Your dream is on the drawing board. You're tired of the "golden handcuffs" of a secure job. You want freedom. You need an "Inner Circle" to help you plan your "break" from the corporation.

Which are you? An entrepreneur, an intrapreneur, or an extrapreneur? Whether you already own a business, work inside a business, or dream of owning your own business, you need to learn how to assemble your Inner Circle—a small group of people to help you cultivate your idea seeds into a full harvest of prisms.

There are angels all around you. Some are visible. Some are invisible. Let's talk about the visible ones first. Of the thousands of people you meet or drive by each week, a few possess the angel characteristics you're looking for to form a powerful team. Pull out your personal Enlightened Wealth Statement (see page 62) and scan through the list of the 101 people on your People Capital list. Remember, this list of 101 people is enormously valuable. Each person on your list represents hidden assets—knowledge, skill, experience, connections. Most of your angels will be on this list. Turn on your intuition. Ask yourself, "Is this person one of the angels destined to be part of my Inner Circle?" Here are some of the resources you're looking for:

A sset Capital—financial, property, equipment, tools, etc. (What financial resources do they possess?)

N etwork Capital—a million people surrounding them! (Who do they know?)

G enius Capital—101 talents, gifts, creativity. (What are their abilities, strengths?)

E xperience/Education Capital—101 gifts of knowledge, know-how, schooling, skills, and street smarts.

L ight Capital—loverage, inner wealth, giving, Higher Power, trustee-ship. (Are they enlightened?)

S erendestiny Capital—101 enlightened current and future opportunities. (What does the future hold for them?)

Your Inner Circle will consist of 4 to 10 people with whom you'll meet on a weekly or biweekly basis. In addition to providing support, motivation, and inspiration, your Inner Circle meets to soul-storm million-dollar Great Ideas.

Inner Circles generally evolve in one of two directions. The first coalesces behind a Great Idea and focuses all of their collective energies to manifest that idea in an ongoing enterprise. For example, Michelle Goering of Vancouver, British Columbia, read our book *The One Minute Millionaire* in December. She was excited about the idea of making an enlig*H*tened million and a few weeks later, on January 12, she formed a team that met together for the first time. They called themselves the MillionHares. It took four weeks of incubation for them to come up with a Great Idea. By February 16 they were testing and marketing their idea. By March 11 they had found a buyer for their idea and had negotiated a seven-figure contract. Michelle went from an idea to a payday in 99 days!

Another type of Inner Circle becomes an incubator for multiple million-

dollar ideas. People join the Inner Circle to "bounce around" ideas in preparation to launch their individual business. Each angel maintains control of
his or her own idea. The Circle's members stay together through the start-up
phase of each individual business to guide one another through the learning
phases of growth. They share contacts, resources, service firms. Each returns
to his or her own enterprise to continue growing it and brings back knowledge, experience, and connections to share with the other team members. A
very famous example of this is the historical fri*E*ndship of Henry Ford,
Thomas Edison, and Harvey Firestone. Edison, Ford, Firestone, and other
American leaders spent considerable time together at the Ford and Edison
vacation homes in Fort Myers, Florida, talking about business, philosophy,
science, and personal affairs. The development of their friendship allowed
important ideas to flourish, not only for their own businesses, but for the
advancement of American business and technology overall.

The HOTS Survey

YOU'RE TRYING TO RECRUIT PLAYERS TO PLAY ON YOUR TEAM. OR
they're trying to recruit you. You can't play this game alone, and they can't
play it alone. If you do, you'll both get creamed.

A baseball team wouldn't be successful with only pitchers. A basketball
team wouldn't be successful with five seven-foot centers. A football team
couldn't be successful with only quarterbacks. Each team member fills a certain role. What are the roles of a successful team? A Hare. An Owl. A Turtle.
A Squirrel. We've created a 20-question test to determine which kind of team
member you are. Please go to **www.crackingthemillionairecode.com** to
take the HOTS Survey to determine which strengths you bring to a team.
The ideal is to have at least one Hare, one Owl, one Turtle, and one Squirrel
on your team. Each has a unique way of looking at the world. We want to
thank our good friend, Alan Fadden, for sharing with us this unique way of
organizing an effective team.

Here's a description of each type of team member, comp*L*ete with
strengths and weaknesses.

The Hare

APPROACH. Conceptual/Spontaneous.

DESCRIPTION. The Hare generates concepts and ideas. He or she likes to reframe the problem and look for solutions that may be unusual, unique, and/or outside the boundaries of traditional thought. Hares are good at exploring alternatives and seeing the "big picture." Hares want freedom from constraint, and when a rule exists, they may break it. They may act im*P*ulsively, letting their feelings guide them. They derive satisfaction from the process of creating, discussing concepts and ideas, and overcoming obstacles. When everything is in its place, the Hare may become restless, get impatient, and have a tendency to move from one subject to another.

CONTRIBUTION. Fresh, original concepts that go beyond the obvious and are not constrained by fear of failure.

WEAKNESSES. Because the Hare enjoys generating ideas, this team member may move from one idea to another without stopping to evaluate the consequences. If left alone to refine concepts, the Hare will *S*olve the problem within the problem within the problem, and eventually lose sight of the objective.

INSTINCT. Reframing problems to achieve breakthrough solutions, moving in new directions, examining possibilities without regard to risk.

69144251521182129144419161520

#51

The Turtle

APPROACH. Conceptual/methodical.

DESCRIPTION. The Turtle challenges concepts under discussion. Believing that consequences matter, the Turtle will want to plan how new endeavors are implemented and prepare for surprises. Turtles like to create order from chaOs, by improving the process by which ideas are implemented. The Turtle may play "devil's advocate" to test the soundness of an idea and try to improve it. This team member prefers order and is comfortable being methodical. Turtles derive satisfaction from the mental exercise of the debate and may lead others to examine the merits of an idea, using a systematic process in generating and exploring ideas.

CONTRIBUTION. Making sure that the concept is thought through and examining how it can be improved and impleMented.

WEAKNESSES. If allowed to control the group or the process, the Turtle may lead the team toward choosing low-risk ideas, filtering out ideas that may have greater risks, but also bigger payoffs.

INSTINCT. Prediction of the problems caused by new or unique ideas; improving ideas before implementation.

The Owl

APPROACH. Spontaneous/practical.

DESCRIPTION. The Owl recognizes ideas and nEw directions in their early stages and develops the means to promote or advance them. When presented with an idea, Owls think of how to get it implemented, using insightful planning based on past experiences and successful methods. They may initially respond to ideas with skepticism but will let accepted

—WILLIAM HAZLITT

norms and their feelings guide them. Owls derive satisfaction from instilling a sense of purpose in the team and promoting that purpose with single-mindedness and determination. Their actions are aimed at achieving objectives by the most direct, efficient means, and they are not inclined to let rules and boundaries discourage them. The Owl is able to focus on many things at once and may move from one subject to another. Owls enjoy respect and influence.

CONTRIBUTION. Energetically promoting team objectives. Recognizing the value of a new idea or trend and actively carrying it forward.

WEAKNESSES. If left alone or working only with someone with a strong conceptual approach, the Owl may move ahead to implement concepts that aren't completely thought through, ignOring danger signs and realistic barriers to successful implementation.

INSTINCT. Choosing the highest-priority ideas and moving swiftly to see them implemented.

The Squirrel

APPROACH. Methodical/practical.

DESCRIPTION. The Squirrel, more interested in protecting the system than being in the meeting, follows up on team objectives and implements ideas and solutions. Squirrels focus on eNsuring the implementation process runs in an orderly manner and achieving high-quality outcomes. They prefer proven, familiar ideas over the novel and untried. They pay attention to details and see that plans follow an orderly process. Squirrels are comfortable being methodical. They tend to be cautious in trying out a new approach and prefer to think things over carefully before acting.

CONTRIBUTION. The details. Spotting easily overlooked problems before they occur and minimizing inefficiencies and Errors during implementation.

—THE KORAN • Prosperity is a great teacher; adversity is a greater.

WEAKNESSES. If working without clear and focused objectives or guidelines, the Squirrel may lose sight of the goal and pursue irrelevant strategies.

INSTINCT. To finish what they start and do things right.

Angels for Your Inner Circle

FINDING ANGELS TAKES EFFORT. IT STARTS WITH A BELIEF THAT IF you put the "word out to the universe" like-minded people will gravitate to you. Among the thousands of people who circulate through your life each month, there are a few you were meant to work with. Some of us have vast networks of friends and social contacts. Others are very poor at people skills. If you're not good at acquiring social capital (people), then you need to attract someone on your team who is!

In Chapter 4, you compiled a list of 101 successful people: teachers, fellow employees, employers, service providers, family members, friends, members of groups you belong to. All it takes is a simple telephone call: "Hi, Jim/Jane. You know how we're always talking about doing something together? I don't know if the timing is right for you, but I've decided that this is my year. I'm ready to launch something. I stumbled onto a book called *Cracking the Millionaire Code.* Fantastic book! [We give you permission to gush on for several minutes. ☺] It shows how to form an Inner Circle team of success-oriented people to create a million-dollar business ASAP. I'm forming a team of four or five people. Are you in?" This process can take a week to a year, or even longer.

You are creating a miniversion of the kind of team that the world's greatest inventor, Thomas Edison, assembled. "The man who invented the twentieth century" was actually backed up by an amazing team of "muckers" in his laboratory in Menlo Park, New Jersey. From 1876 to 1881 Edison and his team set the goal of cranking out one minor invention every 10 days and one major invention every six months. Many of Edison's 1,093 lifetime inventions came from a five-year spurt of genius originating in an upstairs room—100 feet long and 30 feet wide with a long bench down the center and shelves along the walls. Edison and his prime 5-member Inner Circle were joined by as many as 10 jUnior team members.

In this environment of creative collaboration, each member of the team played differing roles. One of Edison's business partners, Charles Batchelor, removed many of the day-to-day operations from Edison's shoulders so that he could nap and think and be a media magnet. From behind the scenes, Batchelor still earned 50% of the profits. Some people don't want to be rich and famous—just rich. You don't have to be an Edison. You just need to align your talents with someone like him. Every great partnership divvies up its talents to multiply its effectiveness. Walt and Roy Disney. Bill Gates and Paul Allen. Steve Jobs and Steve Wozniak. And Hansen and Allen.

Once the team is established, the ground rules are set, and the meeting times are arranged, then the doors are open for business. At least once every two weeks, the team should assemble for at least a two-hour meeting. The first item on the agenda is to determine if all the members have privately prepared themselves to receive enLightened ideas. Is each angel following through on the 3B habits of prayer/mediation, sacred study, and exercise?

g-net – h-line r- you r-pert – i-seen: e-tern – r-z-pie

#52 _____

Then, each person is given an opportunity to "educate" the other angels about their own individual Enlightened Wealth Statement—using the letters of the ANGELS acronym. The first pass is to uncover each angel's prime attributes. Each person has invisible strengths. Until you bring them out in the open, you won't be able to use them. In preparation for the meeting, the following questionnaire may help:

A _____ What are your three most important financial resources or assets?

_____ What three financial assets do you lack?

N _____ Who are your top 10 "make-it-happen" people?

_____ Which are your three most difficult relationships?

G _____ What are your three greatest gifts and talents?

_____ What are your three greatest weaknesses?

E ____ What education, knowledge, skill have you acquired?

____ What education, knowledge, skill do you lack?

L ____ What are your three most enlightened characteristics?

(Loverage, Inner Wealth, Giving, Higher Power, Trusteeship)

____ What are your most endarkened tendencies (what stands in the way of your enlightenment?)

S ____ What do you feel your destiny holds for you?

____ What stops you from unlocking it?

Your team is a puzzle. Sharing this in*F*ormation with one another is like dumping all the pieces of your team puzzle on the table so that everyone can see them. Get the blind spots out in the open. Obviously, it takes tremendous courage for people to share their strengths and weaknesses. But the truth will set you free. What is the truth about *your* strengths? (You have more than you might have realized.) What is the truth about your weaknesses? (They may be more valuable than you thought.) All angels comm*I*t to capitalize on one another's strengths and to fortify one another's weaknesses—and do it with class and dignity. Uncover. Discover. Recover.

Soul-storming

AS STEPHEN COVEY TEACHES, THERE ARE FIVE CANCEROUS HABITS that destroy any group activity:

THE FIVE CANCEROUS C'S

Criticize, Compare, Contend, Compete, Complain

We suggest that your meetings should also accentuate the five practices of enlightened soul-storming.

Exchange, Empathize, Enjoy, Encourage, Empower

As with more typicaL meetings, rules are helpful. Here they are for soul-storming: all positive feedback, no criticism, and all ideas are accepted. This just makes good sense. We are all soft and sensitive inside. The greatest fear most of us have is the fear of rejection. Most of us have vivid memories of being ridiculed in some setting . . . perhaps we have memories from school that still sting decades later. One of our major fears is the fear of looking foolish, which shuts down creativity fast. Create an environment where your childlike genius feels encouraged to come out and play.

At our seminars we often ask audience members to introduce themselves to each other in the most foolish manner possible—speaking in fake foreign accents, shaking feet instead of hands, standing on chairs, using voices of the opposite sex, or making funny faces.

This accomplishes two things. First, it's hilarious (and who doesn't need a good belly laugh from time to time?). And second, it brings out the child in us. It Loosens the rigid roles we have settled into. As Einstein said, you can't solve a problem at the level of thinking that got you there in the first place. You have to see things from new perspectives. Soul-storming is about accessing different types of souls: the soul of a small child; the soul of a creaTive genius; the soul of a fearless warrior.

Speaking of soul, when you hear the title *Chicken Soup for the Soul,* what comes to your mind? At the deepest level *soul* is a very spiritual word. Does each team member have a soul? Do you?

> *"Every noble impulse, every unselfish expression of love; every brave suffering for the right, every surrender of self to something higher than self; every loyalty to an ideal; every unselfish devotion to principle; every helpfulness to humanity; every act of self control; every fine courage of the soul, undefeated by pretense or policy, but by being, doing and living of good for the very good's sake—that is spirituality."*
>
> —*DAVID O. MCKAY*

time is money.   —BENJAMIN FRANKLIN   • See everything; overlook a great

It's no secret by now that we believe that business has a spiritual side. Soul-storming is *much* more than mere brainstorming. Soul-storming accesses the w*H*ole you.

How wise is your spirit or soul? Some people believe that the spirit is eternal. Does eternity run in both directions? Is there life *before* life as well as after life? Did you or your spirit exist before you were born? Is your intuition more than just communications from your unconscious mind?

In Joni Mitchell's 1960s anthem, "Woodstock," she sings,

> *We are stardust*
> *Billion year old carbon*
> *We are golden*

Are we stardust? There is actual scientific evidence that the physical part of us *is* made from stardust. But what about the spiritual part—our souls? Are we a billion years old? Were we in training for eons of time—schooled and m*E*ntored in special classes—in preparation to come here? Were we aware that this would be such a short visit?

As you look in the eyes of your Inner Circle, realize that there may be more there than "meets the eye." We've given your teammates the nickname of "angel." There may be some deeper truth to that. At the deepest level, your Inner Circle is a source of unfathomable wisdom, depth, br*I*lliance, and genius.

#53
_____

_____

Right margin (vertical text): —POPE PAUL XXIII • Sharing is having more. —BUCKMINSTER FULLER • Should we

THE SECOND CIRCLE: VIRTUAL CIRCLE

—

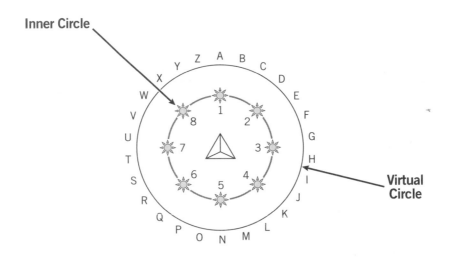

Inner Circle

Virtual Circle

There is so much to learn from the geniuses who have gone before—their yearning for truth, their hunger to discover. We owe our lives, freedom, and happiness to these amazingly focused thinkers. Let's add their help to your soul-storming in the form of some honorary team members. Arranged in 26 chairs around the Inner Circle is an imaginary circle that we call the Virtual Circle. As a way to expand the mindsha*R*e of your team, select geniuses from all ages in all kinds of fields. We know this may sound very arbitrary, but we encourage you to select one member for each letter of the alphabet. For example,

A   Aristotle, Joan of Arc
B   Ludwig van Beethoven, Pearl S. Buck
C   Christopher Columbus, Madame Curie
D   Leonardo da Vinci, Emily Dickinson
E   Edison, Queen Elizabeth I

Do you think that these men and women, with their vast imaginations and experience, could see things *Differently* enough to come up with a revolutionary new slant on things? Without a doubt!!! Scan through the following categories and come up with some names for possible inductees into your Virtual Circle Hall of Fame.

Then, assign team members to prepare short verbal reports each week to stretch the minds of your members. Invite the minds of these great virtual team members to help you. Faced with a difficult problem, ask yourself, "How would Edison approach this?" "How would Florence Nightingale organize this?" See through the eyes of your chosen imaginary mentors. If it were possible, who would you like to invite to your soul-storming s*E*ssion? (If this exercise inspires you to read some biographies of geniuses, so much the better!)

Artist, Architect, Astronaut, Athlete, Author

Banker, Bible Figure, Billionaire, Biologist, Businessperson

Capitalist, Captain, Cartoonist, Celebrity, CEO, Coach, Comedian, Composer

Designer, Developer, Diplomat, Director, Discoverer, Doctor

Economist, Editor, Educator, Entertainer, Engineer, Entrepreneur, Evangelist, Explorer

Farmer, Family Expert, Financier, Founding Father, Friend, Futurist

Game Designer, General, Genius, Guru, Government Leader

Healer, Health Expert, Hero, Heroine, Historian, Humanitarian, Humori*S*t

Illustrator, Industrialist, Inspirational Speaker, Internet Expert, Inventor, Investment Guru

Journalist, Judge, Joker, Jeweler

Kid, King, Knight, Kitchen Guru

Lawyer, Leader, Lender, Lyricist, Literary Genius

Manufacturer, Marketer, Millionaire, Mogul, Money Guru, Mother, Motivator, Musician

National Hero, Naturalist, Negotiator, Ne*T*worker, Newscaster,

Nobel Laureate, Novelist, Nuclear Physicist, Nun, Nurse, Nutritionist

Oilman, Olympian, Opera Singer, Optimist, Orator, Orchestra Leader

Painter, Pastor, Peacemaker, Personal Coach, Persuader, Philanthropist, Philosopher, Photographer, Physicist, Pianist, Playwright, Poet, Politician, President, Prime Minister, Prophet, Psychologist, Publisher, Public Speaker

Quadriplegic, Quality Control Guru, Quality Leader, Queen, Quantum Physicist

Rabbi, Racer, Radio Personality, Real Estate Guru, Religious Leader, Relationship Guru, Researcher, Restauranteur, Rock Star, Rocket Scientist, Royalty

Sage, Saint, Sales Guru, Scientist, Sculptor, Senator, Singer, Sports Star, Spiritual Leader, Statesman, Stock Market Guru, Strategist, Success Guru

Talk-Show Host, Teacher, Technology Guru, Telecommunications Guru, Television Personality, Theologian, Therapist, Th*I*nker, Trainer, Tycoon

Uncles, Ushers, Uncoordinated People

Vendor, Ventriloquist, Video Creator, Virtuoso

Writer, Wise One

X-pert

Youth, You!

CIRCLES THREE, FOUR, AND FIVE:
THE WINNER'S CIRCLE

—

We've asked you to compile a list of your 101 most successful acquaintances on a list called "101 People with Enlightened Capital" (see page 73.) From this list you selected a few members of your Inner Circle. The remaining names on the list make up what we call the Winner's Circle. These are the win∨ers encircling your life. Most of us rarely tap into this power, and for good reason. We have an aversion to exploiting our closest relationships for personal gain. Yet almost every great achievement came when someone overcame fear or reluctance and tapped into their Winner's Circle.

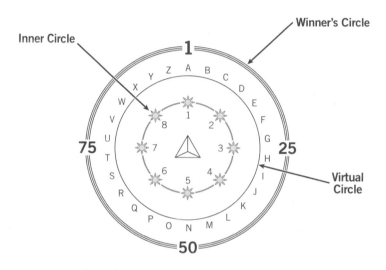

While teaching a class of deaf-mutes at Boston University, a 27-year-old professor became acquainted with one of his pupils, Mabel Hubbard. She was a 15-year-old who had lost her hearing and then her speech due to a childhood bout of scarlet fever. The girl's father, Gardiner Hubbard, hired the professor to tutor her privately. In the course of the tutorship, the professor shared his ideas with Mr. Hubbard for an invention he was working on. Mr. Hubbard agreed to financially support the professor's additional research. Two years later Alexander Graham Bell filed the "most valuable single patent ever issued in any country": the telephone. Alexander Bell and Mabel Hubbard were eventually married and became the parents of four children.

Who is to say that the people in your Winner's Circle aren't there for a

—I TIMOTHY 6: 17–19

reason? A very important reason!! Will we all look back with shock to realize how many opportunities were hidden out in the open for us to seize upon? It was *carpe EVERY diem*. Were *You* too preoccupied with *Monday Night Football*? Were you too worried about a "bad hair day"?

The connections, contacts, and intersections in the lives of 101 successful people are staggering. As we mentioned in a previous chapter, all of these winners have their own Winner's Circle with at least 101 successful contacts. And they, too, are well connected. Each circle knows a circle that knows a circle. Or to use our model, Circle Three is surrounded by Circle Four, which is surrounded by Circle Five. Therefore, *each* person in your Inner Circle has access to over a million successful people (101 × 101 × 101 = 1,030,301).

rsetsandntereepciereoland.

#54 _____

This means that a five-person Inner Circle has access to more than five million people. Let's assume that each of these five million is in daily contact with an average of 10 people. Then, the worlds that rotate around you and your team are in daily contact with 50 million people! Across several continents! For*Get* acres of diamonds!!! It's continents of diamonds.

How Do You Mine the Diamonds in Your Enlightened Database?

Step One. See Them as Diamonds!

The people in your main database are not diamonds in the rough. Each one is brilliantly polished, breathtakingly multifaceted, exquisitely designed. They probably wouldn't label themselves as diamonds—"I'm just an elementary school teacher." But you're n*O*t interested in their labels. You see beneath their labels. Labels are like those wooden Russian babushka dolls, the most popular of all Russian souvenirs—with smaller dolls stacked or

their treasure as a good foundation for the future so that they may take hold of real life.

money, which will soon be gone. But their trust should be in the living God, who

THE ANGEL CODE | *151*

nesting within the bigger ones. Each inner doll represents a different label, until you get to the smallest doll at the interior of the stack and find out, to your surprise, that it's not a tiny doll at all but a 10-carat, flawless, D color, brilliant-cut diamond! Each person has an Enlightened Wealth Statement valued at more than a 10-carat diamond. Besides, one well-placed phone call from someone in your Winner's Circle is worth at least that much to you. You just aren't aware of which person it will be. So you must tre*A*t everyone like the jewel that they are.

Step Two. Assemble and Evaluate Your Diamond Database.

Gather your contact information and maintain it. It's perhaps your most valuable asset. Each angel in your Inner Circle is asked to bring his/her list and be ready to expound on it at the next Inner Circle meeting. Why did you select these people? What makes those individuals special? What do you like about them? How they think? Who they know? What they're good at? The assets they control? What they be*L*ieve? What they know? Using the same ANGEL acronym used earlier (see p. 136), do a preliminary analysis of your Diamond Database.

A   ssets
N   etworks
G   enius
E   xperience/Education
L   ight
S   erendestiny

Step Three. Identify the "Make-It-Happen" People on Your List.

Scan down your list and identify those people who have "make-it-happen power." What does this mean? Here is an example. A boss calls his employees and says the following: "A flash flood destroyed parts of downtown last night. People are hurting. They need our help. So I'm canceling work today. I'm asking a few of you to stay here on a skeleton crew to answer phones, etc.

The rest of you please report to the Red Cross stations to help in whatever capacity you can. You'll receive your regular pay plus overtime for any extra hours. Thank you."

That is make-it-happen (MIH) power. In 10 minutes a whole company can be refocuSed. Some of the people on your list have that kind of power. MIH power gives you *access* to every resource you need—money, encouragement, know-how, endorsements, and so on. According to the old adage, it's not what you know but who you know. But it's much more than that! With whom do *you* have MIH power? Do you have that kind of relationship with anyone on your list? Have you forged lifelong friendships, been on service committees, or played sports with someone? What kind of MIH power (or influence) do you hAve with them? With one phone call from you would they join you in a cause? Would they enlist other people?

This kind of influence comes with respect. How do you earn that respect?

RESPECT FROM ACCOMPLISHMENTS. This comes from what you've accomplished in your life. For example, major authors ask us for endorsements for their books. If we've read their previous books and admire their work, even though we don't know them personally, we often spend extra time reading their maNuscripts and giving them a quote for their book jacket. Obviously, they've earned respect from a lot of people—agents, publishers, readers, media. They've also earned our respect.

RESPECT FROM GIVING. Did you earn respect from what you've done for people personally? It could be a lot of little things. Did you make a contribution to their cause? Did you serve as the soccer coach for their child? Did you step in to substitute for them at a school fund-raiser? Or did you do something major, like pulling them out of a crashed car on a rainy night in California?

RESPECT FROM WHO YOU ARE. You could have earned their respect for who you are. You're a friend, a family member, a lodge or club member. You have a shortcut to their respect. You're a member. You're in. They respect you.

Make a list of the people on your list with whom you've earned enough respect to *D*efinitely "make it happen." What kind of influence do you have with them on a scale of 1 to 10?

UNLIKELY	PERHAPS	PROBABLY	LIKELY	DEFINITELY	GUARANTEED
1	2	3	4	5	6	7	8	9	10

MAKE-IT-HAPPEN SCALE

Then, scan down your entire People with Enlightened Capital list again. The first time you were looking for people with whom *you* had MIH power. This time, look for anyone on the list who has major MIH power with others, even if you don't have major "pull" with them. Suppose someone on your list is the president of a bank. You're in the same service club with her but you're not especially close. She has MIH power with a thousand people. One word from her and there would be *movement*! Unfortunately, with access to all of this power, you haven't yet earned enough respect. It's unlikely she'd drop thing*S* to have lunch with you. She'd likely fit you into her calendar in a month or so.

As you explain your "loose" relationship, another member of your Inner Circle jumps up and exclaims, "My cousin went to college with her. They were sorority sisters. They were on an overnight camping trip and were accosted by some drunks. My cousin hauled off and decked one of the attackers and it so rattled the other guys that they split. My cousin still has a scar on her right knuckle to prove it. She owes me a favor, so if you need to get to the bank president, I can get you in."

There are other people on your list who "know someone" who has that kind of power. For example, suppose two buddies fought in the Gulf War in 1991 and one soldier risked his life to save his friend in a firefight. They went their separate ways, maintained frequent contact, exchanged holiday greetings. But between them there was a deep connection, and on one man's part, a deep sense of gratitude. As he puts it, "If you ever need me, for *anything,* I'm there. Just call and I'll make it happen."

As busy as you are, there are people who "get thr*O*ugh" to you. They have *access* with a capital A. They've earned the privilege. How did they earn it? What are the steps to building that kind of respect? Study your Diamond Database. Ask yourself, "What would I need to do to develop that kind of access?" It's called social collateral or social capital. It's so*M*ething that's earned. The more quickly you earn it, the more power you possess. If used for enlightened purposes it's called Empowerment.

Rewhenize syntheic presixize nondegreesize deoftion
reseparationally premeetsal proserendestinyable—
conthatsion repowize! bipowerton-nonohton-enwowoton!

#55 _____

_____

_____

Step Four. Catalogue the Resources in Your Diamond Mine.

On one wall of your Inner Circle meeting room make two lists:

Top "Make-It-Happen" People   Top "Make-It-Happen" Resources

Have your angels make a list of their top 5 MIH people and what r*E*source they have access to.

At the end of this session, a five-member Inner Circle will have 25 names and 25 resources on the list. This is just the first pass through the Diamond Mine to open your eyes to the power and wealth of the angel resources that exist in your group. At following meetings, try to dig deeper. Sometimes the biggest diamonds are buried deepest in the ground.

Step Five. Keep Expanding Your Empowerment Base.

Now that you're aware of the power you possess, encourage one another to keep growing your MIH power relationships. Let your angels select three people in their Winner's Circle with wh*O*m they have let slide a valuable relationship. Have your angels explain how they intend to move these associations from a 5 to an 8 on the MIH scale. This is one way of expanding your Empowerment base.

THE SIXTH CIRCLE: CIRCLE OF LIFE

—

Tapping into your Winner's Circle is a very organized process. Tapping into the Sixth Circle is much more serendipitous. There are seven billion people on this planet. How can you vibe in a couple of million of them for your Enlightened Enterprise? We're going to spend a lot of time in Chapter 9 teaching you how to crack the Star Code. But besides finding millions of customers, there are dozens, hundreds, or thousands of your fellow huma*N*oids who can provide resources to help you fulfill your destiny. So let's keep our eyes, ears, and hearts open.

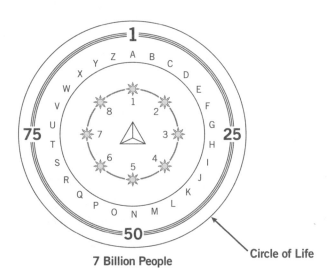

7 Billion People   Circle of Life

Synchrodestiny

REMEMBER THE EXAMPLE OF HOTMAIL CITED BY PO BRONSON ON page 112? Here is how the originators describEd themselves, in their own words,

> *"Two 27-year-old guys who had no experience with consumer products, who had never started a company, who had never managed anybody, who had no experience even in software— Jack and I were hardware engineers. All we had was the idea. We didn't have a prototype or even a dummied graphical interface. I just sketched on his whiteboard."*

Sure, there was plenty of hard work and stress and dedication, but *somehow* the centrifugal forces in the concentric circles around these two men spun off the resources to manifest their dream. Seed money, knowledge, office space, equipment, PR, word of mouth, and a very rich buyer. If you were to connect the chain of destiny dots of this story, it would amaze you. This person bumped into that person who told someone to call his cousin who sent an e-mail to . . . it's mind-boggling. But it still happened!

Why don't you do that? Scan back over the events that led up to one of your major accomplishments. How did you get there? Think about it. Graph it out. Where are the destiny dots—those chance intersections of the trajectories of the people and events? If just one of those dots were eliminated, where Would you be today?

Deepak Chopra, in his book *Spontaneous Fulfillment of Desire,* talks about "coincidence":

> *We can choose to dismiss [coincidence] as a random occurrence in a chaotic world, or we can recognize it for the potentially life-altering event it may prove to be. I do not believe in meaningless coincidences. I believe every coincidence is a message, a clue about a particular facet of our lives that requires our*

attention. . . . When you live your life with an appreciation of coincidences and their meanings, you connect with the underlying field of infinite possibilities. This is when the magic begins. This is a state I call synchrodestiny, in which it becomes possible to achieve the spontaneous fulfillment of our every desire.

What is a coincidence? It is a co-incidence—when events coincide. Co + incident. An intersection of events. A crossing of trajectories. A shared happening. It's s*I*x degrees of separation meets synchrodestiny. Six degrees is when you send out a signal. Synchrodestiny is when it miraculously connects with you. Combine the two theories and you have some serious power. Then, combine this with serendipity—making fortunate discoveries by accident and intuition.

Six Degrees of Separation + Synchrodestiny + Serendipity = Serendestiny

Higher Power is aware of the infinite possibilities. HP is absolutely aware of how to connect the Serendestiny dots. HP knows how each person you meet could connect you to exactly who you need to meet and why. But most of the time we b*L*indly stumble along with our hearing aids turned off. God is there nudging us . . . "Look!" HP points. "The person you were just introduced to knows the brother of the. . . ." But we blow by without noticing. So the entire game changes and the infinite possibilities reshuffle. Higher Power whispers, "OK, if you won't heed that signal, then listen to this one. . . ." And the tumblers of the vault rearrange like a giant, fluid, electronic Rubik's Cube of rotating, revolving, shifting activities. "Here. How does this feel? If you'll just turn it three times here and four times there. . . . OK, this is how we can get you to your destiny."

But are you noticing? An idea flashes across the blank canvas of your mind. Is it a friendly environment? "OK," Higher Power says, "you s*L*ept in and were late for work. So your boss, who was going to promote you, gave the job to Eleanor instead . . . and so we'll have to rejuggle Eleanor's destiny path as well as yours. You could have reached your goal much more easily and faster . . . but here's another possibility." I think when we're done with

158 | CRACKING THE MILLIONAIRE CODE

this life we'll spend another million years watching instant replays, not of what happened, but of what might have happened. What an interesting reality game show that will be!

Aviicoryluarf:ivigylourf.

#56 _____

Speaking of games, do you know the story of Rubik's Cube—the all-time bestselling puzzle toy in history? Twenty-nine-year-old Erno Rubik invented the toy in 1974, applied for a patent in Hungary in 1975, and licensed his idea to a small Budapest company who brought it out in 1977. Sales were sluggish. Would it ever have seen the light of day if a *H*ungarian businessman hadn't spied a waiter playing with it and acquired the rights to introduce it to the West? As they say, the rest is history. Erno Rubik became the first self-made millionaire from the Communist bloc. He has set up a foundation to help promising inventors in Hungary.

Serendestiny? After the fact, it's easy to spot. But what about *before* the fact? In the language of coincidence, there is an incident, a preincident, and a postincident.

How do we notice the signals, before the fact—preincident? How do we hear the still small voice more clearly—preincident? Feel the vibe quicker? Is it possible to be tipped off early?

Do you believe in *E*SP? Do you receive premonitions?

Here's a suggested methodology for preparing yourself and your intuition.

#57 _____

STEP ONE. FIRST, BELIEVE THAT HIGHER POWER IS SENDING SIGNALS.
HP has a destiny for you. Higher Power has already given you lots of signals. Your passions, interests, talents, gifts, values, contacts, connections. The puzzle of your life is a giant Rubik's code to crack. You can try to figure it out by yourself, knowing the odds of solving it randomly are 1 in 43 quintillion. Or you can be mentored by the best Rubik's Cuber in the universe who will help you solve it blindfolded in less than 52 moves and 22 seconds (a recent world record). If you want to do it your way, it might take you an eternity to do it. At any rate, these intersecting concentric circles are infinitely complicated and impossible to unravel without the he*L*p of Higher Power.

STEP TWO. GO BACK AND NOTICE THE PATTERNS IN YOUR LIFE.
The opportunities you seized. The ones that got away. Were you aware of any early warning signs? What were the signals? A feeling? A voice? An aura? These signals are usually very subtle, very delicate. Tune in to them today. Believe that someone you meet today is on your destiny path. Or you are on theirs. You'll exchange gifts. Maybe you'll meet someone at a *P*arty who works in an attorney's office and is aware of a pending foreclosure. The owners need to sell quickly and are willing to take a deep discount to move this albatross off their necks. You'll have the cash and will be looking for a deal. You'll exchange business cards.

STEP THREE. HEIGHTEN YOUR AWARENESS. Your 3B preparation begins to open the flow of messages from Higher Power. Put the Big Rocks in first. Ask to be led to your surest path. It's not my way but the Higher Way.

STEP FOUR. SEE EVERY PERSON YOU MEET WITH MORE HEIGHTENED SENSITIVITY. "Is it you?" you wonder. Instead of noticing the outer person, practice seeing the whole package—their Enlightened Wealth Statement. This is a multimillionaire you're talking to—whether the person knows it or not. Treat all persons as if they were the bearer of the final number of the combination lock of the vault containing everything that you and Higher Power want for you. If they're not part of your Serendestiny, they'll certainl*Y* appreciate the way you treat them. Tell all persons about your prime target—what you are trying to accomplish—in 101 words or less and then listen with your "inner knower" as they share theirs. Give them suggestions on how they can reach their target more quickly. Be a giver, not a taker.

STEP FIVE. GIVE EVERYONE YOUR SERENDESTINY CARD. On one side of your SD card, state what your Great Idea is and exactly what resources you need. On the other side of your SD card, state clearly, in less than 101 words, exactly what your philanthropic goal is. One side is your Hot Idea. The other side is your Heart Idea. If you clearly state what you want, people can sense with their intuition. Give them your enlightened résumé in 101 words or less. Let them know what you stand for, what you're trying to accomplish—your ultimate goal, your enlightened vision, and not your commercial goal. For example:

> *"Hi, My name is XXX YYYYYY. Before I tell you what I do for a living, let me tell you what I do for a loving. What's that? I want to end illiteracy. Why? Imagine living in Russia without being able to read the signs and not knowing what is going on. It limits your life. Over 90 million US adults today are living like that.* How will I go about it? I donate the first 10% of the profits I earn from my XYZ Enterprise. The money goes to finance three illiteracy programs in schools in my city. One person at a time. We've taught a thousand people so far. We're going for a million in five years."*

If they show an interest, teach them about Serendestiny. Tell them that you might be part of their destiny path also. There are no coincidences. Try to discover the hidden reason for your encounter. We're in a giant classroom and the kids are passing notes to each other across the aisles, yet this time the teacher is telling us who to send the messages to. Share with them how you're cracking your wealth codes: Destiny, Prism, Angel, Star.

* "The State of Literacy in America," National Institute for Literacy (www.nifl.gov)

STEP SIX. FOLLOW UP. How many business cards have you received/handed out in your career? How many people ever contacted you again in other than p*U*rely commercial ways? Intuit which of the people you meet should be added to your Winner's Circle. And then, follow up, follow up, follow up. Old-style networking is about commerce—I'll scratch your back, you scratch mine; I'll give you leads, you give me leads; I'll give to your charity, you give to mine. You're creating more than a network. You're creating a soul-net—an enlightened network that will be a primary source of good on the planet in addition to creating profits and products.

Sometime during this process the world and everything in it will become new, alive, vibrant with possibilities. Million-dollar ideas will be revealed to you in magical, mysterious ways.

THE SEVENTH CIRCLE:
THE ETERNAL CIRCLE

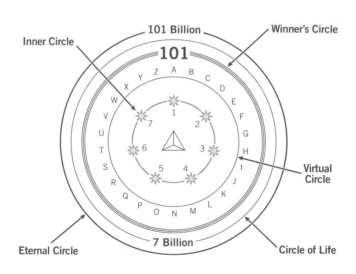

OK, *F*asten your seat belts, we're going for a space ride on an orbiting spacecraft above our magnificent earth. Seven people live down there on that magnificent breathing ball of life. Astronauts who've been out here, in space, return with a deep reverence for our circular spaceship. By one estimate, there have been 90 billion people who have seen a sunrise since the dawn of life. How many more are waiting to come down for their t*U*rn on earth? Another 10 billion? Who knows? That means that perhaps 101 billion spiritual beings (pre- and post-earth) are floating around somewhere in the universe. Depending on your spiritual leaning, some of these beings are in some dark "holding cell" waiting to be sentenced. Some of them are in a delightful place waiting for the "reading of the will" when even more wonderful things will transpire. Are all of these spirits forbidden to check in on us down here? Can any of them take a peek once in a while?

Close Encounters of the Invisible Kind?

EARLIER WE TALKED A LOT ABOUT FINDING "VISIBLE" ANGELS FOR your Inner Circle. Now, a few words about those "invisible" angels. Do angels exist—the spiritual kind? What are angels supposed to be doing?

An ancient Jewish saying teaches that every blade of grass has an angel standing over it, encouraging it: "Grow! Grow!" (Rabbi Nilton Bonder, *The Kabbalah of Money*.)

Is there an angel over you, encouraging you to grow? What about guardian angels? Do you have an invisib*L*e protector? The Old and New Testaments reference the appearance and invisible presence of angels 262 times. Are there angels or aren't there? When we ask our audiences how many of them believe in angels, the vast majority of people in the room raise their hands. The response is the same when we ask, "Do you believe that there are angels in this room right now?" The *F*irst time we asked this question we were actually floored. Here's a purely off-the-wall question: Are any of these angels allowed to help us with our Enlightened Enterprises?

With so much belief in invisible beings, why is there so little talk about divine oversight in business?

Here's why: Because people will think *you've lost your mind*! The same entrepreneurs who think *you're* crazy also think *they're* perfectly sane to launch a traditional start-up business with odds of success that are *Far worse* than the *best* odds in Las Vegas. But if you ask them to consider an alternative approach, they look at you the way doctors used to look at chiropractors. Loony! Sometimes the alternative approach can be better. So this is a book about alternative ways of creating Enlightened Wealth—more specifically Wealth with a capital W. One day, we predict that this "alternative" way of thinking of Enlightened Enterprise will be much more acceptable.

One of the reasons that movies like *Ghost, City of Angels,* and *It's a Wonderful Life* are so popular is because they strike a chord of truth within us. Rather than laughing and crying in a movie theater, let's bring the angels more openly into our thinking about business. Let's operate our enterprises as if angels were watching. Let's invite them in. Let's see the world of business from a Higher perspective.

A Higher Perspective

TALK-SHOW HOST REGIS PHILBIN HOSTED A POPULAR TELEVISION show called *Who Wants to Be a Millionaire?* The contestant who answered all 16 multiple-choice questions walked away with a million dollars in cash.

In real life, there are *real* million-dollar questions that will take you more surely toward earning an extra million dollars in your lifetime. We call them the Enlightened Wealth Questions. Answer these two questions and you're on your way!

Question #1. "What Is the Meaning of Life?"

"What!?" you ask. "Just what does *that* have to do with my desire to create wealth?" More than you might think. So let us ask you, Why *are* we here? On this planet? At this time? Why did Higher Power create this place? Ponder that for a moment.

While you're thinking about the meaning of life, let's take a brief detour into a discussion about mentors and mentorship. People often ask us how they can find mentors. Our answer is simple: Find mentors you admire, hopefully in your own city. Discover what their top three goals are in life.

Then, without asking them to help, without bothering them for their advice, without dogging them for their attention, simply help your mentors accomplish their top three goals. Make it cLear that there is no expectation of reciprocation. Let mentors know that you realize that you may never be able to be tutored by them personally, but you admire their example so much that you'd just like to help them accomplish their top three goals. And then, begin doing just that.

From time to time, people can drop your mentors a note to let them know exactly how you have helped them accomplish their top three goals.

In our experience, good things begin to happen. First, you might be surprised to find out what your mentor's top three goals are. Two, you'll probably be amazed at how much you learn by helping your mentor accomplish his or her goals. And three, after you've given your support, often your mentor will naturally want to help you achieve your goals—maybe not face-to-face, but he or she will naturally want to give you a "leg up" to the next level.

Mentorship, if done right, is magical.

Now, when it comes to mentors, who is the Mentor of mentors—Coach of coaches—Guide of guides—Tutor of tutors—Teacher of teachers—Guru of gurus?

Higher Power is the ultimate mentor.

If this is true, then what are Higher Power's top three goals? If you help Higher Power accomplish His top three goals, Higher Power is obligated to help you accomplish your enlightened goals; in fact, the more aligned you are to Higher Power, the more His goals become your goals. So what is the "meaning of life" from a Higher Power perspective? What is Higher Power trying to accomplish with this seminar called "Life"? What's the bottom line of life?

Come back with us in time . . . 13.7 billion years ago. Why did Higher Power cause the Big Bang? He touched His finger to that infinitesimal singularity at the beginning of time, and a flood of galaxies exploded out over the universe. On the outer spiral of one of those speeding pinwheel galaxies is a nondescript star—our sun. Revolving around that sun at a distance of about 93 million miles is a special blue jewel of a planet . . . inhabited by about six and a half billion living humanoids.

Why?

Was this an accident? Or is it part of a grand design? A plan? There should be no doubt on which side of this debate we firmly plant ourselves. In our humble opinion, there was and is a divine plan.

A plan to do what? What are the three grand goals of this divine design?

Why are these trillions of stars sprink*L*ed throughout billions of galaxies? Are there other earths out there, just like this one? According to one scientific source, it is now estimated that at least 10% of the stars in our own Milky Way galaxy could have planets just like earth—that's 30 billion planets! If so, then ET will have a harder time finding home than finding a specific grain of sand on all the beaches of Hawaii.

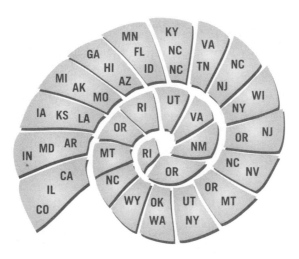

#58

Maybe all of those 30 billion planets in the Milky Way are as dead and lifeless as Jupiter—except for our planet. Maybe it takes an entire galaxy to incubate just one "live" earth like ours. If there were only one earth in each galaxy, that would still mean billions of "live" earths like ours.

At least that's one possibility. Another possibility is that our tiny blue jewel is the only living thing in the cold, swirling vastness of space. Only one in the universe! If so, it took a trillion trillion suns to spawn our magnificent earth. Which makes earth that much more special.

From Higher Power perspective, from out in space, this blue jewel swirling around the sun has no boundaries, no borders, no barriers. Almost 7 billion human life-forms cling to a rotating rock that's revolving around a ball of fire careening through space.

When you get up in the morning and watch a sunrise, it seems so peaceful, so tranquil, so calm. But it's all an illusion. The earth is spinning on its axis at 1,000 miles an hour to make the 25,000-mile round-trip each day. The earth races round the sun at 67,000 miles an hour to make the 500-million-mile lap each *Y*ear. The sun itself is rotating around the center of our galaxy at 558,000 miles an hour. The Milky Way galaxy is speeding away from the Big Bang universe at over a million miles an hour.

Six and a half billion people clinging to this orbiting rock have been placed here for a reason. What are Higher Power's g*O*als with regard to this place and these people?

The heavens are telling of the glory of God; And their expanse is declaring the work of His hands.

—PSALM 19:1

What in the world was He thinking when He organized this experience? There are 101 different answers, but a verse in one sacred text gives us a clue:

Then God said, "Let us make people in our image, to be like ourselves . . . masters over all life. . . ." So God created people in his own image; God patterned them after himself; man and female he created them.

—GENESIS 1:27, *NEW LIVING TRANSLATION*

In His image? Patterned after God? Created from His blueprint?

Yes. We believe that we come with divine DNA. Higher Power wants to mentor us through the experiences of this life to be like Him (or Her, depending on your particular belief). What is Higher Power like? Creative? Yes. Forgiving? Yes. Generous? Definitely. Loving? Absolutely. Omni-everygoodthing? Unquestionably!

He wants us to know Him (John 17:3). That's one of His goals. He wants us to know ourselves. That's another goal. Knowing who He is automatically lets us know who we are—his spiritual offspring. He wants to mentor us to become like Him. That's another of His goals. Frankly, the word *goal* is m*U*ch too narrow, too limited, too finite, too earthly, too time-oriented to be applied to Higher Power. Higher Power doesn't do "goals." He does purposes. There is no end to the purpose of life. It began long before we got here and will go on long after we leave here.

His business is the business of creating mini HPs. Higher Power wants to put us in business—His business. We are His business. He needs apprentices. There's a lot to do. He's processing several billion prayers a day. Lots of pleases—please help me find a job, or a spouse, or to put some food on the table. Lots of thank yous—thank you for my family or my health or my happiness. Lots of prayers. Billions of them.

Which prayers get through? Which ones get answered? Maybe this is a simplistic answer but here goes: Higher Power helps those most who are helping Him *R*each His top three goals. Do that, and Higher Power has an enlightened obligation to help you. He's given you His word on that: "Your heavenly Father already knows all of your needs, and he will give you all you need from day to day if you live for him and make the Kingdom of God your primary concern" (Matthew 6:32–33, *New Living Translation*).

We truly believe that this is the fastest, safest, easiest, quickest, most empowered, enlightened way for you to get rich.

$$15.33.31.24.22.23.44.15.33.15.14$$
$$15.33.44.15.42.35.42.24.43.15 \quad 24.43$$
$$43.35.24.42.24.44.45.11.31$$

Since Higher Power is rich—He owns everything—then one of the meanings of life is to show us how to be more like Him. He's given us all everything we need. It's all around us and in us. He knows precisely the talents, gifts, connections, opportunities that surround each of us. He knows exactly the right combination of ingredients that will make of your life the most delicious gift.

Suppose you want to help Higher Power to support your brothers and sisters. What products, Services, experiences, and information do they need right now?

According to Maslow's Hierarchy of Needs, people first need to survive—1.3 billion humans live on less than a dollar a day. They need help. Now! Some need clothing. Some need shelter. Basic needs. Everybody has 'em. Billions of others have their basic needs handled. For them, there are safety needs and social needs and self-esteem needs and needs for self-actualization.

Higher Power created a seminar called "Life" to mentor us all to the Highest needs. People who've been beyond and back can teach us a thing or two about Higher needs. Pick up any book about near-death experiences—and there have been plenty of books on NDEs since Raymond Moody's jaw dropper *Life After Life* in 1975. Upon their return, people who have experienced an NDE tell of a tunnel . . . and a light at the end of it . . . and a life review in full holographic, multisensory detail . . . and a sense of peace and love, impossible to put in words . . . and of powerful lessons they learned about life. First, there *is* a life after life—beings they met on "the other side" are real. Second, there is nothing to fear in death. It's like walking into another room in your house. Third, nothing is more important than learning how to love. It's the bottom line of all bottom lines.

At each stage, a host of Higher Power helpers is needed to facilitate the growth and progression of each individual. This process will go on long after our need to breathe.

HAOIOL PRUNSI IERIST SOITII AFNEBE WYFPIS

#60 _____

Most people throughout time have lived on this planet without ever getting beyond the survival needs. Does it seem unfair that so many have so little compared to the "so much" of so few? Is there more to life than a new SUV? Higher Power wants to satisfy our Higher needs and take us all to the Highest level. Will there be time enough for everyone to "get it"?

In the cold Northern wastes there is a mountain a thousand miles long, a thousand miles high. Once each thousand years a small bird flies North. A small bird flies North to sharpen his beak on the cold hard stone. When the mountain is thusly worn down, one second of eternity shall have passed.

—TIBETAN POEM

Higher Power needs apprentices. Are you in?

Whew!! That was pretty heavy stuff. Maybe too heavy for a business book. And yet, we warned you. This isn't a book about business in the traditional sense. This book is about Enlightened Enterprise and Wealth with a capital W.

Can you handle one more heavy question?

Question #2. "What's the Meaning of *Your* Life?"

There are needs to meet, people to feed, love to share, esteem to be built, selves to be actualized. Each of us determines which need we are most perfectly attuned to fulfill. Some of us make soup for the homeless soup kitchen. Some of us create clothing for supermodels. Some of us teach self-esteem to teachers. What do you do? What instrument were you destined to play in the symphony of life? You discovered some of the answers to these questions in cracking the Destiny Code. You aligned the meaning of life with the meaning of *your* life.

In the following chapters we'll share with you how to align your destiny with the angels so that you can let the white light flow through your prism to bless the stars. Or something like that.

#61 _____

_____

_____

Chapter Eight

INSIDE THE ENLIGHTENED
ENTERPRISE

I f things go as planned, your new or existing business will soon be growing faster than a rabbit farm on a hormone diet. Whether you're a solo-
preneur on the move or in an expanding enterprise, the challenges of
exploding growth can seem daunting. So before this momentous growth
takes place, take a moment to step back and decide what kind of lifestyle you
want to create for yourself and your loved ones. Look out five years into the
future. Your enterprise is one of the 5% that "made it." WOW!!!

What's your life like here in the future? Where are you living? How are
your relationships? What's your spiritual life like? Are you physically fit?

Donald Harris

Every medical breakthrough is born of a desire to serve. Dr. Donald Harris has shared the dream of every person who wakes up in the middle of the night and stumbles, cursing, to the bathroom, helpless without his or her glasses. Fortunately, Dr. Harris is an optometrist, and when he and his partners set out two decades ago to correct nearsightedness without surgery, they came up with a discovery that may change the way many of us see (or don't see) the world. (Nearly half of all Americans are nearsighted, and that number rises to nearly three-quarters of the population in Asia.)

The process is called corneaplasty, and it works by placing "softening" drops on the cornea, then putting on a corrective contact lens that works like braces to reshape and straighten the cornea. After a stabilizing drop is put on the cornea, the process is complete, although a retainer lens may be required for a week to hold the correction. Corneaplasty works for all people with low to moderate nearsightedness and can fully correct astigmatism. And reshaping a cornea has none of the risks of invasive surgery.

To advance their dream further, Dr. Harris and his four colleagues have created their own way of reshaping corneas, and call it Permasight, a patent pending process. After nine years of research on Permasight, they have two FDA approvals. One day soon all of us who stumble to the bathroom each night may finally be able to throw our glasses and contact lenses in the trash once and for all. And Dr. Harris will have done good while doing well.

David Huffman

David Huffman understands from firsthand experience how debt slavery can debilitate the soul and spirit of a human being. As a child he was devastated by watching his father, a builder of upscale homes in San Diego, California, go from extraordinary wealth to over-

How do you spend a typical day? Are you still putting the Big Rocks in first? How about your planning? You've created residual income and residual philanthropy, but did you create a residual lifestyle—to wake in the morning unpressured and free to invest your time where Higher Power directs you? A wildly successful business can be so intoxicating that it can overwhelm everything. Don't you want the cushion of time to enjoy activities that enrich your life in addition to those that enrich your bank account?

Your dream lifestyle is a Big Rock. If you don't plan for it, you'll never be able to fit it in. Envision it and constantly work toward it and you'll begin to catch glimpses of it moving toward you at the speed of LIGHT.

The key to a residual lifestyle is building a team of people around you who can keep moving the dream forward when you aren't there. (Because one of these days, you *won't* be there.) So you're trying to create an enterprise that doesn't require your presence. Yes, it may take prodigious amounts of your presence to launch this baby, but once it's orbiting, you can go launch other ventures. To borrow Michael Gerber's terminology from his book *E Myth,* you need to spend more time working "on" the enterprise and less time working "in" the enterprise.

This mind-set should permeate the entire organization. Each employee (angel) should constantly be wondering, "How can we permanent-ize this business? How can we make the processes around here work more automatically (residually) so we can spend more time with people—our customers *and* our friends and families?" Every team member should be vitally interested, because the smoother business operates, the more secure everyone's jobs become. Then, each employee has more freedom to plan for his or her own residual lifestyle outside of work.

So before you open a checking account for your new business, plan for the day when things can run on automatic pilot. What makes such a vision possible is people. Teams of amazing, enlightened people.

In his colossal business bestseller *Good to Great,* Jim Collins shares the basic principles gleaned from exhaustive research on how good companies can grow into great ones. In describing the process, he states, "They first got

whelming debt before he died under the crushing weight of $7 million in outstanding loans.

David decided to do something about it. What he found when he looked closely shocked him. America is a nation swamped with debt. The average American has eight credit cards and owes over $13,000, creating interest payments that eat families alive. David found that 97% of people did not even know how much they owed, much less have any sense of how to solve the problem. As he puts it, "Most people owe $1.19 for every dollar that they earn. The average person has car, gas, rent, clothes, utilities, food, and other payments that exceed their ability to pay, and no one has ever given them a class called 'Money 101' or 'Debt 101.' That's why they are broke, and getting deeper and deeper into debt."

The credit card companies don't mind. It's no accident that they promote easy, unsecured credit. Think about it from their point of view. If a customer pays only the minimum payment each month on a credit card debt of $20,000, the customer is paying at an interest rate of 20%. This means 10 out of 12 payments a year go just to interest; only two payments pay off the principal, or original credit card purchases. At this rate it takes 25 years to pay off the average credit card. Last year, Citibank made $1.4 billion each quarter—that's $18 million a day. When that money comes from credit card debtors, it's coming from Americans who can least afford it.

As an alternative, many debtors could only turn to what David calls "debt settlement companies that were merely consumer credit people in disguise." Fortunately, David Huffman dedicated himself to addressing the problem that had destroyed his father's life, and he has made everyone better off in the process.

In 1999, David started his company, the Freedom Group. David and his team work with individuals to get them permanently out of debt in 36 months or less. Together with each client they create a budget, then they hammer out all the indebtedness with creditors one deal at a time. With the help of the Freedom Group the debtor ends up paying only 60 cents on a dollar, which is better than declaring bankruptcy. (Not everyone is qualified

the right people on the bus (and the wrong people off the bus) and then figured out where to drive it."

The right people can help you accomplish amazing things! You learned about the Angel Code in Chapter 7, which focused on how to use the Seven Circles of Empowerment to launch a start-up. Once that business is up and running, new teams need to be organized. Even if your corporation is 100 years old, the ideas in this chapter can help expand your business into the next century.

OUTSOURCED ANGELS

The Angel Code extends to all of the players that your enterprise interacts with in the "outer" world—suppliers, government agents, vendors, service providers, manufacturers, advertisers, distributors, consultants and coaches, and so on. These players are part of your enterprise's Winner's Circle. Just as individuals have their own Inner Circle—a list of 101 successful contacts—so, too, your enterprise has concentric circles of successful people who help you support and service your customers successfully. The same rules apply to these people as to your personal Winner's Circle that we reviewed in the last chapter. Namely:

> See them as diamonds!
> Assemble and evaluate your Diamond Database.
> Identify the "make-it-happen" people.
> Catalogue the resources in your Diamond Mine.
> Keep expanding your Empowerment base by upgrading your relationships.

In summary, see your support team as diamonds and treat them like diamonds. Why? Because every person on that list possesses amazing current and future resources on his or her individual Enlightened Wealth Statement.

to go bankrupt. To go bankrupt you surrender yourself to a bankruptcy judge. The judge may determine that you have too many assets or too much disposable income. Besides, to go bankrupt costs a minimum of $1,500 for a bankruptcy attorney and blemishes your credit for seven to ten years. If you can get a new credit card at all, its interest is usually slated at 28%.)

Then David and his team teach people how to stop getting into debt, plug the leaks, learn how finances really work, and master the subject as a life skill, while balancing their own checkbooks and starting to live sanely again.

The average client's debt is $25,000. The initial cost to work with David's company is about $475. David has created systems to handle what seemed like impossible tasks and has made them customer-friendly and seemingly effortless. His dad's painful experience taught him early to be nice to people, and clients took notice.

Six months after starting his business, David realized he was earning over $20,000 a month, all while helping people eliminate the suffering caused by debt. Competitors sprang up, but David noticed that they made their businesses more about making money than about the client. David made it his mission and commitment to make the client number one, his agents number two, and earning money number three.

Today the Freedom Group employs 100 agents and has already represented over $100 million in debt. David's business is driven by word of mouth, by his Internet website, where prospective clients can calculate their debt; by ads in phone books; by telephone, where representatives are standing by to provide confidential assistance; by infomercials; and by realtors coming to him in droves trying to help people buy a new home. For David the success is nice, but what he really loves is the fact that his company provides a service that makes people's lives easier, and does it right. He says, "It's easy because we do what we say we are going to do."

Sadly, David's business has a bright future. Twenty percent of Americans desperately need his company's help. Debt is holding Americans hostage. Debt is the number one cause of divorce. So David works on ways to put himself out of business. His dream is to get people to quit borrowing their way to indebtedness, the crushing burden that destroys people's lives.

- **A** sset Capital—financial resources or assets
- **N** etwork Capital—a million people surrounding them!
- **G** enius Capital—101 talents, gifts, creativity
- **E** xperience/Education Capital—101 gifts of knowledge, know-how, schooling, skills, street smarts
- **L** ight Capital—enlightened ideals: loverage, inner wealth, giving, Higher Power, trusteeship
- **S** erendestiny Capital—101 enlightened current and future opportunities

Not every one of your "B keepers" has every one of these attributes, but you're looking for the most enlightened "outside" enterprises you can find to support your Enlightened Enterprise.

Your Winner's Circle is made up of enlightened spaceships that hover over your planet to help you ferry goods back and forth to the population that you serve. They may serve other worlds but when they arrive in your airspace they want to feel welcome. They want to be drawn to the enlightened aura that glows out from your core.

ENLIGHTENED LTV

Now, before you think we're getting too carried away with this right-brain *every-person-is-valuable* mantra, let's come back down to earth with a concept that is championed in the halls of finance. It's called LTV—the lifetime value of a customer. We realize that we're not talking about customers right now (that's Chapter 10), but we're going to borrow the LTV concept first, and then reverse it. So, just what is LTV?

Business leadership guru Tom Peters says that every time a Federal Express courier comes into his office, the driver should see $180,000 stamped on the head of the secretary. His executive firm of 30 people has a $1,500-a-month courier bill. That's $18,000 a year times 10 years for a total

LTV of $180,000. If the secretary can convince just one other customer to start using FedEx, this LTV doubles. But most mail couriers think that the value of the customer is just the $20 or less they spend today. Each of your customers is worth thousands of dollars if you'll take care of them. That's LTV.

But let's take this LTV concept and turn the tables. How should the secretary see the FedEx driver? Is the courier just a glorified messenger boy or girl? What is the FedEx driver to her company—$20 bucks or less? The secretary also needs to see a number stamped on the courier's forehead— $1,000,000! And here's why.

The courier who picks up your packages every day is a roving Diamond Mine. Could he or she help you uncover the missing piece to the puzzle of expanding growth for your enterprise? Delivery people meet hundreds of people each day. Could they become privy to an idea, some bit of know-how, a clue, a piece of information about a competitor, a Serendestiny opportunity that they became aware of driving around your city?

Why would they provide you with a piece of your puzzle? The better question is, Why wouldn't they? Do you treat them like a diamond or a FedEx driver? Do you make them feel like family? Do they know you? Do you know them? Are they on your Inner Circle or are they in your Outer Space? When you see them, do you just see the 25% of their limited, visible value to you—as in, "Make sure this package gets there tomorrow"?

Or do you see the 75% of their unlimited, invisible value to you—as in, "You sure have a great attitude. We'd like to honor you as one of the valuable winners on our company Winner's Circle. We have a quarterly banquet where we honor our winners. We'll pick you up in a limousine and treat you like the diamond you are."

If you honored them this way, do you think they'd remember you? Would you be at the top of their list? **A**bsolutely! They'd most likely honor you back with their best. What would their extra ounce of superior service be worth to you? One idea, one tip, one connection, one lead, one rescue, one disaster averted, one "in-the-nick-of-time" solution, one "take the first class line vs. the coach" line, one "I'm not supposed to do this but for you,

I'll make an exception." If you add up all of those little extra "goodies," it could add up to tens of thousands of dollars.

.מהצאההח מף עצמדסטצ החף הסא פמר

#63 _____

And we've only just begun. Your courier has hidden value today, but what about future potential? Perhaps this low-level FedEx driver is just biding time until he or she can become an ex-FedEx driver—and launch his or her own enterprise. Success may be just around the corner, and who will they look to when they've "made it"? To their own Winner's Circle. They'll automatically think of all of their friends and start showering business on those who've showered business on them.

Your FedEx courier, your advertising account rep, your hotel catering manager, your travel agent—every winner in your Winner's Circle has a huge value sticker on their forehead representing current and future serendipitous value. *Huge.*

YOU CONTROL THEIR VALUE TO YOU

——

You are completely in control of how high that number can go. If you treat them like 20 bucks, they'll give you 20 bucks' worth of value. If you treat them like a million bucks, eventually—and it may take decades—they'll return the honor you gave them. And if they forget, Higher Power will do it for them in ways that are secretly connected but impossible to discern.

Why? Because that "outside" employee valued by the world at 20 bucks is a highly prized son or daughter of Higher Power. You take care of His kids and He'll take care of you. How you treat Him is a model for exactly how you'll be blessed by the boomerang you tossed. Guaranteed. It's the "windows of heaven" principle.

Just exactly what are the windows of heaven? This is how it works. If two companies have equal quality and service, but one company gives prodigious amounts of time and money to residually philanthropic endeavors and the other doesn't, then you vote with your wallet for the more enlightened one. You want to reward them for "good business" practices every bit as much as you would hope that your customers would reward you. You want to give them good word of mouth. Why do you bless the "better" business with more of your business? There is a statement in the Old Testament about the power in giving. It states:

> *"I will open the windows of heaven for you. I will pour out a blessing so great you won't have enough room to take it in! Try it! Let me prove it to you! Your crops will be abundant, for I will guard them from insects and disease. Your grapes will not shrivel before they are ripe," says the Lord Almighty.*

> —MALACHI 3:10–11, *NLT*

A large portion of the blessings that come from Higher Power actually come as a result of His "apprentices" doing nice things for the family of humankind. The windows of heaven are opened through other people. In other words, *you* are the windows of heaven. When you are "touched" and feel like doing something nice for someone, it's as if the windows of heaven are opening through you.

As you shower business on other enlightened businesses, you become the fulfillment of prophecy. You are the "proof" that Higher Power promised. You hold that power in your hands. You're a "spotter" for Higher Power, trying to determine toward whom the windows should be opened. You're on the lookout to protect enlightened businesses from hazard. Higher Power has promised prosperity and protection to those who put Him first. Most of that prospering and protecting is going to flow through you. You'll just feel right about things.

Being heaven's window and heaven's shield now makes you more enlightened—and qualifies you to be the recipient of windows and shields from someone else. Where you treat Enlightened Enterprises in enlightened ways, the floodgates of Serendestiny open wide. Every outside service provider—every electric meter reader, every attorney who handles your claims, every nurse who works in the offsite day care center, every advertising representative, and so on—becomes "activated." When you treat everyone like diamonds, you never know when they'll use their MIH power with the friend of a friend of the cousin of the sister of the president of the company who will buy everything you can manufacture for the next 10 years.

Treat your network—or more accurately, your "soul-net"—like family because that is how Higher Power views them. They are your spiritual brothers and sisters in the seminar of life. They're trying to learn how to love and give and serve and grow and take care of their friends and family, just like you are. They have hierarchy needs that they're trying to satisfy, just like you are. They also have Higher-archy needs—spiritual deficits to pay down, spiritual opportunities to pursue, just like you.

The enterprise you operate is just a *front*—a front with a store attached that is set up to provide services to children of Higher Power. It's a family-owned business and a family-run business. Enlightened dollars flow in and out. Some of those enlightened dollars flow out to support other enlightened service businesses (like the company that handles your outsourced manufacturing). Some of those enlightened dollars flow in from enlightened customers who, like you, are looking for some good people to bless with their business. They need to spend the money anyway—it might just as well be with family. If you operate this way, the strange and mysterious wheels of Serendestiny begin to turn. "Chance" meetings and happy "coincident" happenings start to occur with increasing frequency. Remember, you are part of the Serendestiny path of others—so why not be a refreshing moment on their superhighway of life. And every once in a while, one of these people comes into your life with the final number for the combination lock that you've been trying to unlock for 20 years.

IT'S MUCH MORE THAN MONEY

—

Serendestiny is more than money. Let's take a look. Suppose one of your employees has a child who is dying of leukemia. Your FedEx man also picks up and delivers to a world-famous oncologist who specializes in leukemia. How would you know that? The only way you're going to uncover this essential connection is if you try to create a database of your winners that's cross-referenced to their resources. Then, after you've done all you can, turn it over to Higher Power to connect the Serendestiny dots. The answer to almost every problem that anyone in your company is dealing with—family issues, health issues, spiritual issues, money issues, recreation issues, time-management issues, people issues—is walking in and out of your business (figuratively or literally) every single day.

Invisible Serendestiny capital is piling up in huge mounds all around you every day, but it's like manna. It spoils if you don't gather it.

ANGELS ON THE INSIDE

—

Inside your Enlightened Enterprise, the same is true. Partners, employees, associates, stockholders—every single one of them is also a diamond, from the least to the greatest. Frankly, each one has an Enlightened Wealth Statement, and no one knows where the next Great Idea could come from. It could just as well originate from the clerk in the mailroom as the vice president of sales. In most corporations it rarely comes from the rank-and-file employees because they are viewed as just that—employees of lower rank who file by to get their checks on the way out the door. And we wonder why so many businesses fail? The ideas to pull them out of the red are walking the halls with "minimum wage" stamped on their foreheads. They're so much closer to the solution than those in the "soon-to-be-vacant" executive suite.

Remember the Harvard research from Chapter 4 indicating that 75% of a company's assets are invisible? It's time your company turned those hidden resources into cash. The power to double your business rapidly resides in your Seven Circles of Empowerment.

So here is a four-step plan for enlightening your enterprise.

1. Buy a Copy of This Book for Each of Your Employees (Bulk Prices Available ☺).

OK, WE KNOW THIS IS SELF-SERVING, BUT WE BELIEVE IN WHAT we're doing! And if you're benefiting from this book, so will your employees. Give them an assignment to read it. If you're really sold that this is the way to higher profits, then pay them to read it in the next 30 days. Get your entire team on the same page as quickly as possible.

#64

Most of your employees have lots of ideas for improving things.

Every day, all over the world, millions of working people see problems and opportunities that their managers do not. With little chance to do anything about them, they are forced to watch helplessly as their organizations waste money, disappoint and lose customers, and miss opportunity after opportunity that to them are all too apparent.

—ALAN G. ROBINSON AND DEAN M. SCHROEDER,
IDEAS ARE FREE.

The way to tap into this hidden resource is a program that our friend Marty Edelston uses with his publishing business, Boardroom. It's called "I" Power. We'll share the details of this program with you on page 187.

Some of your current employees are natural-born intrapreneurs. They're sitting on ideas *right now* that could make you serious money if they just got the green light. 3M, the Fortune 500 company, operates this way. It gives employees dedicated time each week to let people tinker with their own ideas to find something where all could win.

Some of your employees already have a business on the drawing board and are just waiting for a time to leave. Let them go with your blessings. That's their destiny. Hopefully, when they've succeeded they'll come back and return the favor.

2. *Be on the Lookout for Enlightened Employees.*

The former CEO of Circuit City, Walter Bruckart, was asked the top-five factors that catapulted his company from mediocrity to greatness. He replied, "One would be people. Two would be people. Three would be people. Four would be people. And five would be people. A huge part of our transition can be attributed to our discipline in picking the right people."

The goal is to find talented people who are also "enlightened." It's not proper to discriminate on the basis of religion, and that's not what we're proposing. But during the interview, have candidates show you their enlightened résumé. Not just the things they've done professionally, but, even more important, the activities they've participated in to "give back." You're trying to determine if your potential hire is a Higher Giver. That is a sure sign that they're due to have a "windows of heaven" shower. Competence is obviously essential; do they have an enlightened glow?

Here are two sample interviews: Candidate #1 is an extremely talented, hardworking, honest, and creative individual. Candidate #2 is someone who has all of those things *plus* a measure of enlightenment. Choose #2. As the baby boomers age, spirituality takes on a greater importance. They'll be looking for you as much as you'll be looking for them. Bring a "spiritual" flavor to the way you do business. Do it sensitively, with class, never overbearingly. But definitely let Higher Power be welcome in your enterprise. The ultimate goal is to assemble on your team a group of competently empowered, spiritually enlightened people.

3. Divide Your Enterprise into Inner Circle Zones.

Executive Inner Circle

Every employee can be, and should be, part of an Inner Circle. The primary focus of the Executive Inner Circle is to crack the Angel Code for the enterprise—uncover the hidden value in the Seven Circles of Empowerment and strategize ways to enlighten the enterprise. You'll find procedures for this in Chapter 7, but here is a review of the major steps:

Complete and explore the Enlightened Wealth Statements of all
Inner Circle members (see p. 62).
Share information on the ANGEL questionnaire (see pp. 142–143).
Have each member take the HOTS survey (see p. 137).
Learn the process of soul-storming (see pp. 143–145).
Choose the 26 players on your Enterprise Virtual Circle (see p.
146).
Have Inner Circle members prepare their personal Winner's Circle
of 101 Diamonds (see p. 149).
Have a soul-storming session to determine your Enterprise Winner's
Circle.

be done. We have faith in lack rather than abundance but there is no lack of faith. Faith is a law.

—ERIC BUTTERWORTH

As you implement these meetings, there may be resistance from some players. As the old saying goes, "The only thing better than a short meeting is no meeting at all." And most of the time, that's true. But done properly, with enlightened intent, these soul-storming sessions will be viewed as indispensable enrichment experiences. Since they will be conducted companywide, it's important that everyone buys into the process and understands the power it can represent.

Sector Inner Circle

Depending on the size of the company, there may be dozens of Sector Inner Circles. These are not your normal department meetings to coordinate day-to-day activities. These Inner Circle meetings are much more like interactive "training." They should be fun and rewarding. And they can be extremely profitable.

Spirituality is not a department of your business—such as marketing, human resources, accounting, or sales. Spirituality is the whole business. It's the blood that flows through your enterprise. It's the spirit that infuses everything. When the spirit is gone, the body is dead. It's very difficult to resurrect it. So cultivate that spirit. Make your enterprise a model of giving and Higher principles.

Just as in the Executive Inner Circle, Sector Circles are encouraged to complete the launch activities. The Executive Inner Circle will ask each Sector for a list of their winners to nominate for the companywide Winner's Circle. Working with the Executive Inner Circle, the Sector Circle will create a process for recognizing and rewarding the winners. The ultimate goal is to attract enlightened suppliers to bless with your business and vice versa. It's all part of an ever-widening series of enlightened circles surrounding your enterprise.

4. Reward Your Sector Circles for Developing Great Ideas.

THE GOAL OF THE SECTOR CIRCLE IS TO LAY THE FOUNDATION FOR enhancing three areas of the enterprise: people, processes, PRISMs.

Who? People are the most valuable asset. Focus on building Angel and Diamond values.

How? Processes are how the enterprise operates. Focus on improving systems.

What? PRISMs are the products, related products, ideas, services, and media that produce the revenue streams.

Using the Millionairium, run all processes and prisms through the exercises outlined in Chapter 5. The goal is to have each sector of the enterprise work in the pattern that Thomas A. Edison and his colleagues used to create a minor invention every 10 days and a major invention every 6 months. The Executive Inner Circle can review all minor and major ideas to adopt those ideas that have the greatest probability of success.

I - Power!

What if there were a formula for turning raw ideas into money? Over 1,200 companies are using such a formula. Would you like to know about it? Called I-Power, it was designed by Marty Edelston CEO of Boardroom, Inc. Edelston and his coauthor, Marion Buhagiar, explain:

> *Everything any company needs to process the work it already does*
> *far more efficiently is already in the minds, hands and experience of*
> *the workers who now handle the work. They know where the waste is.*
> *And they are often the first to recognize new opportunities for the*
> *company to pursue.*

> —MARTIN EDELSTON AND
> MARION BUHAGIAR, *"I" POWER:*
> *THE VERY SIMPLE SECRET OF*
> *BUSINESS SUCCESS*

It all started out when Edelston invited management guru Peter Drucker in for a day of consulting. One idea that came from that meeting has made Boardroom, Inc. millions of dollars—from $25 million in annual sales, it went to over $100 million in four short years. The idea is so simple it's easy to dismiss. Here it is, in Drucker's words:

"Have everyone who comes to a meeting be prepared to give two ideas for making his/her own or the department's work more productive . . . ideas that will enhance the company as a whole."

—MARTIN EDELSTON AND MARION BUHOGIAN

Employees must attend weekly management meetings and bring two ideas with them. The ideas are anything that can improve the company, starting with their own job, using their own power—a product, service, or process. Employees who don't contribute their two weekly ideas are not eligible for quarterly profit sharing, which can be serious money, so few employees miss the opportunity to think up an idea or two for each meeting.

al ty I tu I spir ment part de I ness bus bus ness I. a of your your is is it not

#65 _____

_____

For example, Edelston's company sells a million and a half hardbound books per year. Escalating shipping costs were hurting sales. They tried cheaper bindings and thinner paper, but it sacrificed the quality that they wanted to represent. One employee saved them a half million plus per year with a little, workable idea recommendation to shave one-sixteenth off each edge of the book's paper. It reduced the weight of the book and was a little, yet significant idea that yielded a giant savings.

Edelston and his management team were inundated by so many ideas that they had to create a process to manage the flow.

Where the average North American corporation receives an average of one idea per year for every seven employees, Boardroom receives 100 ideas *per employee* per year!

"I" Power rewards ideas even if they aren't implemented because it creates a culture of creative thinking. In 1991, Boardroom had 66 employees and received 7,000 ideas. Of these, 5,500 were approved, although only 3,000 were implemented. It caused greater profitability, savings, focus, higher motivation and participation, better results, and happier, more thoughtful personnel. See **www.crackingthemillionairecode.com** for more information on this simple yet revolutionary program.

E Power Ideas

Ask each person to bring to Inner Circle meetings one "enlightened" idea that can improve the 3P's of the business: people, processes, and PRISMs. How should these ideas be rewarded? It is generally thought that paying high cash rewards and percentages of profits for Great Ideas is a way to foster creativity. Frankly, the opposite is closer to the truth. People can be demotivated if the process of rewards is too complicated or is perceived as unfair. Rarely is one person the originator of an idea. Often, it comes from groupthink, so singling out one person to receive a major reward can cause jealousy and conflict.

The truth is, thinking creatively should be part of every employee's job description. The biggest reward is to be part of an Enlightened Enterprise that is growing and blessing the world. Job security and opportunities for growth need to be the ultimate goal. However, it *is* important to have a system for recognizing, valuing, and appreciating enlightened ideas, no matter how small or seemingly insignificant the reward may appear.

Napoleon is quoted as saying, "My life changed when I realized that a man will risk his life for a blue ribbon." As Edelston discovered, an immediate small reward (from $1 to $10) for any idea—good or not so good—had the effect of letting people open up and have fun. Criticism is banned. Creativity is celebrated. Having small ideas that can be implemented immediately causes immediate improvement to be noticed. This encourages even more creativity. We highly recommend you obtain your own copy of *"I" Power* to learn more details. Another great book we recommend is *Ideas Are Free* by Alan G. Robinson and Dean M. Schroeder.

E Power Ideas from Outside Firms

Create a process whereby outside visitors—customers and outside service providers—can pass on their ideas to you. Every time a supplier interfaces with a sector of your enterprise (e.g., the FedEx courier) have them receive, as part of the invoice, perhaps, a Serendestiny card with a request to have them contribute ideas for improving the 3P's of your business. Each month, select one Great Idea and reward the contributor.

Do the same with customer contacts. Give them lower prices if they turn in a Great Idea. If the idea is implemented, send them a nice reward check.

Where Are the Giants Hidden in Your Enterprise?

Systems of rewarding small ideas are just camouflage for what you're really trying to accomplish—to flush out a really GIANT idea. Perhaps the most amazing story along these lines occurred at the turn of the last century when the president of a large company threw a banquet for his employees in New York City in 1896.

One of his employees, an engineer from Detroit, brought along the schematics for a unique project he had been working on after company hours in his garage. Everyone he'd shown the idea to was negative. After the banquet, the engineer rolled out the idea on the dinner table and asked the president for his opinion. After studying the papers, the company president pounded his fist on the table and exclaimed, "That's the thing!"

"He was the only person who gave me any encouragement up to that time," the young man said years later.

The engineer eventually resigned his post and forged ahead with his Great Idea through two bitter bankruptcies. Finally, in 1908, down to his last few hundred dollars, the first Model T Ford rolled off the assembly line. Henry Ford sold 6,000 cars that first year. The next year he sold 14,000 cars. By 1914 he was cranking out 230,000 cars a year. His Great Idea became a Colossal Idea.

Two years later, in 1916, Henry Ford bought a property in Fort Myers, Florida, next to that of his old boss, Thomas Alva Edison, who had encouraged him 20 years earlier at the Edison Illuminating Banquet.

Millions of dollars are walking through the halls of your current or future enterprise. They are buried deep in the minds, hearts, and DNA of the people who flow through your life: partners, associates, suppliers, and customers. The ideas can be small or huge. It's your task to uncover them.

Oh wow, they often have visions here ... 13 9 14 4 18 21 7 2 21 19 21 19!

#66 _____

CAN WE TALK? AN OFF-THE-RECORD CONVERSATION WITH EMPLOYEES

—

"Pssssssst. Over here. Can we talk? Yes. You."

You probably already know this, but your job is in jeopardy. Maybe not tomorrow, but let's look 10 years down the road. Whether your corporation has been around for more than a century or for less than a decade, the options for you are pretty much the same: It's up or out. Corporations work just like your body—there are anabolic processes and catabolic processes— systems that build up and tear down. On the outside, your division is being chewed on by some Chinese competitor. On the inside, someone is on your heels with better skills or smarts or style, ready to outflank you any minute. It's either "up" or "out."

But going up is not that easy. In many respects, work life is like a down escalator that you're trying to walk up. You walk in place without seeming to go anywhere. You double your efforts to try to reach the next landing, but it's exhausting. Debts start to pile up, and you've got to get a second treadmill. The more money you make, the higher tax bracket they throw you into, so you've got to walk even faster to stay in the same place. And if you stop, it's all the way back down to the bottom to start over again.

New jobs are like start-up companies. The chance that you'll stay at that same job for a year are less than 50%. Within five years 95% of the employees will be gone. They'll either go up or out. Some of them will move to another company, where they'll start the same game—up or out.

In a world that's so volatile, what's a person to do to gain some security?

Our answer is the same for employees as it is for start-ups. Since the failure rate of new companies is so high, we encourage you to adopt enlightened principles. Higher Power has an escalator that puts you on the fast track.

Higher Power knows exactly the right career path for you. Higher Power is intimately aware of your talents, gifts, and skills and is anxious to have you put yourself to your Highest use. Wherever you go, work to enlighten yourself and your position.

Enlighten Yourself

PULL OUT THE LIGHT PRINCIPLES AND BEGIN TO LIVE THEM. GET your 3B in every day. Put the Big Rocks in first. The angel standing above you is urging you to "Grow! Grow!" Take the HOTS test online and do the Destiny Code Clue Finder on page 86 to figure out where you'll grow the fastest.

Then, bring that attitude to work. "Plant me where I can grow."

Your First Job Is to Make Yourself Indispensable

FOR MANY EMPLOYEES, THINKING LIKE AN INTRAPRENEUR IS FOREIGN. They come to work, do their job, collect their paychecks, and go home. If they keep thinking like that, soon they may not have a job. The world of work is increasingly volatile. The incredible speed of information, lower trade barriers, international competition, short product life cycles—in this whirlwind of change, employees are increasingly dispensable.

When the "higher"-ups in your company start thinking about cutting costs (as they always have and they always will), you want to make sure that your name is never on the chopping block. You *must not* allow yourself to be viewed as an expense item! You must make yourself indispensable. Period. How?

Activate your Enlightened Wealth Statement and start to prove your worth. Prove to your company that you are a creative source of ideas to improve the bottom line. Instead of viewing you as an expense, they must view you as an extremely valuable, revenue-generating, enlightened associate who is on the move *up*.

You've got to start thinking like the boss. Activate your dormant entrepreneur genes. Start assembling your own group of soul-stormers at work. Many larger corporations already have procedures for creating ad hoc committees to explore ways to improve the company bottom line. But if no such procedures exist, take the initiative to start your own Inner Circle of like-minded people and meet once a week during lunch. The goal is to soul-storm ways to improve the company's existing product line or come up with suggestions for new products or services.

The ideas in the next chapter are exactly the fuel you need to fire up your company's bottom line.

Up you go!

Chapter Nine

THE STAR CODE

L et's assume you've cracked the Destiny Code—you've figured out what "song" you were destined to sing. You've cracked the Angel Code and assembled a group of players to play with you. You've produced the CD of your songs and all the prisms to go with it. You've stacked a whole warehouse full of inventory. How are you going to move this stuff out the door—the enlightened way?

MARKETING DRIVES BUSINESS

The lifeblood of business is marketing. Marketing is the process of directing eager-to-buy people to your enterprise with cash in hand. Traditional businesses use a myriad of strategies and techniques to accomplish this, some more enlightened than others: market research, targeting the customer, creating a USP (Unique Selling Proposition), figuring out the lifetime value of the customer, devising an advertising and PR strategy, and creating a product to market to them.[Se]

Traditional marketing is much like a carnival. The townspeople are drawn by curiosity and marketing spends money "barking" them into the tent. Once

Earl Bakken

Enlightened Entrepreneurs create enlightened businesses and enlightened philanthropic activities, inspiring others to do the same. Dr. Earl Bakken is one of the most enlightened of enlightened individuals.

In 1957, working in his garage, he created the first wearable, battery-operated, transistorized cardiac pacemaker. This became the basis both for a relationship between Dr. Bakken and the University of Minnesota that has helped millions of people, and for the creation of an international company, Medtronic, based in Minneapolis, that grows at an annual rate of roughly 15%, generates about $5 billion a year, and has 25,000 employees. Medtronic's mission has never changed: "To contribute to human welfare by application of biomedical engineering in the research, design, manufacture, and sale of instruments or appliances that alleviate pain, restore health, and extend life." The company has been involved in creating, manufacturing, and selling over 1,400 cardiological and neurological devices.

Dr. Bakken's love of innovative enterprises and philanthropies led him to found a unique hospital, Five Mountain Medical Community, in Waimea on the "Big Island" of Hawaii. It is the facility of the future, a $100 million, 50-bed hospital that offers multiple medical modalities from allopathic medicine to having a Hawaiian shaman work on you to effectuate healing. Medical doctors have to have their "chronobiology" tested to ensure that they are physiologically at their peak before going into surgery. (Chronobiology is the study of the relationships between our minds and bodies to time, to the cycles and the rhythms of our activities. It has been proven that half of the treatments for high blood pressure in the United States are unnecessary because the people are measured at the wrong time of day.)[e] Dr. Bakken's vision is that conventional medicine and complementary ther-

→

they're inside, the sales team takes the lead and "closes" them. Customer service takes over to deliver the product and keep them happy. The bottom line? Sell bunches of things to bunches of people and make tons of money.

Marketing and selling have often been viewed as pushy and aggressive and—can we say?—sometimes less than enlightened. And yet many principles of influence are truly enlightened. We call them Heart-Sell™ as opposed to Hard-Sell. The fundamental principles of the Heart-Sell system form the basis for this chapter. More techniques will be found on the 101-Day Plan at **www.crackingthemillionairecode.com.**

Good solid marketing is based on scientific formulas and techniques that have worked for a thousand years, and they'll work a thousand more. There are shelves of books on the subject. We've listed the top 101 marketing books of all time on our website. Here are a few of our favorites:

> *Jump Start Your Business Brain: Win More, Lose Less and Make More Money* by Doug Hall
> *Permission Marketing: Turning Strangers into Friends, and Friends into Customers* by Seth Godin
> *Guerrilla Marketing: Secrets for Making Big Profits from Your Small Business* by Jay Conrad Levinson

And here is another one by one of America's greatest marketing minds, a gentleman who has helped the two of us generate millions of dollars—no, tens of millions—over the past 20 years: *Getting Everything You Can Out of All You've Got: 21 Ways You Can Out-Think, Out-Perform, and Out-Earn the Competition* by Jay Abraham.

Let's flex your marketing muscles by pulling a few key marketing principles from these excellent books. Then we'll overlay these fundamentals with enlightened marketing ideas.

Hhaarrtdeeellllsston

#67

apies such as chiropractic, massage, acupuncture, herbal therapy, and clinical therapy can work together to enhance the well-being of the patient.

Dr. Bakken is a pioneering visionary who starts every day at 6 A.M. and works tirelessly in hopes of making the world better through his inventions, companies, and many philanthropic activities.

Jay Abraham teaches that any marketing machine consists of three simple buttons:

1. Bring more customers in the door.
2. Have each customer buy more as they enter.
3. Have each customer return more often to buy even more.

All marketing systems teach you different ways to push those buttons. In *Guerrilla Marketing*, Jay Conrad Levinson shares the "Thirteen Most Important Marketing Secrets."

1. You must have *commitment* to your marketing program.
2. Think of that program as an *investment*.
3. See to it that your program is *consistent*.
4. Make your prospects *confident* in your firm.
5. You must be *patient* in order to keep a commitment.
6. You must see that marketing is an *assortment* of weapons.
7. You must know that profits come *subsequent* to the sale.
8. You must aim to run your firm in a way that makes it *convenient* for your customers.
9. Put an element of *amazement* in your marketing.
10. Use *measurement* to judge the effectiveness of your weapons.
11. Establish a situation of *involvement* between you and your customers.
12. Learn to become *dependent* upon other businesses and they upon you.
13. You must be skilled in the *armament* of guerrillas, which means technology.

A large portion of the success of any business is found in those key marketing principles. Doug Hall (this guy is a master!), in his excellent and well-documented book *Jump Start Your Business Brain,* shows how a focused, simple approach to marketing can make a huge difference. If you want to increase the number of customers walking into your "tent" and sell them more while they're there, you must master three laws of marketing physics.

First Law of Marketing Physics: Overt Benefit

SIMPLY AND FORCEFULLY PRESENT AN **OVERT** **BENEFIT** *TO DISTINGUISH your product from all others.*

How much difference does this make? It can increase your sales by up to 300%. For Federal Express, it's overnight delivery.ea For Volvo, it's safety. For Domino's Pizza, it's fresh, hot pizza in about 30 minutes.

If you keep your overt benefit as clean and simple as possible, sales can increase even more.

A simple taste test proved this convincingly. Researchers held two different taste tests at a supermarket. Test #1 gave shoppers a choice to sample any of 24 delicious confectionery jams. Test #2 gave shoppers a choice of only 6 jams. Which test created more sales? Test #2 increased overall sales by 600%! Keep it simple.

Second Law of Marketing Physics: Real Reason to Believe

CUSTOMERS WON'T PULL OUT THEIR MONEY UNTIL THEY PERCEIVE A real reason to believe *that you will deliver on your overt benefit.*

Let people have a personal experience with the product, show them your credentials, use testimonials, offer a guarantee. How much of a difference does this make? Products with few or none of these reasons have only an 18% probability of success. Those with a high reason to believe have a 42% probability of success.

Oh, Vert, Be Tifen

Reel Be Lie Victoryability

Drama Tictoc Differecne

XPlow Sive Sails nad pro-fits

#68

Third Law of Marketing Physics: Dramatic Difference

AN OVERT BENEFIT PLUS A REAL REASON TO BELIEVE *PLUS A* dramatic difference = *an explosion of sales and profits.*

In other words, make your product revolutionary and new-to-the-world. How much difference does this make? Your chances of success increase 353% when you have a dramatic difference. Makes good sense, doesn't it?

Seth Godin, in his groundbreaking book, *Permission Marketing,* explains how to increase the frequency of purchase—how to get people back into your tent over and over again. Godin states:

> *Fire 70% of your customers and watch your profits go up. Instead of focusing on how to maximize the number of new customers, the focus should be on keeping the best 30% of your customers longer and getting far more money from each of them over time.*

Principles of marketing can and ought to be studied and mastered by all business owners. We love the science of marketing, but this chapter is not about traditional marketing. Although smart marketing may be responsible for up to 97.5% of your success, this chapter is about the other 2.5%. This chapter is about the small, enlightened differences that can make a huge impact. We call it cracking the Star Code.

The goal of this chapter is not to change marketing, but to transcend it by overlaying the time-honored principles of business success with a system of enlightened practices. Let's take a closer look.

ENLIGHTENED MARKETING OVERLAY

Suppose you work hard and smart and succeed in getting your business off the ground and into the profit column. What would have to happen to cause a tidal wave of new demand for your products? Ponder that while we share some seemingly unrelated statistics.

In the 2004 Olympics in Greece, the Men's Swimming—Butterfly competition pitted the world's top eight swimmers against one another.

1	USA	PHELPS Michael	51.25	OLYMPIC RECORD
2	USA	CROCKER Ian	51.29	+0.04
3	UKR	SERDINOV Andriy	51.36	+0.11
4	GER	RUPPRATH Thomas	52.27	+1.02
5	RUS	MARCHENKO Igor	52.32	+1.07
6	BRA	MANGABEIRA Gabriel	52.34	+1.09
7	CRO	DRAGANJA Duje	52.46	+1.21
8	AUS	HUEGILL Geoffrey	52.56	+1.31

Snap your fingers. That took about a second. In this race, the gold medal winner, American swimming phenom Michael Phelps, broke an Olympic record by swimming four one-hundredths of a second faster than the silver medal winner, who swam seven one-hundredths of a second faster than the bronze medal winner._{ch} The fourth-place finisher missed the bronze by less than half a second.

All eight hands touched the wall within 1.31 seconds of each other. What could this minuscule time differential be worth to them? The gold medal winner can parlay his experience into a lifetime of paid speeches, endorsements, business deals, and coaching assignments—many millions of dollars, if properly handled. The last-place finisher, one snap of your fingers slower, will have parlayed four years of hard work into some nice photos of Athens, and a few memories. You'll probably never hear from him again. From everything you've ever wanted to a few memories in 1.31 seconds. The difference between first and last is a margin of roughly 2.5%. Hold that thought for a minute.

Now, think about how a few *tiny* adjustments could propel your business from last place to first place. One well-worded ad, one well-connected angel, one well-researched product improvement, one well-respected endorsement, one well-placed PR event, one well-heeled partnership. Just one. Think of it. One. Uno. Un. Eins. Ichi. One tiny little tweak.

Where might that one nudge come from? You can trace scores of fortunes to that one integral spark that ignited the entire enterprise. Hard work, yes. Risk, of course. Dedication, definitely. But remove the spark? The spark can come from almost anywhere—luck, coincidence, or serendipity. And don't forget, the convergence of a fortuitous surprise with the providence of Higher Power.

High, higher, highest, pow, power, powerful,
powerfully, ignite, ignites, igniting, ignition, the, a, an, spark,
sparks, sparkling, sparkle, sparkles.

#69

But Higher Power still isn't going to carry us to the finish line. Higher Power expects us to put in the 97.5%. There still will be heaps of work, discipline, training, and sacrifice. This isn't get rich quick in the traditional "lottery ticket" sense. But what if you got a tiny nudge at exactly the right time? A phone call here, a recommendation there, a suggestion here, a contact there. Just a breath in the sails at the right time.[5] A nudge when you need it. What could a 2.5% bump in the right direction be worth to you?

Will you ever "know" if Higher Power is *really* supporting and protecting your enterprise? Perhaps it's really just a matter of luck after all. But happily for our thesis there has been a lot of research to show how spirituality, prayer, or willful attention can actually affect a lot of things, including the flip of a coin.

DOES COMMUNICATING WITH HIGHER POWER REALLY WORK?

Larry Dossey, MD, in his 1993 book entitled *Healing Words: The Power of Prayer and the Practice of Medicine,* became curious about a number of studies showing the effectiveness of communicating with Higher Power through prayer. As a medical doctor, he had to overcome some initial skepticism.

> *. . . the experimental data on prayer that I turned up caught me off guard. I really wanted nothing to do with it. Meditation was acceptable, but the thought of "talking to God" . . . I thought I had laid to rest. Yet the results of the prayer experiments kept forcing themselves into my psyche. . . . Experiments with people showed that prayer positively affected blood pressure, wounds, heart attacks, headaches, and anxiety. . . .*
>
> *Remarkably the effects of prayer did not depend on whether the praying person was in the presence of the organism being prayed for, or whether he or she was far away; healing could take place either on site or at a distance. Nothing seemed capable of stopping or blocking prayer. Even when an "object" was placed in a lead-lined room or in a cage that shielded it from all known forms of electromagnetic energy, the effect still got through. . . . The evidence is simply overwhelming that prayer functions at a distance to change physical processes in a variety of organisms,*

from bacteria to humans. These data ... are so impressive that I have come to regard them as among the best-kept secrets in medical science.

What does this research on prayer in healing have to do with spirituality in business? It is our belief that if prayer—or meditation, if you will—can positively affect your physical health, it can positively affect your financial well-being. But perhaps you're still harboring doubts. If so, read on and see how remote intention—just willing something to happen—can cause positive and statistically significant results. In other words, if you won't believe in Higher Power, then at least believe in yourself![T]

Wayne Dyer, the bestselling author and psychologist, endorsed an excellent book by Lynne McTaggart entitled *The Field: The Quest for the Secret Force of the Universe.* In this book McTaggart relates the research of Robert Jahn, a Princeton University professor, and Brenda Dunne, a developmental psychologist from the University of Chicago. The two researchers joined forces in the late 1970s to design a scientific project (called PEAR: Princeton Engineering Anomalies Research) to determine whether or not ordinary humans had the ability to exert "mind over matter." They designed an electric device that, in essence, randomly displayed a heads or tails scenario. Statistically, the odds of getting a heads or tails answer were 50/50.

To test if mind power worked, the researchers placed participants in front of the "heads or tails" machine to conduct three simple tests. In one test, the participant would "will" the machine to produce more heads than tails. In the next test, the participant would "will" the machine to do just the opposite—produce more tails than heads.[A] In the final test, the participant would not attempt to influence the outcome in any way.

Year in and year out, Jahn and Dunne carried on the tedious process of collecting a mountain of data—which would eventually turn into the largest database ever assembled of studies into remote intention. ... In one 12 year period of nearly 2.5 million trials, it turned out that 52 percent of all the trials were in the intended direction and nearly two thirds of the

materialized. —ROBERT G. ALLEN • Unless the Lord builds a house, the work of the builders is useless. Unless the

ninety-one operators had overall success in influencing the machines the way they'd intended. . . . Although (this) doesn't sound like much of an effect, statistically speaking it's a giant step . . . the odds of this overall score occurring (randomly) are a trillion to one.

—LYNNE MCTAGGART,
*THE FIELD: THE QUEST FOR THE
SECRET FORCE OF THE UNIVERSE*

When two or more people joined together try to influence the outcome, the results were even more dramatic. Couples of the opposite sex (friends) had three and a half times the effect of single individuals. Bonded couples in relationships had the most profound effect—nearly six times as strong as that of single operators.

The PEAR studies provided strong scientific support for the power of human intention.

#70

Now, let's pull together all of these apparently unrelated concepts to make our point. In the Olympic swimming competition, the time difference between the gold medal winner and the last-place finisher was approximately 2.5%. In both the prayer studies and the "mind over matter" experiments, the participants were able to affect the outcome through sheer force of will between 2 and 4% of the time.

The differences seem insignificant, but the end results can be as different as a gold medal finish and last place. You have the ability to influence events and other people's behavior through your prayers and thoughts. When you add a team of congruently focused and committed people, you possess amazing power. Your influence may appear to be insignificant—1 or 2%—but sometimes this is all you need.

"OK," you say. "How do we do this? What is the system? The nitty gritty. The details. Cross our t's. Dot our i's. You tell us, 'If you build it, they will come.' How will they come?"

This is how.

Here is a six-secret plan for getting that extra 1 or 2%.

Secret One. Replace Your Marketing Director (Even If It's You)

TRADITIONAL BUSINESS IS LIKE TRADITIONAL MEDICINE. THE human body has more than a dozen unique systems that regulate life—the circulatory system, the nervous system, the immune system, the digestive system, respiratory system, and so on. Physicians spend 10 to 15 years studying these systems to get their medical degree. Business also has its systems—marketing, accounting, manufacturing, shipping,[R] and so on. When it comes to business, it takes at least six years to get an MBA or CPA degree, beginning from high school.

As it is in medical school so it is in business school. There are years of training on how the body or the business functions but almost *zero* discussion of one of the most important life systems—the spiritual system. Every system is essential, but the spiritual system is preeminent. Without spirit, there is no life. But do doctors talk about it? Not until recently. Do business professors talk about it?[th] Isn't it worth at least 2.5% of the course curriculum? According to a recent Gallup Poll:

95% of North Americans say that they believe in a Higher Power.

95% said that they pray to a Supreme Being.

95% of those feel their prayers have been answered.

93% have a Bible or some other scriptures in their home.

76% feel a closer connection to God after reading scriptures.

82% are sometimes very conscious of the presence of God.

82% feel a need to experience spiritual growth.

79% believe in miracles.

78% of American adults believe there is a heaven.

76% of U.S. teens believe in angels.

To quote from George Gallup Jr.'s book, *Surveying the Religious Landscape,* "With nearly four fifths of the population giving ample reflection on their relationship to God, it is not surprising that the United States is regarded as the most religious nation of the industrialized world. Despite recent clamor about the nation's indifference to matters of faith, the vast majority of Americans demonstrate interest in the divine-human relationship."

So what is the system for bringing Higher Power into business and operating business from Higher Spiritual Principles? The "god" of the traditional marketer is statistics. Probability is the Holy Grail. With six and a half billion people on the planet, what is the probability that a large group of motivated people could be convinced to need/want your product? Fairly high. What is the probability that a database can find them? Good. What is the probability of creating a message that hard-sells one-half of 1% of them to buy your product? Fair. But with 6.5 billion people to market to, one-half of 1% is about 35 million people! There is enough business even considering that a large group of them don't have any money.

$$19 = 5\ 5$$

#71

Business is a numbers game. Marketers don't need God, or so they believe. They just need to test their marketing premise on enough people. Find a tiny percentage of a huge number of people and they're rich. That's how it works.

Most of the money spent in marketing chases this tiny percentage. This drives advertising and marketing costs sky high, pushing profit down. This leaves less money available for enlightened activities such as helping the 20%

progressive narrowing of the personality and prevents exploration and experimentation. There is no

THE STAR CODE | *209*

of the world family who can't afford *any* products and are subsisting on less than a dollar a day.

What we're proposing is radical. It's heretical. It's crazy. It's unscientific. Let's let Higher Power be VP over marketing. Higher Power knows where the customers are. He knows what they want and what they need. He knows how much they can afford. He knows which products, ideas, people, experiences, and services will bring them closer to Him and which ones will divert them from Him._{ro} He knows exactly which products will enlighten His family. Frankly, that's the essence of an enlightened idea: It brings someone closer to Higher Power instead of diverting them away. Higher Power likes that. That's the name of His game—to bring people closer to Him, to be more like Him.

Higher Power does not play probabilities. He knows where 100% of us live, the best ways to reach us, and just the right words to motivate us. He doesn't need to send a junk mail letter to 100,000 of us in order to find 500 consumers. He wouldn't allow 99,500 letters to be thrown in the trash this way, impoverishing the earth by denuding it of trees.

Higher Power would send a "Highly" targeted letter to 500 people and have 100% of them respond. The marketing costs would be almost zero, allowing the Enlightened Enterprise to slash its prices dramatically (in comparison with those junk mail marketers) and drive up profits dramatically so that more money could be given away. And there would still be plenty of money left over for personal toys and trips and treasures and trinkets, if those things turn you on. (Like the bumper sticker says: *I know that money doesn't bring happiness, but I'd like to find out for myself.* OK. Find out for yourself, just as long as you give away the first 10%.)

And that's precisely how you bring Higher Power into your enterprise. You live the LIGHT principles: Loverage, Inner Wealth, Giving, Higher Power, and Trusteeship. Now *there's* a foundation to build an enlightened skyscraper on! You just flat-out make the decision that Higher Power comes first. Call it what you will—prayer, meditation, focused attention, enlightened intention, commitment to Higher values, socially responsible business—just do it.

$$\setminus \div \diagup \setminus \propto \| \quad \in \equiv \leftarrow \propto \| \quad / \equiv \| \sim \neg \rangle - \; = \; \bullet\bullet \% \; \div \approx \sum \in \div \| - \infty \div \equiv \approx$$

$$\updownarrow \% \quad \in \propto \| \sum \in \div \| - \infty \div \equiv \approx$$

#72 _____

Secret Two. Pay it Forward

FIRST, LET US SHARE THREE STORIES.

Story #1. A preacher is driving along a country road, passing field after field, until he sees an unusually rich crop of billowing waves of ripe grain. He sees the farmer there, in the field, and approaches him.[ug] "That's a fine, fine crop you and the Lord are growing there together." The crusty old farmer thinks on this a moment and says, "You shoulda seen it when the Lord had it all by Himself."

Story #2 comes from the movie *Tin Men,* starring Richard Dreyfuss and Danny DeVito, about the lives of some low-life aluminum-siding salesmen. One of the salesmen, Tilly, played by Danny DeVito, is sitting with his partner at a crowded bar celebrating their big sale. And his partner says to Tilly, "You know somethin', Tilly? I'm beginning to believe in God."

"Yeah, me too," says Danny DeVito, who is thinking about his huge commission check.

"No, no. You don't know what I mean. I'm beginning to give God more thought."

"Well, you were never one of those atheists, were you?" asks Tilly.

"Look, I'm not saying that. I'm just beginning to believe in God more, that's all."

"What'd you do . . . have some kind of religious experience?"

"Yeah. Well, I took my wife for lunch yesterday. Went and had some smorgasbord and it kinda happened."

"You found God in a smorgasbord!!?"

"Yeah."

"That's a nice place to find God," Tilly smirks.[hH]

"Well, I go there. I see celery, I see lettuce, tomatoes, cauliflower and I think—all these things come out of the ground. They just grow outta the ground. I mean, they had corn outta the ground. Radishes outta the ground. And you say to yourself, 'How can all of these things come outta the ground?' You know what I'm talking about? All these things are outta the ground. I mean, how can that be? Outta the dirt all these things came. And I'm not even getting into the fruits. I'm just dealing with the vegetables right now. With all of these things coming outta the earth . . . there must be a God."

"You know," Tilly says as he glances around at the girls in the bar, "I'm not getting the same religious effect that came over you. I don't feel like running to a church to pray right this second. You know what I mean?"

"You gotta admit, it's amazing. Nature. Outta the ground. Anything you can name, it's outta the ground."

Story #3 is a true story. When we were young we watched a television show called *The Millionaire.* (Remember, you baby boomers?) A man showed up at the door, unannounced, with a million-dollar check . . . no strings attached. This was back when a million was serious money. How would that money change the recipients' lives?[i] That was the premise of the show.

Now, suppose you heard a doorbell ring. You walk to the front door, and there is an official but kindly looking gentleman. He's holding an envelope *for you*! You open it . . . and there is a crisp, green legal-looking check made out to you in the sum of . . . that's right . . . *one million dollars.* Your mind is awash with all of the possibilities.

But wait, there's a catch. (Isn't there always?) The gentleman informs you that in order to receive this gift of one million dollars, you have to give the first 10% of the money back.

"That's it?" you ask.

"Yes," he says. "Here is how it works. First, I give you one million dollars. Then, before you buy anything for yourself, before you invest it, before you buy a new home or a new car or a new set of clothes, even before you pay off any of your debts—before you spend a penny of it for yourself—you give me back the first $100,000. And then, you may spend the remaining $900,000 in any way you choose."

"Wow," you say, "that sounds fair."

"Wait," he says. "There's more.

"My benefactor has instructed me that from time to time I'm to send you more checks in the mail—$100 here, $1,000 there, sometimes $10,000, and so on.gh The rules are the same. You give back the first 10%, and you can spend the rest of it in any way you choose. And I'll keep sending you more. But there's a caveat. If you stop giving back the first 10%, all the money will just sort of disappear. Like manna that spoils in the wilderness."

"Wow!" you say.

"Yup, that's the way it works," he says. "My benefactor has instructed me to keep giving money to only those who learn to give back. If they don't give back, the streams of money dry up."

The Law of Real Money

Most of us were never taught the real reality of money. No wonder we have a hard time with this idea of sharing some of our hard-earned money with others—especially with those who haven't worked as hard as we did to earn ours. "It's my money. I earned it. I sacrificed for it. I saved it." Like the attitude of the farmer standing in his field, saying, "You shoulda seen it when the Lord had it all by Himself."

That's the way the two of us used to think, and then "reality" hit. Both of us lost everything—bankrupt. An early frost wiped out our crops. "And you shoulda seen it when *we* had it all by *ourselves*!" It wasn't pretty.

During those dark times each of us decided, independently, to try something different. We decided to be givers instead of hoarders. And that's when everything began to change. Starting with our attitudes. We became slowly aware of a bigger picture—what that farmer standing in his field hadn't even considered. Yes, he had worked hard—planted, weeded, fertilized, and harvested. But Higher Power had done the truly miraculous things—the seed, the soil, the sun, the rain, and the changing of the seasons—and the harvest grew. *Right outta the ground. How can that be? Outta the dirt all these things*

pride above that which any other experience can bring to him? Discovery! To know that you are

THE STAR CODE | *213*

came. And we're not even getting into the fruits. We're just dealing with the vegetables right now.

ˈak-ˈtɪ-vat thə ˈsi-kəl əv ˈləv

#73

We learned a new way of looking at giving. We began to share out of the abundance of gratitude for the things we had already received. Instead of waiting for the millionaire to knock on our door with our million-dollar check, we began to realize that he had already come. We'd already deposited the check. The windows of heaven had already been opened. The floodgates had already been released. Not for anything we had done and worked and saved for. It was a gift.

But sometimes we forget, kinda like teenagers. You try to get them to clean up their rooms, and they come back with, "You don't own me. You can't tell me what to do!" As a parent, you say, "Who do you think pays for the roof over your head, that fridge full of food? Who do you think pays for the cars, and the phones, and the clothes, and the running water. Who do you think changes the toilet paper? Who do you think worries about you and prays for you, night and day. Who wants the best for you?"er

We imagine Higher Power listening in on this scene and chuckling. His adult children have also been acting like teenagers. "It's my money. I worked for it. I saved it. You can't tell me what to do with it!" And He replies, "Who do you think created this whole universe just for you, with a sun to warm you, with a fridge full of food that grew *right outta the ground*? Who do you think ponders about you and plans for you? Who wants the best for you?"

We learned the hard way, but now we're sold on giving. We used to be hoarders. We'll never, ever make that mistake again!

We looked up at the sky last night, at the smorgasbord of stars, and it kinda happened. We saw stars; we saw planets, moons, comets; and we

—SANDY M. BUSHBERG

thought, All these things grow right outta the sky. And we said to ourselves, "How can that be? From outta space all these things came. And we're not even getting into the galaxies. We're just dealing with the stars right now. With all of these things coming right outta the sky . . . there must be a God."

Oh, by the way. Edison was wrong. He said it was 99% perspiration and 1% inspiration. The truth is that our contribution to wealth is the tiniest part of the equation. Higher Power contributes almost all of it. All He wants us to do is acknowledge Him and to learn to be a giver like He is.

Can you be successful using this model?[P]

Have you ever heard of eBay? Everyone knows that the young founder of eBay, Pierre Omidyar, and his wife have already pledged to give away 99% of their multiple billions. Pierre's original goal was to create a "founding culture" using the moral principles he learned in childhood. "My mother always taught me to treat other people the way I want to be treated and to have respect for other people," he says. "Those are just good basic values to have in a crowded world." That's the motto of eBay: "Empowering people and helping them be the best they can be."

So transform your enterprise into a giving machine. It's the least you can do. And let Higher Power do the heavy lifting.

Secret Three. Lighten Up Your Enterprise

IMAGINE A CONTINUUM OF ENDARKENED TO ENLIGHTENED BUSINESSES on a scale of 1 to 10—with 1 meaning completely endarkened and 10 meaning completely enlightened.

The sun has one kind of glory, while the moon and stars each have another kind. And even the stars differ from each other in their beauty and brightness.

—I CORINTHIANS 15:41, *NLT*

Very few businesses are completely endarkened—except maybe those operated by the Sopranos.ow In the lowest world, it's "take and take." In the middle world, it's "give and take." At the highest level, it's "give and give." Dog feed dog works better than dog eat dog.

Businesses operate with various visions, but most businesses are honest, ethical, efficient, and helpful. The top 10% operate in the rarefied air of purpose, heart, class, excellence, civic-mindedness, commitment to "good" values, employee satisfaction, environmental sensitivity, and philanthropy—where brothers and sisters feed each other in the banquet of life. This is the ideal.

#74 _____

_____

Make the decision that you'll be the gold-medal-winning enterprise. The white light from Higher Power beams through your prism to the world. Try to lighten up each stage of the process. Is your soul-storming enlightened? Are your support companies enlightened? Are your manufacturing processes enlightened? Are your angel employees enlightened? Any negative, unethical, or pushy process blurs, diffuses, and distorts the message. How would Higher Power rectify and purify the conduit?

Scour your enterprise from top to bottom. Enlighten the darkest corners of it.

existence of a Higher Power. People who believe in God believe Him enough to do what He says.

—ROBERT G. ALLEN

TRADITIONAL BUSINESS		ENLIGHTENED ENTERPRISE	
CEO	Chief Executive Officer	CEO	Chief Enlightenment Officer
P&L	Profit and Loss statement	P&L	Purpose and Love statement
USP	Unique Selling Proposition	USP	Universal Soul-ing Proposition
LTV	Lifetime Value	LTV	Light Time Value
ROI	Return on Investment	ROI	Return on Inspiration/Intuition
ROE	Return on Equity	ROE	Return on Enlightenment
CPM	Cost per Thousand	CPM	Compassion per Thousand

(M being the Roman numeral for 1,000)

Secret Four: Feed Them Exactly What They Want

HAVE YOU HEARD THE TALMUDIC TALE OF THE MAN WHO IS GRANTED a glimpse of the afterlife? First he is shown a vision of hell. Groups of hungry, miserable people are gathered around a banquet table laden with beautiful, deliciously exquisite foods.er It's a feast! Unfortunately, the elbows of every person are locked so they can't bend their arms to get the food on their forks into their mouths. The room is filled with the sounds of weeping, wailing, and gnashing of teeth.

Then the man is shown a vision of heaven. Here happy people are gathered around a similar banquet table laden with an equally magnificent feast. Their elbows, too, are locked. But rather than impotently complain, they reach out and feed each other! Each person feeds someone else . . . selecting for them exactly what they want in exactly the right amount until the other person is fully satisfied. And then, the person who has just been served returns the favor by feeding someone else. Thus, everyone is fully fed. The room is filled with the sound of joy, rejoicing, and celebration.

The world of Enlightened Entrepreneurship, at the highest levels, is a world where each member introduces new members to the banquet of prosperity. If you've made it to the millionaires' table, you'll also be expected to feed as many as you can. It's not just trying to sell them a bunch of stuff. Since they're family, you want to show them those parts of the banquet you were destined to share with them—resources, connections, ideas, experience, wisdom, and energy to help them "make it happen" in their own lives.

Higher Power planted in your mind and heart the idea for an enlightened product. It's your job to take care of your customers—to feed them. But what should you feed them? Ask them exactly what they want, and feed them exactly that. This may seem obvious, but it is overlooked by 99% of businesses.

Traditional businesses dream up a great product and then go look for a market to sell it to. Along comes a little-known marketing guru, Jeff Paul, who counsels people to do exactly the opposite. "Don't dream up anything," he says. "First, find the hungriest schools of fish in feeding frenzy, drop in your bait, and watch the explosion of sales.$_e$" To prove his point, he markets to one of the most voracious schools of fish on the planet—golfers. His direct-mail letter selling an exclusive set of golf clubs contains no pictures of the clubs he's offering. You might be shocked to learn that these golf clubs cost $6,000 per set! And he has sold millions of dollars' worth of them! These piranhas were hungry!

We're in agreement with Jeff if all you're trying to do is make some serious cash fast. That's not what this book is about. But we'll share with you how we would adapt Jeff's brilliant marketing conclusions to create the Enlightened Enterprise. You see, as an Enlightened Entrepreneur you are the conduit between Higher Power and your customer. It's the Serendestiny trinity: you, your neighbor, and Higher Power. All three parts are essential. *What do you want me to say? How do you want me to say it? Who do you want me to say it to?*

Perhaps that is exactly what Jeff Paul is describing—a pure entrepreneur with talent to create and market, being guided to the right hungry markets, and feeding them exactly what they want. We would just put more emphasis on the "being guided to" part of the equation. But feeding them exactly what they want is *so* important. Imagine yourself at the banquet table with a hankering for asparagus and someone comes up to you with a fork dripping with pickled herring. You politely decline and they insist that you "try it." They love pickled herring themselves and they can't understand why more people don't like it. You're craving asparagus and they're force-feeding you herring!

But isn't that the Golden Rule?

Do for others what you would like them to do for you.

—MATTHEW 7:12, *NLT*

No, that's not what it really says. At the deepest level, the Golden Rule is saying, "Love people just as you love to be loved." In marketing it's how you love those people that's important. We call it the Star Rule: *Do for others exactly what they want you to do for them.*

What do they want? If they want asparagus, feed them asparagus.[y] Treat them like stars, as if they were Higher Power in disguise.

ArBAlCf CfBrCmCaBk AtCf Cm ClAmBeBe-
CAtBiAmAl, ClAmBeBe-BrBeAlDbAmAl, ClAmBeBe-
BiAmCaBhAtBhAr AtBhCsAtCfAtDsBeAm BhCeAlArAm
AtBh CAsAm CaAtArAsC AlAtCaAmDbCAtBBh.

#75 _____

_____

Most businesses only see "customers"—people who buy stuff—and that is the problem. So we've come up with a new word to describe them—STARS. Are you tired of all the acronyms in this book yet? (Hang in there just a little while longer.) The word *STARS* can have plenty of meanings, but rather than tell you how to treat an enlightened customer, we'll let you create your own acronym. What does the word mean to you?

S _____
T _____
A _____
R _____
S _____

Make up your own word based on how you feel your customers—your STARS—should be treated.

Secret Five. Activate the Seven Circles of Empowerment

READ THE LAST CHAPTER AND THIS ONE OVER AGAIN. ACTIVATE all Seven Circles of Empowerment from Inner Circles, Virtual Circles, Winner's Circles, and the Circle of Life to the Eternal Circle. Turn 101 billion eyes on the opportunity of taking care of your STARS in such a way that they can't stop talking about you. Put the STARS through the Millionairium and explore ways to sparkle your understanding of how to serve them.

Secret Six. Treat Them Like STARS!

THE ENTREPRENEUR WHO WANTS TO OPERATE THE MOST ENLIGHTENED Enterprise on the planet needs to see each customer through Higher Power eyes. That's not a "piece of meat" wandering through the store, with a price tag around its neck. That's God-stuff embarked on a special mission through life.

> *Love every person that you meet for they are*
> *my children and each is priceless to me.*

The value of that customer is more than the few dollars he or she spent today. The lifetime value (LTV) of that customer equals what a loyal customer would purchase from your enterprise in a lifetime. Let's assume that you're selling life insurance. If a customer continued buying insurance from your firm at the rate of $200 per month for 40 years, the LTV (gross revenue) of that customer would be $96,000. If that same customer recommended your service to two friends at the same level of buying, it could triple the LTV of that customer.

SSAADNHERI.TRAETRCEBELGTNDAKTN.ARTTYIEMEG

#76

Now let's add the enlightened business overlay. Instead of LTV, let's calculate the Love Term Value of one enlightened customer. The difference between a business that struggles and an enterprise that thrives may be *one extra referral per customer every month*. Let's repeat that again. What if every single one of your customers were to enthusiastically rave about your enterprise to just one extra person per month? Let's try that one more time. What if each of your STARS were to personally bring you one new member of his or her Winner's Circle every single month? That would double your business every month. Could you handle that?

When we view these customers with traditional eyes we see only what they can buy. When we see them through enlightened eyes, we see what they can contribute other than direct revenue. There is hidden revenue, secret revenue, invisible revenue. Perhaps just one phone call from this customer could connect you to a large corporation that could hundredfold your business.

Yes, you'll continue your normal marketing activities, casting your nets to find that tiny percentage. But when you find them, you'll see them through Higher Power eyes because . . .

You replaced your marketing director with Higher Power,
You lightened up your enterprise,
You started paying it forward,
You fed the fish exactly what they wanted,
You activated the Seven Circles of Empowerment,

and

You began to treat them like STARS!

Then, what begins to transpire is hard to describe. It's irrational, unbelievable, unscientific, foolish, crazy, ridiculous, and absurd.[es] At the same time, it's amazing, miraculous, marvelous, indescribable, wonderful, grace-ful, and incredible.

Fish start swimming into your nets voluntarily! They even jump into your boat! And what's more, they bring schools of other fish with them! Why? Three reasons.

REASON #1. The fish are fed up with the get-rich fix that the world is hooked on: chase the lead, close the sale, swipe the card. Next! They know something is missing.

REASON #2. What you're doing is so refreshingly different . . . so rare, so special. You're not the normal amusement park. You're Disneyland! And this is exactly what Walt Disney said: "Do what you do so well that when people see what you do, they'll want to come again and bring their friends."

Look at the billions that have flowed to the Disney Enterprise as a result of that philosophy. It's called Enlightened Word of Mouse. Now trace it back to the moment when it all started. Walt said:

> *I only hope that we don't lose sight of one thing—that it was all started by a mouse. . . . He popped out of my mind onto a drawing pad . . . on a train ride from Manhattan to Hollywood at a time when business fortunes of my brother Roy and myself were at lowest ebb and disaster seemed right around the corner.*

Now *that* was a Higher-Powered idea! Is there a "Mickey" idea scurrying around in your brain?

REASON #3. Are you ready to receive floods of enlightened customers into your life? Are you ready to take care of them? Are you ready to love them? Are you ready to contribute to their prosperity? Can the windows of heaven be opened through you?

Enlightened customers intuitively know where to give their business. They intuitively know that once they give you their business, some of that profit will flow through you to bless the lives of others. Higher Power broadcasts a silent signal to exactly those you're destined to reach. They become aware of your presence where before you were invisible to them, below their intuitive radar screens. They'll notice your ads now and something will just "speak to them," beckon them. And they won't know why. Your switchboard will just *light* up.

In Chapter Two we shared the story of *Field of Dreams,* where streams of cars began flowing to a solitary baseball diamond in a far outfield in Iowa.

They'll come to your Field of Dreams for reasons they can't even fathom. They'll turn up your driveway, not knowing for sure why they're doing it. They'll arrive at your door as innocent as children longing for the past. "Of course, we won't mind if you look around," you'll say. "It's only 20 dollars per person." They'll pass over the money without even thinking about it. Where it is money they have and peace they lack. And they'll walk out to the bleachers in shirtsleeves on a perfect afternoon and find they have reserved seats somewhere along one of the baselines where they sat when they were children and cheered their heroes and they'll watch the game and it will be as if they dipped themselves in magic waters. The memories will be so thick, they'll have to brush them from their faces . . . Oh, people will come, Ray. People will most definitely come.

Cracking the Star Code is difficult to explain, but you'll know when you've cracked it. People will start telling you how much they love the "asparagus" you're feeding them. They'll love the way you do it exactly the way they like it. They'll have a difficult time expressing what they're experiencing or feeling. There's just something special about your enterprise. They feel at home. Because they are home. They're family.

The principles and the goals of an Enlightened Enterprise are very clear. Give love to Higher Power. Give love to yourself. Give love to every team member in the enterprise. Love every single person whom the enterprise serves. Give love through the profits of the enterprise to bless other people. In fact, the entire enterprise sails on winds of love—guided toward the very people it is destined to serve.

Now let's learn how to take your Enlightened Enterprise and hundredfold it.

#77

Chapter Ten

HUNDREDFOLDING

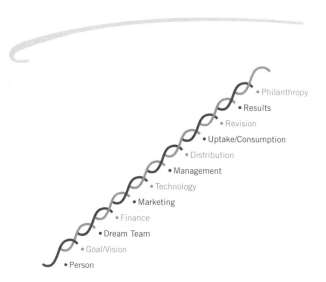

- Philanthropy
- Results
- Revision
- Uptake/Consumption
- Distribution
- Management
- Technology
- Marketing
- Finance
- Dream Team
- Goal/Vision
- Person

Hundredfolding!!! Are these guys off their rockers?!! Growing my business by 500 or 1000% would be a huge stretch. But multiplying my sales by 10,000%!!!? There's no way!

That's the point. There's no way you can do it alone. This is a goal that is bigger than you. Maybe bigger than everyone in your current company combined. But it's a goal that is doable. Maybe even essential.

Can any business do it? Of all the 24 million businesses in North America, 98% of them earned less than a million a year in gross income. That's 23,500,000 businesses, many of which won't be around in five years, by the way, and many of which have trouble keeping the doors open, let alone multiplying their business by a hundred.

A typical business that, let's say, grosses $800,000 a year in sales, if hundredfolded, would be bringing in $80 million. *"Yeah, right!! Maybe in fifty years . . . but not in five."*

Dick Marconi

Dick Marconi loves people. As a young man he came to California with only $500 in his pocket and a job working as a salesman for Pfizer Pharmaceuticals, Inc. After seven years Dick got tired of selling prescription drugs that only offered symptom relief. He wanted to help people to keep from getting sick in the first place, so he began to work with herbs, vitamins, minerals, and other nutrients.

When Dick visited Mongolia in 1980, he discovered *Schizandra chinensis.* Fascinated by the ability of this ancient plant to prevent premature aging, Dick dedicated himself to bringing it to the West. When Dick Marconi learned that lutein, a substance found in marigold flowers, helps retard macular degeneration, an ailment that robs millions of Americans of their eyesight, he devoted himself to making it widely available. Dick believes that there is a natural solution to most health maladies—and that he has an obligation to bring those solutions to the public.

"My dad taught me to learn, earn, and return," says Dick. He and his wife, Bo, are passionate philanthropists. Dick says, "Kids are 20% of the world's population, but 100% of the world's future. I want to help them be smart, healthy, well-adjusted, and hardworking. Doesn't it make sense to mentor a child and serve children through charities that will make an instant impact and have a lasting effect?" With this goal in mind Dick created the Marconi Automotive Museum in Tustin, California, filled with over $30 million worth of exotic cars. This nonprofit organization, with Bo at the helm, often helped by Dick's son John and daughter Kim, charges an admission fee and also rents the museum for events and conventions. From the museum's revenues the foundation has given away millions of dollars to children at risk. The Marconi Automotive Museum and Foundation for Kids will serve children now and in generations to come.

The Marconis have also turned their estate, Villa Marconi, into an African wild animal park, home to giraffes, camels, zebras, elands, and other

→

Yet some have done it! Thoroughbreds that raced out of nowhere and blew by the 24 million other horses as if they were standing still.

Amazon did it.
eBay did it.
J. K. Rowling did it.
Beanie Babies did it.

Every year the accounting firm Deloitte & Touche publishes the Fast 500—a list of the 500 fastest-growing technology companies over the previous five years. There are hundreds of other sectors of the economy—groceries, auto, clothing, medical—that could produce a similar list of 500 thoroughbreds. The slowest-growing company on Deloitte's Fast 500 (**www.fast500.com**) had increased its annual sales in five years over 300%—from annual sales in 1998 of $70,000 to $300,000 in 2003. That was the worst on the list!

要求更大的功率是您的企業CHO

#78

The best one opened its doors in 1998. Its revenues in 1999 were $220,000. Within five years its *annual* revenues were just shy of *one billion dollars*! That's growth of 473,000%, which, you'll agree, is substantially higher than our hundredfolding goal of 10,000%. The name of this company is Google, adapted from the mathematical numeral "googol"—the number 1 followed by 100 zeroes.

On the Fast 500, the top 30 companies all hundredfolded their annual sales in five years. Most of these companies you may have never heard of—TheraSense, STSN, Cardiac Science, PriceGrabber.com, Kyphon, Magma Design Automation, Align Technology, HouseValues, InterMune.

We're not suggesting that just because these companies hundredfolded that they are automatically enlightened. But they certainly are providing solutions for millions of customers. For example, the second company on the list was TheraSense, Inc. Its sales were $85,000 five years earlier and grew to

animals native to Africa. Dick and Bo want to make sure that these beautiful animals survive to enrich the diversity of our biosphere and to inspire future generations.

At 70 years young, Dick is still building businesses. He says: "God will tell me when to quit; until then, I am in the fast lane and enjoying every second of it." Perhaps his most visible success was helping a young man named Mark Hughes launch a company called Herbalife. Dick supplied Mark with the product, intelligence, and supplier financing to start what has become a $2 billion company.

Dick puts the underlying reason for his remarkable success this way: "God always makes me feel bigger and more capable. God gives me stability and purpose. I just want to make the world a better, healthier, and safer place and then I can say I have done God's work."

$212 million—a growth rate of over 249,000%! TheraSense provides equipment to help diabetics monitor their blood glucose levels. Does Higher Power receive a lot of prayers every day from the 20 million diabetics in North America? Higher Power knows that diabetes is an epidemic and solutions are needed immediately.

Each year *Inc.* magazine publishes the *Inc. 500* list of the fastest-growing privately held companies (**www.Inc.com/resources/inc500**). The top three on the list had annual revenue increases of 30-fold to 60-fold—that's 3,000% to 6,000%! In just one year!

How did they do it?

By now, you've probably guessed what our answer will be. Higher Power, right? Well, yes, that's the first part of the formula. But hundredfolding is not as exotic as you might think.

Bees do it. Sunflowers do it. Watermelons do it. Apples do it. Strawberries do it. Rabbits do it. Wheat and corn do it.

Sunflowers	up to 3,000 seeds per plant
Watermelon	up to 1,000 seeds per melon
Papaya	up to 500 seeds per fruit
Corn	up to 560 kernels per ear
Apple	average 10 seeds per apple and 384 apples per tree on average
Wheat	up to 100 kernels per head of wheat
Strawberry	from 150 to 200 tiny seeds on the surface of a strawberry
Honeybee	the queen lays 1,500 to 2,000 eggs per day and up to 200,000 per year
Rabbits	5 to 8 bunnies per litter and 4 to 8 litters per year— up to 64 rabbits

Hundredfolding is *not* rare. Hundredfolding is happening all around you in nature and in business. One of the most quoted parables in the world also teaches hundredfolding very clearly. In fact, in about 100 words, this simple story tells you everything you need to know to hundredfold your Enlightened Enterprise.

230 | CRACKING THE MILLIONAIRE CODE

> *A farmer went out to plant some seed. As he scattered it across his field, some seeds fell on a footpath, and the birds came and ate them. Other seeds fell on shallow soil with underlying rock. The plants sprang up quickly, but they soon wilted beneath the hot sun and died because the roots had no nourishment in the shallow soil. Other seeds fell among thorns that shot up and choked out the tender blades. But some seeds fell on fertile soil and produced a crop that was thirty, sixty, and even a hundred times as much as had been planted.*

—MATTHEW 17, *NLT*

The very first people to hear this story didn't get it. They **w**ondered why the Teacher always disguised His te**a**chings in stories. He had to break it down for them:

> *Now here is the explanation of the story I told about the farmer sowing grain: The seed that fell on the hard path represents those who hear the Good News about the Kingdom and don't understand it. Then the evil one comes and snatches the seed away from their hearts. The rocky soil represents those who hear the message and receive it with joy. But like young plants in such soil, their roots don't go very deep. At first they get along fine, but they wilt as soon as they have problems or are persecuted because they believe the word. The thorny ground represents those who hear and accept the Good News, but all too quickly the message is crowded out by the cares of this life and the lure of wealth, so no crop is produced. The good soil represents the hearts of those who truly accept God's message and produce a huge har-vest—thirty, sixty, or even a hundred times as much as had been planted.*

#79 _____

_____

FOUR KINDS OF PLANTINGS WITH FOUR DIFFERENT RESULTS

—

Seed on hard path	Someone talked them out of it.
Seed on rocky soil	Started strong but quit at the first sign of problems or criticism.
Seed on thorny ground	Got diverted by daily stuff and by the lure of get-rich-quick.
Seed on good soil	Finished strong! They "got it" and produced a huge harvest.

Your enterprise, if enlightened, *is* a spiritual crop. Your Great Idea, if enlightened, is *good seed.* Your enterprise, if enlightened, is *good soil.* If you'll just keep weeding and watering (and working like crazy) Higher Power does everything else (the hundredfolding) that is impossible for you to do.

THE SIGMOID CURVE

—

In his book *The Age of Paradox,* Charles Handy demonstrates how almost everything—product life cycles, biological life, companies, countries—can be plotted on a scale called a sigmoid curve.

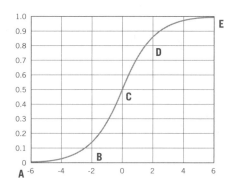

At first there is a base-building/introductory phase (A to B), followed by a spurt of exponential growth (B to C), followed by linear growth (C to D), then plateauing stable growth as it reaches saturation (D), and finally a phase of steady decline (D to E).

Obviously, the best time to create a surge in new growth is to start another growth curve at the top of the sigmoid S as it reaches point D. See the graph on page 231.

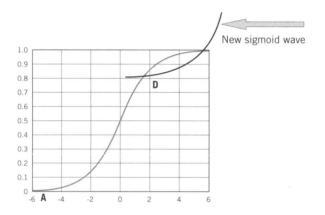

New sigmoid wave

Hundredfolding occurs from A to D. Then, sales usually plateau and decline—in some cases collapsing to zero. Hundredfolding is normal in every business but rarely sustainable—unless something comes along to spark a new sigmoid surge. Google and all the other surging companies had multiple sparks to keep their revenue surging forward.

Where is capitalism on the sigmoid curve? We believe that old-style capitalism is reaching its plateau at point D. It's time to start a new curve, and we believe that Enlightened Entrepreneurship is the spark to spur a new surge to world abundance. We believe you're already beginning to see the trend gaining momentum. Enlightened Entrepreneurship is the next big thing, economically speaking. Doing well by doing good. It just feels right. It transcends the few parts of capitalism that don't work—the selfishness, the greed, the unbridled environmental damage, the waste, the focus on short-term results, the unfulfilled lives of employees everywhere, the pressure, the materialism, the complexity and the purposelessness of modern life.

Neiman Marcus on the phone and say, "Just send me something you think I might like."

HUNDREDFOLDING | *233*

DFZ

The problem with the sigmoid curve of any growth enterprise is the belief that things will only get better. We get complacent and settle into patterns of our comfort zone. It's human nature to want to coast. Unfortunately, it is during peak growth that scouts need to be sent out into the uncharted territory to discover the new opportunities. These new opportunities provide the next surge upward and keep the hundredfolding going.

The leap to a new level is risky. It actually can appear to be a step backward. We call this process the DFZ. Let us explain.

New product
line beginning

DFZ

Darn Failure Zone

Old product
about to wane

The dip occurs because the team has to add new skills and sometimes these skills take time to learn. Just like learning a new golf swing. This dip in progress is what we call the DFZ. It's a very scientific term that you might have difficulty understanding; we call it the Darn Failure Zone.

The DFZ is where most people give up on the future. It is a period of time when things don't appear to be going as planned. In truth, things are going exactly as needed. But most people don't plan for this dip, so it is unexpected, even scary. If you learn the new skills required for a new sigmoid spurt, then

You'd be specific—color, size, style. It's the same with manifesting. —EDWENE GAINES • You will always gravitate to that which

you secretly most love. Men do not attain that which they want but that which they are.

your Enlightened Enterprise enjoys a dramatic new surge of growth. Then, in retrospect, the DFZ turns out to have been a Dynamic Future Zone.

This is the essence of hundredfolding—keeping the growth moving upward through successive sparks of growth.

#80 _____

_____

HUNDREDFOLDING SPARKS

—

Every business book talks about how to recognize hidden opportunities for massive growth. Andy Gove, in his book *Only the Paranoid Survive,* calls them "Strategic Inflection Points," where the rules of the game suddenly change, causing a massive shift in the way business is conducted. Gove, as the president of Intel, the world's leading maker of computer chips, saw how the PC and the Internet were going to dramatically change the business world.

• Your problems are good. They are power in disguise. —MARK VICTOR

HUNDREDFOLDING | *235*

Peter F. Drucker says that opportunities for sudden growth are often hidden inside sudden change. He states that a great leader should first ask the question, "How can I best serve?" A follow-up question is, "How can we exploit this change as an opportunity for our enterprise?" Here is his list of seven changes that can be converted into opportunities:

1. An unexpected success or failure in your own enterprise, in a competing enterprise, or in the industry
2. A gap between what is and what could be in a market, process, product, or service (for example, in the nineteenth century, the paper industry concentrated on the 10% of each tree that became wood pulp and totally neglected the possibilities in the remaining 90%, which became waste)
3. Innovation in a process, product, or service, whether inside or outside the enterprise or its industry
4. Changes in the industry structure and market structure
5. Demographics
6. Changes in mind-set, values, perception, mood, or meaning
7. New knowledge or a new technology

In his wonderful book *Getting Everything You Can Out of All You've Got*, Jay Abraham calls these hidden opportunities "breakthroughs."

There are an unlimited number of breakthroughs out there . . . just waiting for you to discover them. Marketing breakthroughs. Innovative breakthroughs. Creative breakthroughs. Operations breakthroughs. Source breakthroughs. Technology breakthroughs. Systems breakthroughs. Process breakthroughs. Selling systems breakthroughs. Product breakthroughs. Distribution breakthroughs. So many breakthroughs, so little time to discover them all.

We call them hundredfolding sparks. Why? Because Higher Power loves enlightened hundredfolding.

HUNDREDFOLD YOUR BUSINESS
AS OVERSEEN BY HIGHER POWER

—

We decided as business builders to discover how great entrepreneurs hundredfolded their enterprises. First, we began to examine our experience
through different eyes.

Bob's Hundredfolding Story

ROBERT ALLEN, THE COAUTHOR OF THIS BOOK, STUMBLED ONTO
his path by being rejected by 30 top corporations while trying to find a job after
graduating with his MBA from Brigham Young University. Serendestiny happened. An enlightened mentor took him under his wing. Bob began buying
real estate with little or no money down (because that's all he had) and eventually created a fortune using the real estate investment system he developed.

Then, the Great Idea for a title of a book popped into his head one day on a
business commute. *Nothing Down.* He decided to launch a one-day seminar
while he was writing his book. His first seminar, by the same name, was
launched with a $25 classified advertisement offering the seminar at a charge of
$100 a person. To his astonishment, around 100 people paid to attend and his
gross revenue was approximately $10,000. Bob had more than hundredfolded.

He hundredfolded again—to $1,000,000 in revenues—when he began
running full-page ads in major cities.

He hundredfolded again after his book appeared and the title attracted
huge interest. His publisher, Simon & Schuster, asked him to approve the
wording for an advertisement they wanted to run in the *Wall Street Journal*
and other major newspapers. Allen objected to the headline and when they
asked him for something better, an amazing thing happened. The words
began to flow from his mouth as if "downloaded" from out of the blue. They
ran the ad with his headline:

> Send me to any city. Take away my wallet. Give me $100 for living
> expenses. And in 72 hours I'll buy an excellent piece of real estate
> using none of my own money.

invigorator of the body is exercise, and of all the exercises walking is the best.

HUNDREDFOLDING | *237*

This was followed by a formal challenge from a skeptical *Los Angeles Times.* They flew him and an *LA Times* reporter to San Francisco, where Allen proceeded to buy six properties in 57 hours with $20 left over from the original $100. The headline for the article read, "Buying Homes Without Cash: Boastful Investor Accepts *Times* Challenge—and Wins." This single PR event was picked up in syndicated newspapers all over the country and within a few short years—and a million copies later—*Nothing Down* became the all-time bestselling real estate investment book, helped along by the first major infomercial.

The road from a hundred million to a billion is not as important to Bob now as the hundredfolding of the human spirit. He learned this through a Serendestiny detour through a personal bankruptcy that slowed him down long enough for him to reach down to pick up some humility and to reach up to thank Higher Power for miracles he hadn't fully appreciated. Higher Power distanced Himself so that Allen could learn how silly it is to try to grow crops "all by himself."

Since then it's been a steady Serendestiny display of fireworks.

Fund bed hold sore his tess band pour pill pan go T's

#81

Mark's Hundredfolding Story

MARK VICTOR HANSEN, THE COAUTHOR OF THIS BOOK, STARTED his career upside down, digging himself out of personal bankruptcy after trying to sell geodesic domes. (That was a dome idea!) The Great Idea for Mark was to be a speaker—to use his inborn ability to weave together stories and ideas to excite and inspire audiences all over the world. But first he had to apprentice to mentor Chip Collins, who taught him the speaking ropes. In his first few years, Mark's hourly fee went from $25 a talk to $50, $100, and then to $2,500 a talk and on up to $25,000 (that's thousandfolding!). Because of what he was learning, earning, and returning in useful immediate value to his audiences (his marketplace), Hansen went on to make a fortune.

—THOMAS JEFFERSON • Life doesn't require that we be the best, only that we try our best.

—H. JACKSON BROWN JR. •

Then, one day in the early 1990s, Mark's friend and fellow public speaker, Jack Canfield, shared an idea with Mark about compiling a book of short stories—the kind that great speakers use to give goose bumps to their audiences. Mark knew an inspired idea when he heard one. He immediately joined the team and the two men each put their speaking careers on hold to write the book, piling up personal debts of hundreds of thousands of dollars. They just knew it was going to work out—somehow.

After the book was written, the title just wasn't right. They both pondered and prayed to "vibe in" a title that would rock this book into the stratosphere. Jack shares his version of how the title actually came:

> Another example of asking for help from a Higher Power came when Mark and I had finished our book but we didn't have a title. So we went into meditation and prayer and we asked God to give us a title. We felt that the work we were doing was God's work. It was inspirational and uplifting and bringing the higher values to people, making the world a better place. We said, "God, we need a title that will make this book a bestseller so we can get it out to as many people as possible." So Mark and I used two different techniques. He went to bed every night saying, "Mega bestseller, Mega bestseller, Mega bestseller" as a way to prime his unconscious mind to open up to the possibility of a title.
>
> Every morning I would close my eyes and ask God to give us a title and I would just wait for an answer. It was about Wednesday of the week I started doing that that the words *chicken soup* just wrote themselves across my visual field as my eyes were closed.
>
> At first I didn't understand what it meant. Chicken soup? That doesn't make sense. This is just a book of stories.
>
> Then I remembered when I was a kid, whenever I was sick, my mom or my grandmother would bring me chicken soup. Chicken soup was supposed to heal whatever ails you. It's often been referred to as Jewish penicillin. I started thinking, "Rather than physical sickness, there is sort of a spiritual sickness that pervades our culture—a disease of the spirit, a disease of the soul. People are living in resigna-

tion and cynicism and despair. They've given up hope. They're living in hopelessness."

After a few hours of contemplation, *Chicken Soup for the Soul* evolved as the title. Everyone with whom I shared the title—with my wife or Mark or people in my office—they all got instant goose bumps.

Even with a great title, spouses were getting nervous. Bills were piling up, and so were rejection letters from dozens of publishers—33 to be precise—prompting their literary agent to tell them, "You're fired." They were turned down by 134 more publishers at Book Expo America, the annual booksellers' convention. Finally, a small publisher, Health Communications Inc., in Deerfield Beach, Florida, agreed to take on the project if the authors guaranteed to buy the first 20,000 copies.

Gulp. Is this what you want us to do? Yes, came the soft-spoken answer.

The book appeared in 1994 but didn't hit its first bestsellers list until after 14 months of almost nonstop work and promotion by Mark and Jack. It hasn't been off the bestseller lists somewhere in the world ever since. *Chicken Soup* is the top-selling series of nonfiction books in history, with over 100 million books in print and over a *billion dollars* in combined sales!

Does this qualify as hundredfolding? How about ten thousandfolding!!? This is the power of a Higher Power spark.

#82

These sparks come **d**isguised in countless shapes and sizes.

PERSON. Sometimes, the hundredfolding spark is a person or a special mentor.

Start with yourself. Jim Rohn, business speaker and author, says: "Work harder on yourself than you do on the job." Make yourself ever more valuable to yourself, your job/occupation/profession/business, your marketplace, and your future.

We all start out naked, helpless, and ignorant. What we do to make ourselves indispensable is up to us. Lee Iacocca helped launch the Mustang automobile and made a fortune for the Ford Motor Company, only to get fired for outshining the boss, Henry Ford III. Lee then accepted the chairmanship of the dying Chrysler Corporation. Because he intuitively knew what it took to hundredfold a company, he resurrected a moribund company with a new product called a minivan.

After hundredfolding several businesses, he decided to turn his attention to hundredfolding philanthropies. As an enlightened capitalist, born of Italian parents, he wanted to acknowledge all self-sacrificing immigrants for their great contributions to America. Lee was asked to help raise $60 million to rebuild Ellis Island near the famous Statue of Liberty.

At 80+ years young, out of unconditional love and total respect for his wife who died early because of diabetes, he began raising $100 million to end diabetes.

Will you learn to be a hundredfolder?

VISION. Sometimes the hundredfolding spark is a unique vision.

Where there is no vision, the people perish.

—PROVERBS 29:18

With vision we flourish. Either you need vision or you need to team up with someone who has a vision that inspires you. Are you the one to "make it happen" or does someone on your team have MIH power? *Chicken Soup* was originally Jack Canfield's idea. Jack shared his dream with Mark.

Our awareness is the key. It is our awareness more than our work effort that gets the

HUNDREDFOLDING | *241*

Together, they made it happen against all the odds. Their vision is to sell one billion *Chicken Soup for the Soul* books by A.D. 2020.

Chicken Soup's great success came by stacking several hundredfolding sparks one on top of the other. The first *Chicken Soup* bestseller was compounded by publishing *A Second Helping of Chicken Soup for the Soul,* then *A Third Helping of Chicken Soup for the Soul,* and so on. The series hit stardom by creating a legalized monopoly in niche markets with *Chicken Soup for the Woman's Soul* and *Chicken Soup for the Teenage Soul,* the last of which has sold over 19 million copies alone.

We have been teaching Multiple Streams of Income for years. Now we see that an Enlightened Enterprise needs to have multiple sigmoid curves stacked in a chain reaction to create current and future results. It is possible for an enlightened visionary enterprise leader to have multiple ideas and product chains working in concert to gain vast wealth or hundredfold seemingly overnight. That's what sparked eBay, CNN, Virgin Records and 400 Virgin companies, Evergreen Airlines International, and Google.

LE THIG HERPO WERS PARKY OURS IGMO IDSUR GE

#83

Even one sigmoid curve can potentially hundredfold a business. When Russell Simmons and his brother Reverend Run, one of the original musicians and hip-hop artists of Run-DMC, brought out Phat Farm Footwear, they created a $100 million business in the first year, which is now licensing to Adidas for a billion dollars.

What is less well known is how Reverend Run came to be enlightened.

Run's turn to religion came after what he calls a day of extreme consumption while on tour with Run-DMC. He was in the hotel tub, eating French toast, smoking dope, and getting his hair cut while waiting for his Rolls-Royce. "I was sitting there with syrup and ashes in the tub and realized there had to be more to life than this." He soon founded Zoë Ministries Community Congregation. He would say the church found him. "Giving up everything is not going to bring you closer to God," the Reverend says. "When you give, you keep receiving. My company is all about the assist. My life is all about giving."

Different strokes for different folks.

DREAM TEAMS. Sometimes the hundredfolding spark is a powerful team.

Dream Teams used to be called "Master Mind Alliances" in the days of Andrew Carnegie, who'd put together teams to "manufacture and market steel." Today, Enlightened Entrepreneurs create working partnerships, joint ventures with corporations and organizations, to do the impossible. Google is an example of two students at Stanford University deciding to put together the fastest, most user-friendly search engine on the Internet. Google grew so fast and so widely that "to Google" has become a verb.

FINANCE. Sometimes the hundredfolding spark is about money.

Alexander Graham Bell borrowed money from his future father-in-law. That was the spark that allowed his idea to hundredfold.

How do we fund the start-up? Do we use sweat equity to self-finance and bootstrap the operation? Do we get investors—family, friends, angel investors, or venture capitalists? Do we finance the customer? Is there a back-end, profitable product that will allow us to lose money on the front end and still win and prosper?

There are myriad ways that financing can serve as the hundredfolding spark. Get sage consultation and coaching to make it smooth and ensure that you keep the lion's share of ownership like Bill Gates did when launching Microsoft.

Bill Gates is the world's richest man and also the world's best saver. Gates's vision is "a computer in every home." He wanted enough money saved to be able to keep every employee working if he got no new sales for one year. Gates has over $60 billion tucked away in the Microsoft Banks in Reno, Nevada. The Bill and Melinda Gates Foundation has given away over $25 billion to charity and plans to give it all away over time, which we feel guarantees Gates's ever-expanding future success.

MANAGEMENT. Sometimes a change in management or management philosophy can hundredfold a stagnant enterprise.

Look at what happened to IBM when Lou Gerstner took the reins in 1993. The stagnant enterprise we're talking about had revenues larger than many small countries like New Zealand or the Philippines. Yet, it lost $16 billion that year. Big Blue was dying. The new CEO had to turn around this ship and fast. It took the better part of a decade but when he retired in 2002, many believed that Gerstner and his amazing management team had pulled off the business turnaround of the century. Here's what he had to say about why it was so important to him:

> *Every now and then, a technology or an idea comes along that is so profound, and so powerful, and so universal, that its impact changes everything. The printing press, the incandescent light, the automobile, manned flight. It doesn't happen often, but when it does, the world is changed forever. . . . Now, I joined this industry and IBM because I believe that information technology has that potential. I'm more and more convinced that IT is the defining technology of the end of this century and will be well into the next century.*
>
> —DOUG GARR, *IBM REDUX: LOU GERSTNER AND THE BUSINESS TURNAROUND OF THE DECADE*

MARKETING. Sometimes the hundredfolding spark is a unique way of marketing.

Marketing is storytelling. Whoever tells the best story gets the sale. Classical marketing has four P's: product, promotion, price, and place. Obviously, you need a great name for your product and a great product. Promotion via an effective media campaign in television, print, radio, and on the Internet can make your launch successful. A perfect promotion can hundredfold your product, get it going, and keep it growing.

IERSEINZ LNEETSNI ETNIEVEP NETSAIR HERRNLRS GDPCIBEE

#84

TECHNOLOGY. Sometimes a new technology can spark a hundredfolding.

Do you remember how life used to be only 20 years ago—before faxes and cell phones and the Internet? Now take this dizzying transforming change and project yourself out 20 years from now.

We are entering a time when hundredfolding will seem commonplace. You will be the one to bring it to pass because Higher Power is waiting to transform the world. Time is running out. People are dying. Hundredfolding is a time whose time has come, none too soon.

If you'd like a trivial example of technology hundredfolding, take the recent trend of "café swarming." Hip Generation Xers spread instant messages on their cell phones to hives of networks—and in minutes a restaurant or café or dance scene or concert or other hot spot is swarmed with hundreds, sometimes thousands, of people.

You won't believe what's coming.

DISTRIBUTION. Sometimes a new method of distribution can spark hundredfolding.

Michael Dell of Dell Computers launched a totally new way of building computers. He adapted the Japanese concept of "just in time delivery" and built a company that could build computers overnight with no retail outlets. The financing is handled by using the component suppliers' money. He ships via UPS. Dell outsources all its service contracts to Unisys, where Dell computers get priority repair over all other manufacturers because Michael has the biggest vision and because he asked for it. By the way, this simple hundredfolding idea made him the world's youngest billionaire.

VELOCITY OF CONSUMPTION. Sometimes hundredfolding happens when consumers ignite word of mouth.

The twofold goal of every business is to find new customers and keep the old ones. Bringing new customers in the door is important, but treating them like stars is essential. Enlightened word of mouth is exponential.

REVISION/REINVENTION. Sometimes a product is hundredfolded by reinventing it.

Everything eventually needs to be reinvented. Every product has what is called a shelf life—its own sigmoid curve. Products like McDonald's hamburgers have been reinvented numerous times, the most famous reinvention being "Happy Meals" with a toy inside for children. How much was that reinvention worth? Billions. Hamburgers are now being reinvented as "no-carb burgers," meaning without a bun. Without constant, insistent, and persistent revision a product gets old and falls out of vogue.

PHILANTHROPY. Sometimes an enterprise can be hundredfolded by partnering with philanthropy.

The enlightened way calls for everyone to become a philanthropist, a giver, and a contributor. All of us have so much to give. Give without hesitation or reservation. Sharing means having more. When each of us gives a little, a lot gets done.

Enlightened philanthropists start by giving 10% of their earnings from every form of their incomes. At their best, they create or participate in great charities, churches, causes, or the equivalent. They involve their friends and everyone that they can reach out to through whatever media to help and contribute generously.

Americans are the gold standard of givers, in both gross amount of dollars contributed and percentagewise. We don't give it because we have it; we have it because we give it. We want *you* to become a great and inspired enlightened giver, who inspires others to do the same or more. You will be glad you did.

Your Inner Circle becomes the source of other hundredfolding ideas, and there are many. Ask yourselves the question, "Where is the next idea to hundredfold our enterprise?" Is it a new mentor or consultant? A new global market? A new feature? A new process? A new application? A new form of visibility? A new strategy?

Which sparks hundredfolded the following enterprises?

Working Assets

This socially responsible financing company went from 0 to 10,000 customers in one summer in 1997.

Enterprise Rent-A-Car

Andy Taylor took over his father's business in 1980 when the company was worth $76 million, and it is now valued at over $7 billion.

Sir John Templeton and Templeton Funds

If you had invested $100 in the Templeton growth fund in 1954 it would have been worth $55 million by 1999. Templeton was known for starting mutual funds' annual meetings with a prayer. He explained that the devotional words were not pleas for financial gain in the mundane world, but rather meditations to calm and clear the minds of managers and stockholders.

Schlotzsky's Deli

From 1989 to 1999 Schlotzsky's Deli grew earnings after tax a hundredfold from $60,000 to $6,200,000.

The Scooter Store

This company was founded in 1991 and had sales of $254 million in 2002.

The Outsource Group

Founded in 1997, this company's 2003 sales were $402 million.

#85

Usight

Founded in 1999, this company almost went bankrupt in 2000. It provides do-it-yourself website building. In 2003, it had sales of $27.6 million.

Zappos.com

Established in 1999, this company has experienced sharp growth, as annual sales reached $1.6 million in 2000, $8.6 million in 2001, $32 million in 2002, and over $70 million in 2003. Zappos expects to double its yearly revenue again in 2004, to over $175 million.

Liquidnet

Founded in 2001, Liquidnet had 2003 sales of $50 million.

Set up your Millionairium to be a catalyst for hundredfolding. On each wall of your office place four large, blank pieces of poster paper. On each page draw a large upside-down triangle. Each triangle represents one of the codes you've been cracking: Destiny, Angel, Prism, Star.

Inside each of these triangles is hidden the next idea that will hundred-fold your business. There's a breakthrough in there. Your goal is to figure out what it is.

WHAT STOPS A COMPANY FROM HUNDREDFOLDING?

Before we end this chapter, let's put on our dark glasses and ask ourselves a different question. What if something goes wrong? What's Plan B?

As entrepreneurs, we often get blindsided by our own optimism. What is the downside? Where could you lose? How could a competitor steal your idea or beat you to the punch? What if you're not protected? What if someone filed a patent infringement lawsuit? What if your profit projections were

#86

too high? What if your designs were impossible, impractical, or too expensive? How would you recoup?

In his excellent book *Getting It Right: The Second Time,* Michael Gershman describes how 49 marketing failures were transformed into some of the most successful products in history. He analyzed 12 factors that turned these "losers" into amazing "winners." You might be surprised to learn the names of some of these losing products. Did you know that Wheaties, Kleenex, Kotex, Jell-O, Marlboro, Life Savers, Tupperware, Pepsi-Cola, Cracker Jack, Aunt Jemima, Pampers, and Post-it Notes were all colossal failures until they were remarketed?

So don't be discouraged if your idea doesn't fly at first. Frankly, we'd be surprised if it did. Here are some of the main reasons, according to Michael Gershman, why products don't get it right until the second or third or fourth time around. Shield your hundredfolding sparks from these dousers.

Don't pitch it the wrong way.

Don't rule out a ride via a piggyback.

Don't underestimate public perception.

Don't incorrectly position your product.

Don't overlook the package.

Don't sell it in the wrong place.

Don't price it wrong.

Don't fail to consider using a premium.

Don't skimp on promotion.

Don't underestimate the power of publicity.

Don't launch a product without a promise.

Don't quit. Have perseverance.

IS THIS THE FINAL WORD ON HUNDREDFOLDING?

———

No, we believe this is the beginning of a new and exciting level of awareness. We believe that you, our faithful readers, will share your stories and insights with us about your favorite hundredfolding idea. Our website will be an open database of hundredfolding ideas from around the world. Come and make your contribution.

Dr. R. Buckminster Fuller, the comprehensive anticipatory design scientist, said: "Real Wealth = Ideas × Energy." Energy can neither be created nor destroyed; therefore, your real wealth is forever increasing so long as you keep generating ideas. We want to have you help us accelerate the process until everyone is fed, clothed, sheltered, educated, and taken care of sufficiently, until they can take the initiative themselves to serve others in an enlightened way.

#87 _____

Now that you have read ten chapters, go back to page xvii of the Introduction and crack code #4.

Chapter Eleven

RESIDUAL PHILANTHROPY—
GIVING YOUR WAY
TO WEALTH

R esidual is a term that comes from show business. It refers to "additional pay given to a performer for reruns, repeated use of a film, radio or TV commercial, or the like, in which the performer appears." For example, actors receive a salary for performing in a commercial, plus every time that commercial runs some actors receive additional fees—called residuals—even though they've long since left the set where they did the filming. Weeks, years, or decades later, as long as the commercial keeps playing they can be earning money in their sleep.

The same is true for writers of advertising jingles—the music that plays on commercials. One of our friends has earned over a million dollars from one single jingle—"Have you driven a Ford lately?" He did the work once and keeps getting paid over and over. In fact, if set up properly, residuals flow in even after a performer is dead. *Forbes* magazine publishes a list of top-earning dead celebrities. Here are the top 20 "deceased" income earners. The numbers represent millions of dollars per year.

Del Smith

As an infant Del Smith was placed at Sacred Heart Orphanage. At the age of two he was adopted. Shortly thereafter, Del's adoptive father died in an accident, and his adoptive mother, "Grandma Smith," whom he calls a "saint on earth," raised him in Centralia, Washington. She taught him by setting the example. He was taught early on about God's importance in finding life's purpose. Poverty only enhanced his appreciation for rewards from hard work and for grasping any opportunities present—she did it, and he modeled it. She taught him the basics: a solid work ethic, honesty, integrity, and the importance of education. She encouraged him to be a student of the Bible and to study and master Benjamin Franklin's "Plan for Attaining Moral Perfection" (of which there are thirteen rules). But the most valuable lesson she taught him was that regardless of money, life was rich if it was filled with love.

As his mother was not in good health, he went to work at an early age to help her and provide for their well-being. Their home in Centralia was near the railroad tracks, where he collected coal that fell from the trains and sold for a nickel a bucket—bartering a product for cash. At the age of seven, he took out a loan of $2.50 from the local bank to buy a lawn mower. He mowed lawns, had three paper routes, set pins in a bowling alley, delivered ice, caddied on golf courses, and worked on farms during the summer. By the time he was 11, he had earned enough to make a down payment on a home for himself and his mother. His vigorous and untiring self-initiative convinced the bank to give him a thirty-year home loan at 2% interest. Little did he know that he was becoming an inspiring, lifelong, award-winning entrepreneur who would make history.

Del's interest in aviation started when he was a boy. He was an airport enthusiast as a youngster. He would hang around airports the way some guys would hang around street corners. At the age of 16, he earned his pilot's license by trading work for lessons, bartering his labor for services.

→

1	Elvis Presley	40
2	Charles M. Schulz	35
3	J.R.R. Tolkien	23
4	John Lennon	21
5	Theodor "Dr. Seuss" Geisel	18
6	Marilyn Monroe	8
7	George Harrison	7
8	Irving Berlin	7
9	Bob Marley	7
10	Richard Rodgers	6.5
11	George and Ira Gershwin	6
12	Jimi Hendrix	6
13	Alan Lerner and Frederick Loewe	6
14	Cole Porter	6
15	James Dean	5
16	Dale Earnhardt Sr.	5
17	Jerry Garcia	5
18	Freddie Mercury	5
19	Tupac Shakur	5
20	Frank Sinatra	5

Mzndypvg Kcdgviocmjkt dn ocz mzndypz amjh tjpm gjqz

#88

There are lots of ways to create residual income other than being the "King of Rock and Roll." Residual income is actually commonplace. Interest earned on money in your checking or savings account is residual. It flows into your life 24/7—small trickles of income, perhaps, but residual income nonetheless. Dividends from stock investments; real estate that's

Del enrolled in the University of Washington, where he joined the United States Air Force Reserve Officers Training Corps. While still in college, Del was flying fixed-wing aircraft to dust crops and even started piloting helicopters. Upon graduation in 1953, he was commissioned as an officer and went overseas as a pathfinder with a combat control team, the forerunner of today's Air Force Special Operations Command. While in the USAF, Del became a believer in vertical lift and the extensive capabilities of helicopters. Del had a vision that helicopters could be used as industrial workhorses and as angels of mercy. That vision has guided Del Smith throughout his aviation career.

In 1956, Del began flying helicopters for Dean Johnson, who was based in McMinnville, Oregon. Flying Hiller two-seat machines, the two men became innovators by putting helicopters to use in the timber industry in planting seeds, applying herbicides, and fighting fires. After Johnson's death in a crop-dusting accident in 1957, Del carried on, combining the Dean Johnson company and Evergreen Helicopters of Sweet Home, Oregon, into one new enterprise based in McMinnville. Incorporated on July 1, 1960, Evergreen Helicopters, Inc., quickly grew. The Evergreen Aviation corporate family now includes the helicopter company, an all-cargo airline, a transport-category aircraft maintenance company, an airport ground handling services company, an aircraft sales and leasing operation, and a group of agricultural enterprises. Thanks to his strengths—visionary imagination, leadership abilities, people skills, negotiation talents, understanding of business, and a fervent desire to make a difference—Del Smith has built Evergreen Aviation into the world's most diversified aviation services company.

Del has bartered to billions. Del says: "Of the nearly 200 countries recognized by the United Nations, 76% have no liquidity, and in some cases poor credit. But they all have resource capital, people capital, intellectual capital, physical capital, and product and service capital. They just don't have cash. Barter can help everyone meet their needs. Barter deals have to be profitable for everyone involved when conceived, contracted, and exe-

$\rightarrow$

appreciating in value; ownerships in businesses; network marketing down-lines; websites that generate sales 365 days a year; franchising opportunities. All these are forms of residual income.

rusttay niay igherhay owerpay akesmay ouyay aay rusteetay foay ouryay nterpriseeay.

#89 _____

_____

One of the primary goals of an Enlightened Enterprise is to set up processes, systems, and strategies to perpetuate the longevity of that business. You want your enterprise to first survive and, then, to thrive for 100 years or more. Will there be income flowing into your estate long after you're here? What should that income be earmarked for? Are you going to leave it to your heirs? Will they continue to operate the business? Will the business survive after your heirs have divvied it all up? Will they be as philanthropic as you were?

The concept of earning residual income strikes a chord with almost everyone—who wouldn't want streams of income flowing into your life "while you sleep"? It's when we start talking about residual philanthropy that we often get "glazed" stares from audiences of entrepreneurs. Frankly, ordinary entrepreneurs are extraordinarily driven, independent, focused, committed to what they want, and—how can we say this gently?—self-centered. So all of this mushy "give the money away" conversation can be very off-putting to someone who just wants to get a Bentley, a beach house, and a million bucks in the bank.

We hear you. We've been there. Yes, you can have all of that. If you want it. We have and do. But if you want to get it fast and, more important, if you want to *keep* it, you've got to be a Higher Power giver. Simply got to. If you don't believe us, then go after your dreams your own way and check back with us in 10 years. If you set out to hoard as much as you can, without letting it flow through you in the cycle of wealth, we'll be surprised if you've got any left by the time we touch base in 10 years.

cuted. The transaction has to be fair for everybody. It just needs to be traded and bartered in the absence of cash. Learning to barter fairly allows you to deal with all the countries on this planet. If you know how to barter you just have a lot more markets."

The only requirement is to develop your bartering skills. Del's talent for bartering with companies and countries is in high demand and low supply. Recently, Del teamed with a Chinese principal to build a power line from Hong Kong to Guangzhou. The Chinese did not have available cash so Del accepted coal as payment, which he sold to Exxon for cash.

Del says: "No one thinks of barter. Barter is trading something of value for something else of value; it's the original form of commerce that precedes money and currency. Barter can be done between individuals, companies, countries, governments, nonprofits, and institutions. A good barterer could easily do a hundred million in business a day and take a percentage of it. There is no school that teaches it. While the rewards are extraordinary, the learning curve is immensely expensive and fraught with danger. The first commandment of barter/trade is to have the product or service presold before you commit to the deal."

Del is the recipient of the Horatio Alger Award, the Wright Brothers Memorial Trophy, the Napoleon Hill Gold Medal Award for Entrepreneurial Achievement, the Helicopter Association International Lawrence D. Bell Memorial Award, the Museum of Flight Pathfinder Award, the Kaman Heroism Award, the World Vision Contributor Award, the Free Enterprise Award, the Boy Scouts of America Silver Beaver Award, the B.P.O.E. Leadership Award, the Optimist Club Leadership Award, the Chamber of Commerce First Citizen of the Year Award, and the National Transportation Award.

Del has two American headquarters that are well worth a visit. In McMinnville, you can visit not only Evergreen Aviation Inc.'s headquarters but also the Evergreen Aviation Museum—The Captain Michael King Smith Educational Institute. The museum is home to Howard Hughes's Flying Boat, the *Spruce Goose*. The world's largest aircraft also creates a

→

It's a paradox. The more you give, the more you get. Really! And the more you hang onto it, the slipperier it becomes. Really! We wouldn't wish any of this on you, but maybe after a few divorces or disagreeable lawsuits or backstabbing incidents you'll figure out that you might have been better off to give more of it away right from the get-go. At least, there might have been an orphanage with your name on it. You'd have something to show for all the sacrifice.

RP = Hacer Bien Haciendo Bueno.

#90

But it's your life. Play it like you see it. If you're one of the few lucky enough to pass unscathed through the gauntlet of greed, we wish you well. More than likely after you've bought a bunch of nice cars and jewels and houses (as we have—and still do, by the way), you'll discover your innate urge to give to something that fulfills you. Just look at the wealthy and see how much giving they do. It's amazing. Why should you wait until you're 65 to be bitten by the philanthropy bug? Ask anyone with money and they'll tell you that they wished they'd started giving earlier. So start earlier. Start when you have nothing. Plan to give away the hundred million when you haven't got a hundred thousand.

And plan to make it residual. The enterprise you launch is going to have to run without you someday. So make a 101-year plan. Go out 101 years from now and envision it.

For some, it's like this. You see your corporate headquarters there with your name on it. Your portrait is in the front lobby. The street in front of the building is named after you. The employees talk about you in reverent hushed tones. "What a guy/gal he/she was! If it wasn't for him/her we wouldn't have been able to send our Johnny/Janet to Harvard/Stanford." You float into the boardroom and eavesdrop as they discuss the hospitals that are open today because of the profits that flow from the enterprise you founded. You feel so proud (in a humble way) that because of you so much

dynamic backdrop to a fabulous collection of 60 vintage aircraft. The second site is the headquarters of the Evergreen Air Center, a maintenance, repair, and overhaul facility located in Marana, Arizona. Here you will find one of the largest aviation dry docks in the world.

While Del Smith is little known to the public, he is a legend in the aviation industry. Among his colleagues he is revered, applauded, and respected.

good is being done. Not to mention the secret good works that nobody knows about. Nobody knows but you and, well, Higher Power. Truth is, none of this would have happened without Higher Power anyway. And by now you're absolutely certain of that.

How does this vision become reality? The business needs to be established with residuality in mind. You're not just trying to sell a bunch of stuff. You're setting processes in place to give permanency to your enterprise. That's the theory, and here are three practical ways to residualize your profits—to make money flow to you now (even when you don't want to be there) and to flow to your chosen philanthropic causes (when you can't be there).

1. *Don't launch any new product or initiative that doesn't have a residual plan.* A single sale is how most businesses operate. Smart businesses go for a stream of sales. In short, if it's not residual, don't do it.

2. *Send a search party out for the hidden streams of income in your existing business.* In other words, empower your employees to search for hidden opportunities for residual streams of income. If you're an employee, then you are the search party. Maybe there are licensing opportunities for some of your successful operational processes (like employee training, or your fast-track order system) for a residual stream of hassle-free, employee-less income. Maybe you could franchise your ideas, or create territories of distributors, or affiliate programs on the Internet, where other entrepreneurs are rewarded for marketing your best ideas and sending you back a steady and increasing revenue stream.

Ôòä óçä 4 Ó'ò îå Æèõèíæ.

#91 _____

Always have these questions in the back of your mind: "What percentage of my day did I spend creating residual income?"

"If I walked away today, could this business survive without me and still send streams of income to the causes I love?"

3. *Make your charity a partner in your business marketing.* Involve your charity in helping you succeed, because the more you succeed, the more they succeed. Let them endorse your business by informing their patrons that their success is directly tied to your success. They'll help you get the word out.

But, remember, philanthropy isn't just a smart business-building strategy—an investment you're making as a part of your marketing budget. You're absolutely committed to this charity. You're passionate about it. If your business doesn't make it—God forbid—you'll still be writing checks out of your personal funds to make sure that the homeless are fed or the battered women are sheltered or that the word about diabetes is getting out.

Giving often falls under the heading of a charitable tax deduction, as in, "I decide where my money goes, not the government!" But eventually your thinking matures. Giving begins to feel so "right" that you would do it without a deduction. It's *that* important to you. It defines why you breathe. If breathing were tax-deductible and they passed a new law removing that deduction, would you stop breathing because the government disallowed it? You do it because that is your "calling." If you haven't found a charity like that, ask Higher Power and be patient. One will be sent your way. You'll know it when you see it.

Won't it feel wonderful to realize that people's lives will be transformed by the generosity of your wisdom? Unborn generations can benefit from your largesse, just like you have been the recipient of the generosity of untold forebears.

Residual philanthropy—doing well by doing good—is smart business. If you invested $100,000 in January 1990 in Domini Social Index Fund (businesses with a social mission), it would be worth $540,000 today compared with $470,000 for the S&P 500.

Oh, please place openly right there unhidden, not in the invisible embryonic self

#92 ⸺ ⸺ ⸺ ⸺ ⸺ ⸺ ⸺ ⸺ ⸺ ⸺ ⸺ ⸺ ⸺

YOUR LEGACY

—

Somebody else paved the roads we are riding on now and dug the wells that we are drinking from; we need to do the same for others behind us.

The only lack we have in the world is consciousness. The only shortage is awareness. That's why we're here—we're working on ourselves and inspiring others to do the same or better. One of your goals, should you choose to embrace it, is to sculpt yourselves into a masterpiece. Self-work multiplied by six and a half billion people can make the world a great place for 100% of humanity. Yes! It's an idealistic goal, and that is fantastic.

Our vision is to help inspire a million Enlightened Entrepreneurs to earn an extra million dollars in this decade. Imagine if each Enlightened Millionaire gave away a million to his or her favorite church, cause, charity, or philanthropy. That would generate a million times a million dollars, or a trillion dollars! With a trillion, could we alleviate many of the social ailments on the planet? We want to create an army of social artists who want to save and improve the world.

Tun ty hap por pro go op to er i fit pi like and and ness health geth

#93 _____

You were DNA-coded at birth to do something great. The Teacher said: "The greatest amongst you is servant of all." You've got some issue you're supposed to solve and then help everybody else solve it, too.

RESIDUAL PHILANTHROPY!

Residual philanthropy is the natural extension of residual income. A residual philanthropist creates an ongoing income source that will serve philanthropy, as a gift that keeps on giving and giving.

In Chapter 1 we shared the story of Paul Newman, our poster boy for what we call residual philanthropy. Starting in 1982 with the famous Newman's Dressing, Newman's Own has contributed hundreds of millions of dollars to charities like the Make-A-Wish Foundation, the Hole in the Wall Gang, Make a Difference Day, and many more. Their motto is "Out of dressing all blessings flow."

Paul created what we call a virtual business. He created the model once and has proceeded to duplicate it repetitively, which is what we are recommending to every reader. Paul "outsources" the manufacturing and distribution and "in-sources" the money/profits. One hundred percent of the profits are contributed to charities. They now have over 70 products, with more on the drawing board. This Enlightened Enterprise will be spinning off enlightened profits for centuries!

A friend of Paul Newman's started Stonyfield Farm in 1983 with seven cows and a mission to create an organic product and give away the first 10% of its profits. Today it's the number three yogurt brand in the United States, with $150 million in sales.

What's the point? Can anyone do this? Touch yourself at heart level and say to yourself, "I can do this." You just have to discover what your "salad dressing" or "yogurt" is.

Will your residual "salad dressing" idea be some form of intellectual property? In our book *The One Minute Millionaire,* we look at over a dozen forms of intellectual property, such as books, tapes, videos, CDs, consultancies, franchises, audios, inventions, copyrights, patents, licenses, songs, registration marks, trademarks, seminars, and so on. We believe each of you has one or more of these in you. Once you create your self-perpetuating wealth, we then encourage you to create a residual philanthropy to solve one or more

Planning is everything
plans are nothing.

#94

_____

problems that have been gifted to you by Higher Power to solve. Entrepreneurs were born to discover how to solve problems profitably and cost-effectively. As you create vast wealth using the principles of this book, you can take on the projects and challenges that no one else can afford to.

THE FOUR T'S OF GIVING

——

Giving has four basic aspects, called the four "T's." You can give or donate your thinking, your time, your talent, and/or your treasures (i.e., your money). The greatest of all of these is your thinking, which almost no charity or church asks for, yet is the greatest source of gifting on earth. (These concepts are more fully explained in *The Miracle of Tithing* by Mark Victor Hansen. Go to our website to download your free copy.)

For example, when the American Red Cross needed blood, they asked Mark to help out. He was told that they need 38,000 pints of blood a day. Mark appealed to his friend, Dr. Fabrizio Mancini, who is universally loved and respected in the chiropractic profession as president of Parker Chiropractic Seminars and president of Parker Chiropractic College in Dallas. Dr. Mancini has MIH power. He was in possession of an e-mail contact list with all 62,000 practicing American chiropractors. Together with Alex Mandossian, inventor of the Audio Generator, Dr. Mancini and Mark created an e-audio postcard campaign to reach every chiropractor to inform them of a way to help solve the Red Cross problem. The solution the trio came up with could be a way to reactivate old patients and generate new patients while giving great publicity for the chiropractic profession.

The chiropractors were encouraged to call 1-800-Give-Life and request that Red Cross bring a bloodmobile to their practice. They were also encouraged to register willing patients to give blood at the local Red Cross blood-receiving center. This inspired hundreds of doctors to schedule blood drives. Realizing that each pint donated saves three or more lives, the doctors, their employees, and their patients rolled up their respective and collective sleeves and gave blood to save the day.

Выберите четырех человек são da mesma opinião em isso Sie wollen machen Zij willen maken

#95

One flight attendant who also worked as a nurse decided she could do something with her skills and her ability to fly free anywhere in the world. She went to Haiti to help sick people there and recruited help from her talented nurse/flight attendant colleagues at the airline. Her efforts gave birth to a new organization that is catching fire called Airline Ambassadors (**www.airlineamb.com**), a nonprofit organization that now is affiliated with the United Nations. Volunteers are ambassadors of goodwill at home and abroad. Their compassion in action helps to hand-deliver humanitarian aid to children, orphans, clinics, and people in remote communities to make a difference.

We launched *The One Minute Millionaire* in Orlando, Florida, where a husband and wife, both in wheelchairs, were in attendance and were inspired by what we had to say. We met them six months later when they rolled up to Mark at an event where he was signing books. They said: "You guys really got to us." The gentleman shared how his life had been transformed:

"I wasn't always in a wheelchair. But at the time I heard you both, I had a cloud over my head. I felt like a victim. You see, I was a PA, a physi-

cian's assistant, in Kansas City. On the day my life changed forever, I was working with a patient on the eighth floor. Across the street was a ball and crane just ready to wreck and tear down the building next door. A tornado passed through our city and the 160-mile-an-hour wind whipped the ball straight through our building, killing the patient in front of me, and dropping me eight stories. My spine was badly crushed by the fall. There was no insurance on the ball and crane company, no insurance on the hospital, and I had no disability income insurance. I felt like my life was over. Then we heard you say at your seminar that each person has been given an issue to solve for themselves, and then to solve for others. For the last six months, because of your teaching, we've been earning $15,000 a month. As of yesterday, we gave away 26 wheelchairs to people who couldn't afford them and had no way of getting them, all because you both gave us a new perspective, a new reason for living, and a new lease on life."

Each person is DNA-coded to solve something for themselves and others.

Odnrpolcetetariayelhyvroigxrodnrcalneriayeperaexrodnrwatboecmnetariayhlegs

#96 _____

The next section describes seven basic models of enlightened residual philanthropy. Please write us and tell us of other models you discover that you think would work. (Our address is: P.O. Box 7665, Newport Beach, CA 92627.) In future editions of this book we will attempt to include them and make them available on our website. We know that this will vastly improve lives, earnings, and futures for everyone.

THE RESIDUAL PHILANTHROPY MODELS

—

Enlightened residual philanthropy comes from enlightened wealth builders. Why give once, when you can give continuously? We're here to help give you a new, bigger, more generous perspective and possibility. The flow of abundance is infinite, but you must turn it on with giving. You can't take a breath until you give one. Here are a few philanthropic models you can use to enlighten your enterprise.

Model One: Just Ask.

EVERY MONTH, WE AUTHORS DO DOZENS OF RADIO "PHONERS"— radio shows on stations all over the country that we can conduct right from our home offices. Our publicist sets up all these radio interviews, usually one day a month. One day Mark was doing his first interview with a station in Kansas City. The night before, he had watched the TV news footage of a tornado that vacuumed up 367 Kansas City homes.

#97 _____

The radio station owner began the call by saying: "It's bad. My tower was down and 58 farmers came out with their chains, ropes, tow trucks, and tractors to straighten it up. Mark, you're the first one to go on air and you'd better have some good *Chicken Soup* stories, because my listeners are hurting real bad." Mark said, "We've got 7,700 stories and I know six great tornado stories that will inspire, uplift, and give renewed hope to your listeners."

The station owner said: "I've got to tell you what's happening here locally. I've got six people sleeping on the floor at the radio station. No one has died, but their homes are gone, their cars are gone, and their trucks are gone. We've got 2,000 folks sleeping on the floor in a mall next door. We've got nowhere to put them. The tornado knocked out both the Red Cross and Goodwill. Our people need clothes, bedding, and blood." Mark spent the rest of the interview giving hope and encouragement to the listeners.

arepoyttnurioppoypseyednanielihw plehuoyeesehtelbisivretteb[2] sessalg[4]

#98

_____

The next scheduled radio talk show of the day was scheduled with a station in Seattle. It was a call-in show. When the host asked, "Do you have any new *Chicken Soup* stories?" Mark told him about what had just happened in Kansas City. Mark asked people to call and give blood, clothes, prayers, and whatever help they could to Kansas City. What happened next amazed him: The station's 12 phone lines lit up like a Christmas tree.

The first caller said: "I have a Fleetwood RV and I'm going to drive right now to Kansas. Just give me the station owner's phone number. Those six people sleeping on his floor will have a place to sleep in my vehicle until they sort things out." The next 12 callers all donated the use of their RVs and they were on their way to Kansas, too.

Americans love to give. All you have to do is ask.

Model Two: Sell Yourself.

NORMAN LEAR CHARGED ALL OF HIS FRIENDS AND COLLEAGUES $2,000 each for the privilege of coming to his 80th birthday party. His friends could easily afford the extravagant fee and raised $2 million for charity. Fundraisers like this happen in hundreds of cities every single day of the year. When's your next birthday party?

Model Three: Partner with a Charity.

WHEN MARK WAS SIXTEEN, THE BEATLES CAME TO AMERICA AND appeared on *The Ed Sullivan Show*. They wowed his soul. Mark called his best friend, Gary Youngberg, and announced that they were starting a rock group called The Messengers. In two weeks, they were earning $17 an hour as enthusiastic musicians. The YMCA had space on weekend nights and needed funds. Mark worked out an agreement with the YMCA to use their space for "sock hops" and split the proceeds. Mark took out an advertisement in the Waukegan, Illinois, Township high school paper and said that The Messengers were performing a charity event on Saturday night for five dollars a person. They had a thousand attendees and raised over $2,500 for the YMCA that night. They duplicated this phenomenon successfully at other Ys. They were happy, and the Y was happy.

yoneyatrixIaginizeandillionizeinyonuentalillionairiuicrocosbyir
roringanyarvelousen(woen)withacrooralsagnificentannersighty
ethodsanduchoneytoiraculouslyanifestyassivelyagnifiedegaillio
nsIediately

#99

_____

_____

_____

_____

We believe there are thousands of potential niches like these that desperately need your ability to create new opportunities. Every time you see a PBS fund-raiser with Suze Orman or Wayne Dyer, realize that these events are carefully orchestrated to raise millions of dollars for Public Broadcasting. It's a model that could work for hundreds of other worthy causes.

Model Four: Sell Your Other Talents.

STEPHEN KING IS THE KING OF HORROR. DAVE BARRY IS THE BEST-selling humor author alive. Amy Tan writes elegant fiction bestsellers. These great writers, and many others, put together a band called Rock Bottom Remainders. They raise a million dollars every year for literacy, and they switch some of the band members in and out so they can keep playing. Wouldn't it be fun to go see the world's bestselling authors playing music, having fun together, and wowing audiences—all for charity? Talented people often have more than one talent and are willing to share it generously for charitable purposes.

Model Five: Pick a Different Charity for Every One of Your Products.

CHICKEN SOUP BOOKS PICK A DIFFERENT CHARITY FOR EACH OF OUR books. The Campbell Soup Company consented to have three *Chicken Soup* stories put on the inside label of 400 million cans of soup, along with request that people bring in one can of nonperishable food to their local bookstore on May 17. If they did, the post office would pick it up free and take it to a local distribution center, where Campbell's generously doubled the gifts. The cans then went to people in need through the good work of the Union Rescue Missions, Abuse Centers, and Second Harvest so that 15 million people got fed.

Model Six: Turn One of Your Hobbies into a Philanthropic Cash Cow.

DICK MARCONI, WHOSE STORY IS ON PAGE 226, HAS HAD A LIFE-long interest in car racing. He built the Marconi Auto Museum in Tustin,

California, and filled it with magnificent antique cars and amazing automobiles. He and his wife, Bo, have fund-raising events there; because the museum is debt-free, all ticket sales go directly to charity. His museum will continue to do this after he's gone, because it has been established in perpetuity.

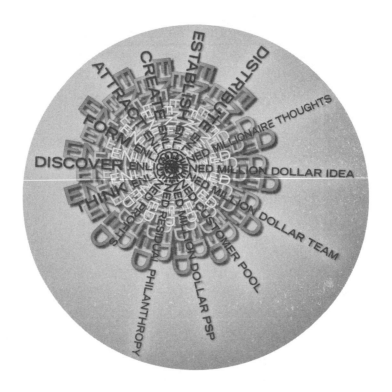

#100 _____

_____

_____

_____

_____

_____

Model Seven: If He Can Do It,
Anyone Can Do It.

DEL SMITH, OWNER AND FOUNDER OF EVERGREEN AVIATION International in McMinnville, Oregon, runs the Children's Free Enterprise Fund, which lends money to any American kid under 19 years old, not for college, but to help them launch their own enterprises. When Del was an infant he was orphaned; his grandma took him in and inspired Del to become an entrepreneur. When he was 11 he went to the bank to borrow $2.50 to buy a lawnmower and then went across the street to another bank and borrowed $2.50 more. When he first told Mark this story, Del said, "You know, that couldn't happen today. Children can't borrow money from banks anymore." Mark said to Del, "Why don't we start a bank for kids?" What happened then was truly inspiring. Mark describes it this way:

I was talking in Orange County when a child came up to me. He said, "Mark, I want to borrow money from your kids' bank. I'm six years old. My name is Tommy Tighe."

I said, "Great, Tommy. I want to lend it to you. What do you want to do with it?"

He said, "I want to create a bumper sticker that says:
Peace Please. Do It for Us Kids, Signed Tommy."
I asked him for his 10-point business plan and he said,

"1. Meet Mark Victor Hansen.
2. Hit him up for a loan.
3. Offer baseball cards as collateral.
4. Sell one million bumper stickers."

Tommy's dad drove over to my office and whispered in my ear, "If my son doesn't pay you back, are you going to foreclose on his bicycle?" I said,

"Mr. Tighe, every kid's born honest, ethical, and moral. They have got to be taught to be crooked and go sideways. I don't think we have to worry about Tommy. Kids all pay back with interest."

Tommy got inspired listening to my tapes and had his dad drive him up to former President Ronald Reagan's home, just after the president had left the White House. Tommy rang the doorbell and sold a bumper sticker to the gatekeeper for a dollar fifty. The gatekeeper said, "Hold on, kid, let me get the president." Ronnie came out, shook his hand, and said, "I understand you're causing peace in the world." Tommy said, "That'll be a buck fifty, Mr. President."

I asked Tommy, "Why did you ask him to buy?"

Tommy said, "You said to ask everybody to buy."

Tommy also sent one unsolicited to President Mikhail Gorbachev with a bill for a dollar fifty. Gorbachev sent him back a dollar fifty and a signed autographed picture that said, "Go for peace, Tommy."

I said, "Tommy, I collect autographs. I will give you $500 cash for that."

Tommy said, "No thanks, Mark."

I said, "You're the best little salesman I've ever met. When you're older I want to hire you."

Tommy said, "When I'm older, I'm hiring you."

We believe that every reader can become rich and also create residual philanthropies. There's a flood of opportunity from which philanthropy can emerge at levels that no one has ever considered before. The rest of the world can play their favorite game—"take and take" or "give and take." For us, "give and give" is the fastest formula to enrichment.

Give, said the little stream
Give, oh! Give
Give, oh! Give
Give, said the little stream

As it hurried down the hill.
I'm small but I know that wherever I go
The grass grows greener still

Singing, singing all the day,
Give away, oh! Give away
Singing, singing all the day.
Give, oh give, away.

—"'GIVE,' SAID THE LITTLE STREAM,"
FANNY J. CROSBY AND WILLIAM B. BRADBURY

Chapter Twelve

MONEY!

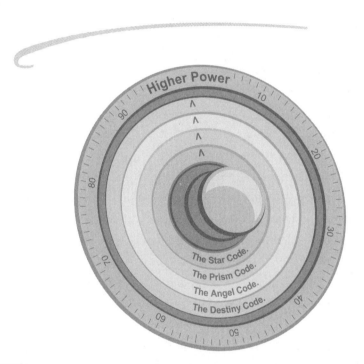

Eckhart Tolle begins his wonderful book *The Power of Now* with a story. We feel this story is an excellent way to end our conversation together.

A beggar had been sitting by the side of the road for over 30 years. One day a stranger walked by. "Spare some change?" mumbled the beggar, mechanically holding out his old baseball cap. "I have nothing to give you," said the stranger. Then he asked: "What's that you are sitting on?" "Nothing," replied the beggar. "Just an old box. I have been sitting on it for as long as I can remember." "Ever looked inside?" asked the stranger.

"No," said the beggar. "What's the point? There's nothing in there." "Have a look inside," insisted the stranger. The beggar managed to pry open the lid. With astonishment, disbelief, and elation, he saw that the box was filled with gold.

—ECKHART TOLLE, *THE POWER OF NOW*

The "box of gold" that each of us is "sitting on" is part of the message of this book. But there is much, much more. We've shown you a system for tapping into your own vast personal wealth vault filled with prosperity, happiness, joy, and fulfillment. We've shared with you how to launch Enlightened Enterprises with enlightened products destined to improve the lives of enlightened customers, and thereby your own.

We began our journey together, at the beginning of this book, with the image of two "prosperous-looking gentlemen" (that's us) standing at your front door announcing your selection to participate in the ultimate reality TV show—the one called Life. The prize, as always, is unlimited access to all this world has to offer. The annals of history prove beyond question that millions of people have cracked the code and opened their personal wealth vaults. If they can do it, why not you?

The fact that you have read this far—that you have completed this book—is the first proof that you have what it takes to succeed. So few people have the discipline to read a book from cover to cover. Kudos to you. Now comes the next phase of your journey—to apply the lessons you've learned despite the challenges life throws you. Do you have what it takes to apply these lessons? Will you set this book on a shelf and say, "Someday maybe I'll do something about this"? Or will you say to yourself, "My 'someday' is NOW!"?

Which voice will you listen to? Will you listen to your "Inner Critic" as it tries to talk you out of your dreams ("You don't have enough money, or brains, or connections. You can't do it!")? Or will you listen to your "Inner Knower" as it whispers to you: "Your destiny awaits. You can do it. Do it. Do it. Do it"?

The voice you heed today will determine what you'll be saying to yourself in five years from now—"I'm sorry I didn't take action sooner" or "Thank heaven, I did it!"

WHICH WILL IT BE?
LET'S LOOK INTO YOUR CRYSTAL BALL

If five years from today you're saying to yourself, "Thank heaven, I did it!" it will be because you succeeded in cracking the four codes of personal wealth. Let's go out five years from now and see what you were able to accomplish.

You cracked your Destiny Code. You pondered and prayed about your own place in the universe. You searched your soul to find the talents, passions, and values that set you apart. You learned to follow your intuition by doing your 3B (Body/Brain/Being) process every day. You began to see the power of putting in the Big Rocks first. You began to live the principles of Enlightened Wealth: Loverage, Inner Wealth, Giving, Higher Power, and Trusteeship. You may not have fully realized your destiny but you sense you're heading in the right direction.

You cracked the Angel Code. You found a group of like-minded people who decided there is a better way to wealth. You've each prepared your Enlightened Wealth Statements to reveal the hidden value of each member of your team. You each took the HOTS Survey online to discover your innate talents. You listed your angels' capital resources—attitude capital, network capital, genius capital, experience/education capital, light capital, and Serendestiny capital. You came to the realization that all the answers you sought were found in the Seven Circles of Empowerment around you.

You cracked the Prism Code. You discovered an idea that interested you. With your angel team you processed your Great Idea through the Millionairium. You saw your Great Idea through multiple eyes—futurize, billionize, childize, and so on. Then you differentiated your Great Idea with the WOW—the Wheel of Wealth—by asking 21 questions to add, subtract, multiply, and divide your Great Idea into a unique and enlightened million-dollar idea. You divided your million-dollar idea into the PRISM of Products, Related products, Information, Services, and Media.

Yes, it took time to assimilate this new vocabulary and this new way of thinking, but a hidden world of opportunity began to reveal itself. You began to realize that with your newfound tools and your newfound team, you could millionize almost anything.

Finally, you cracked the Star Code. You learned how to attract a growing number of customers through enlightened word of mouth. People started to flood into your Enlightened Enterprise because of the way you treated each new customer as a star. They came again and again and brought their friends with them. Serendestiny of increasing proportions began to magically occur as Higher Power began to open up new doors for your Enlightened Enterprise in sudden and magical ways.

In short, the vault of ever-expanding prosperity and wealth was finally opened to you, and you realized that the enormous effort and concentration and dedication was worth far more than you had invested. You did it!

Having cracked open your vault, you felt compelled to find others who were still struggling and show them how they could model what you had done.

And how did you achieve all this?

It all started with reading *Cracking the Millionaire Code* five years earlier. You remember reading the final chapter and a strange assignment that the authors gave you in the final four pages. You remember how energized you were by those final words—how they inspired you to action.

Here is what you read.

FINAL THOUGHTS AND ASSIGNMENTS

—

Think back over the series of Serendestiny dots that brought you to this place in time, when you are ready to read these words at this very moment. How did this book "fall" into your hands? Do you feel that it was an accident that you "stumbled" across these pages? Did someone "give" it to you? Did you "bump" into it at a bookstore? Did you "catch" one or both of us doing a media interview? Did one of our ads or infomercials "grab" you?

It was pure Serendestiny!

There is an enlightened window of opportunity open for you. Your future five years from today depends on what you do in the next 24 hours.

Assignment 1. Give Away Some Money ASAP.

DO YOU BELIEVE IN ENLIGHTENED WEALTH? YES? THEN PROVE IT!
Find someone who needs some financial help—even a small amount: $5 or $10 or more. Maybe it's a family member or a friend or a church or a cause or someone on the TV asking for a pledge or a beggar on the street asking for a handout. No matter. Check with Higher Power and ask to whom your windows of heaven should be opened today. Feel it. Follow it. Give it. With no expectation of reward, or even a thank you. Then notice how it feels.

Do it by this time tomorrow. Just do it.

Assignment 2. Crack the First Wealth Code.

DID YOU CRACK THE FIRST SIMPLE CODE HIDDEN IN THE INTRO-
duction (pp. xi–xvii)? It's not too late! Go online and download the Code Checklist. It contains clues that you might have overlooked. Do it before the clock strikes midnight. Just get it done.

Assignment 3. Talk with Your Angel Team.

REMEMBER THE LIST OF 10 PEOPLE WE ENCOURAGED YOU TO CONTACT
at the beginning of this book? Talk to three of them before your head hits the pillow tomorrow night. Invite them to be part of your team. Maybe none of them will be interested. You may need to talk to all 101 people on your Diamond List to find a handful of excited participants, but they're the ones you want!

If you have much, give of your wealth, if you have little, give of your heart.

MCMURTRY • If you have

The sooner you form your team, the richer you all become. Check in at our website, where the complete 101-Day Plan to cracking your wealth code is found. Follow it day by day and watch the miracles happen.

Contact three people in the next 23 hours and 55 minutes. Do you dare?

Bonus Assignment

GO TO WWW.CRACKINGTHEMILLIONAIRECODE.COM AND DOWNLOAD a blank WOW form based on Chapter 6. In the blank space next to each of the 21 icons, we encourage you to dream. Dream up your 21 most memorable future memories. In other words, what are some of the unforgettable memories you'd like to create in your life with your future time and money freedom? There will be sample lists online for you to study, with items such as:

Ride an elephant.

Be a lead for a day in a real Broadway play.

Swim with the dolphins, and/or whales, and/or sharks.

Golf on the world's top 10 courses.

Meet the governor or president or prime minister or
    chairman of the board.

Paint a picture with the world's top marine artist.

Go hang gliding with the inventor of the sport.

Scuba in the world's most beautiful ocean while saving the coral.

Have lunch with Andy Rooney or another famous TV personality.

Explore the Amazon jungle.

Be a circus clown for one day.

Drive a steam locomotive or entire train.

Sit at the controls of the *Spruce Goose.*

Go to Space Camp and simulate real space travel like an astronaut.

Fly in the stratosphere at 100,000 feet above the earth to see the
    curvature of Spaceship Earth and witness an ancient star show
    unknown to earth-based humans.

Go on an archaeological dig in the Mayan ruins of Guatemala.

Meet and chat with America's wisest and smartest woman.

Fly a private plane, a glider, a helicopter, a jet,

    or the space shuttle simulator.

Go on a daylong $25,000 shopping spree.

Race Formula Dodge cars.

Conduct the orchestra for a symphony.

Watch open-heart surgery up close and personal. (But not your own!)

Watch *The Producers* from backstage.

Ride in a submarine and pilot the sub.

Why all of this dreaming? Visit the website for more information. You might be surprised! Now, with all of these thoughts and assignments swirling around and inside you, take a deep breath before you start on your 24-hour experiment.

IT'S A WONDERFUL LIFE

—

How many times have you seen the movie *It's a Wonderful Life*? Of all the movies that Jimmy Stewart starred in—and of all the movies that Frank Capra directed—this was, by far, their favorite. It came out in 1946, just after World War II. It might surprise you to hear that it was not a very successful movie and disappeared quickly from the movie theaters that year. It was only several years later that this "gem" was discovered and became perhaps the most-beloved movie of all time. Watch it again.

Remember how George, played by Jimmy Stewart, was getting ready to jump off a bridge after the collapse of his small savings and loan company? His suicide attempt was thwarted by Clarence, a bumbling angel trying to "earn his wings." Clarence lets George see what life would have been like had George never been born. George is stunned to realize that even though his finances were in chaos, his Enlightened Wealth Statement was priceless. Then we watch what happens when George "comes to himself" and enlists the angels in his life. Miracles happen. Can you watch this movie without your eyeballs "sweating"?

Some people might say that it's just a movie. It's just someone's interpretation of a fictional story. It's not reality. But we ask, What is reality? What is real? Look around at the actors in the movie of your professional life. Isn't what you see just the manifestation of someone's idea of the way things should be? Someone (an entrepreneur) wrote a screenplay (business plan) and sold it to a producer (a banker or partner), then hired some actors (employees) and rented some sets (office space) and hired some set designers (interior decorators) and then hired a director (manager) to direct these actors to act a certain way.

Is reality real? Is this just a movie you're acting in? Shakespeare said, "All the world's a stage, and all the men and women merely players." Are you playing a bit part in someone else's movie? How would you like to play the lead?

You are the screenwriter, the producer, the director, and the lead actor in the movie of your life. Someday, someone will see your movie. Will you be the Jimmy Stewart who struggles at first and then triumphs? It's up to you.

The next scene is ready to shoot. You've got 24 hours to get some great footage, and we wish you the best of everything.

Lights! Camera! Action!

#101 _____

ACKNOWLEDGMENTS

We dreamed the impossible dream, then we were fortunate enough to find a Dream Team that wholeheartedly helped us bring it to life in the pages you have just read. For this priceless gift we are humbly and deeply thankful. Our gratitude goes out to everyone who has helped make this book a reality, and we apologize for inevitably overlooking someone in these acknowledgments.

The creation of this book, and indeed anything else we have achieved, would not have been possible without the loving support we receive each day from our wives, Patty Hansen and Daryl Allen. They are the solid bedrock from which we can soar in our flights of breakthrough thinking. They also contributed generously with specific and insights to each iteration of this book. A special thanks to Patty Hansen for her tireless assistance overcoming legal, accounting, and permissions hurdles, and for her brilliant business insights.

We are richly blessed to be championed by the agent of agents, Jillian Manus. Our great friend and tireless advocate, Jillian went the extra mile for us at every turn. As James Bond said: "Nobody does it better." Thanks also to her superb assistant, Dru Gregory. Our lifelong friend and colleague, Chip Collins, worked ceaselessly with us to ensure that readers would have a predictable system to become millionaires. Chip's brilliance and creativity was absolutely essential to cracking the millionaire code. We are forever grateful, Chip!

Our amazing friend and partner, Tom Painter, provides us with invaluable support through the Multiple Streams of Income and our training corporation, Enlightened Millionaire Institute. Tom is a true marketing genius, and we couldn't get our message to the world without him. Thanks ten million, Tom!

Wow! How did we get so blessed as to have the world's most talented and caring editor? Peter Guzzardi inspired us to bring our clearest thinking to this book, sentence by sentence, page by page. Endless thanks also to Julia Pastore, at Harmony Books, who lovingly shepherded our manuscript through the publishing process, to the world's best publisher, Shaye Areheart, and to Crown's president and publisher, Jenny Frost: Their vision and encouragement helped us realize this book's true potential.

Megagratitude to our publicist Imal Wagner. You will always be in our hearts.

Our respective staffs have raised us on their shoulders and carried us through the challenges provided by each new day so we that we could make good on our promise to deliver this project, which we believe will change the economic future of the world. We deeply appreciate Debbie Lefever for her constant, patient revisions and insights on how to have our text read smoothly and effortlessly. Our deepest thanks to Mark's staff: Lisa Williams, Michelle Adams, Dee Dee Romanello, Shanna Vieyra, Jody Emme, Mary McKay, Tanya Jones, Patti Clement, Maegan Romanello, Joel Bakker, and Laurie Hartman. We are enormously grateful to Justine Painter for keeping us focused, and for providing superb logistical support, ably assisted by Teresa Rowe. Bob's staff contributed with equal heroism. Special thanks to Jan Stephen, Steve Carlson, Trulene Hutchings, Sheryl Spencer, Kurt Mortensen, Angii Arderton, Mike Ray, Anton Ewing, Carol Liege, and Tad Lignell among others. We lovingly appreciate Greg Link for giving us his 50,000-foot observations and for keeping the brand pure. Joyce Belle Edlebrock helped us create the Draconian Codes and performed a thousand other miraculous tasks deep into the night. Joyce, you're wonderful!

Our deepest gratitude goes to Pat Burns and her daughter, Michelle Burns, who worked with us to create the Inner Circle program to test, teach, and perfect these principles, strategies, and techniques. Pat worked relentlessly to help make millionaires into billionaires and supergivers. Thank you for showing us, and the world, how pure imagination can be transformed into dramatic tangible success.

We also gratefully applaud the thousands of our students in dozens of cities in North America who served as the true "guinea pigs" for this book. The names of our Inner Circle members are printed on the following pages.

You can read their incredible true stories on the *Cracking the Millionaire Code* website.

We treasure you, our fans and readers, for reading, absorbing, and using the principles in the book and sharing them with those whom you love and care about. We hope this book makes your wallet grow and your soul glow through the principles of Enlightened Wealth. Again, thank you for reading our work.

In the many areas of life, it's customary to save the best for last. Thus, we acknowledge and honor the presence of the Higher Power from whom we receive so many gifts and enlightened insights. As you'll see in this book, Higher Power comes first in our lives.

Mark Victor Hansen
and
Robert G. Allen

Thanks a million to the amazing, creative, courageous members of our Inner Circle who worked closely with us to refine and expand the concepts in this book:

Amae Allen, Jeannie Austin, Rhonda Baines, Diane Baker, Linda Bardes, Karen Nelson Bell, Colleen Berg, Werner Berger, Dr. Linne Bourget, Annette Brandley, Joel Brandley, Barbara Brazina, Michelle Burgad, Sandy Bushberg, Carol Caldwell, Scott Campbell, Beth Carls, Susan Carlson, Larry Chao, Mary Comtois, Paul Congress, James Cooper, Lynn Koon Conrad, Kent Corbell, Kathy Creath, Mary Anne Durham, Jose Espana, Jim Felt, Charles Fleischmann, Pearly Fort, Donna Fox, Scott Freebairn, Martha Friedman, Craig Gibble, Angela Graham, Kym Grant, David Graves, Duncan Guertin, Gary Haggerty, Dahvee Haley, Thomas Hamelin, Reta Harbaugh, Melissa Hatch, Teresa Higgins, J. C. Ige, Hallie Javorek, Marilyn Johnson, Nobuji Kanai, Doug Keeley, Gary Kimmel, Tom Kish, Nancy Klarman, Gerald Kong, Robbie LeBlanc, Maria Leslawski, Sandra Lilo, Elmie Litam, Amy Looper, Travis Loriano, Dr. David Luquette, Teresa Luquette, Art Martin, Steven

Mattos, John McGee, Peggy McGee, Jeannette Monosoff, Cynthia Morgan, Liz Nichols, Crystal Olson, Daniel Oostenbrink, Greg Poulos, Hope Prins, Mike Prins, Michelle Rabin, Jann Roney, Pat Rowan, Paulie Sabol, Ian Sanchez, Ted Schneck, Jim Scott, Heshie Segal, Dr. Joyce Shaffer, Scott Simpson, Mark Smith, Segovia Smith, Cynthia Stipech, Michael Stipech, Marvin Taylor, Julianne Towan, Gary Turner, Arnie Urbick, Rich Van Iderstine, Jennifer Wilkov, Bill Wokas, Steven Wong, Dr. Jean Smith Wooley, Brad Wozny, Jen Wozny, Mary Wozny, Richard Wozny, Dottie Zveibil, Robert Zveibil.

INDEX

288 | **INDEX**

—MARK VICTOR HANSEN • Our greatest glory is in never failing, but in rising every time we fall.

—CONFUCIUS • Out of abundance he took abundance and still abun-

People don't buy with their head but with their heart. The heart is closer

290 | INDEX

WILLIAM HAZLITT

Prosperity is a great teacher; adversity is greater.

THE KORAN

outfit that is dead or dying. —B. F. HARRIS • Some people are motivated by visualizing themselves reaching their

dream. Some people are motivated by the nightmare of not reaching it. Do both.

ABOUT THE AUTHORS

MARK VICTOR HANSEN is the coauthor of the Chicken Soup for the Soul series, one of the biggest-selling book lines in history, with more than 100 million copies in print. He has been a public speaker for thirty years, entertaining and enlightening audiences worldwide. He is the author of five other books and six popular audio programs and is the recipient of numerous honorary degrees and awards, including the Horatio Alger Award.

ROBERT G. ALLEN has probably helped create more millionaires in North America than any other single person and is the author of some of the most successful financial books in history. His first two books, *Nothing Down* and *Creating Wealth,* have each sold more than a million copies, and his other books—*Multiple Streams of Income, Multiple Streams of Internet Income,* and *The One Minute Millionaire* (coauthored with Mark Victor Hansen)—have also been major *New York Times* bestsellers.

Visit them at www.crackingthemillionairecode.com.